D1600106

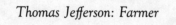
Thomas Jefferson: Farmer

Thomas Jefferson: Farmer

by

Barbara McEwan

McFarland & Company, Inc., Publishers
Jefferson, North Carolina, and London

British Library Cataloguing-in-Publication data are available

Library of Congress Cataloguing-in-Publication Data

McEwan, Barbara.
    Thomas Jefferson : farmer / by Barbara McEwan.
      p. cm.
    Includes bibliographical references and index.
    ISBN 0-89950-633-X (lib. bdg. : 50# alk. paper) ∞
    1. Jefferson, Thomas, 1743–1826 – Career in agriculture.
    2. Agriculture – Virginia – History.   3. Farmers – Virginia – Biography.
    I. Title.
    E332.2.M43 1991
    973.4'6'092 – dc20
    [B]   91-52748
                                                                         CIP

©1991 Barbara McEwan. All rights reserved

Manufactured in the United States of America

McFarland & Company, Inc., Publishers
  Box 611, Jefferson, North Carolina 28640

Table of Contents

Introduction

Thomas Jefferson is known primarily for his political activities. His biographers most commonly portray him as a statesman. Yet this is not how Jefferson saw himself—he was a farmer by choice. His father had been a planter, as had his grandfather and his great-grandfather. A Virginia gentleman might be a lawyer, a doctor, or a politician, but wealth and status in the Old Dominion was synonymous with growing tobacco. Thus, while Thomas Jefferson pursued the law as a student and then as a respected and financially successful member of the legal community, he could not fail to understand that the basis of his social standing depended on his ability to harvest good tobacco crops. Later, farming melted into his philosophical and political convictions so that understanding Jefferson the leader begins with understanding Jefferson the planter.

The Revolutionary War marked the end of Virginia's dependence on tobacco. Soils in Jefferson's native Albemarle County and elsewhere had been destroyed by the weed and by maize as well. Owners of large tracts were forced into wheat. As with his more progressive peers, Jefferson's role as a largely absentee tobacco planter evolved into that of a farmer who had to attend to his land. With America established as an independent country rather than a British colony, his thinking was reinforced by his occupation.

A society of independent farmers, most with small holdings, almost wholly self-sufficient, would anchor a nation of happy individuals, beholden to no one, and uncorrupted by their own greed or that of an employer. While he himself hardly fit the model, with his thousands of acres of Virginia land and his Monticello mansion (and later one at Poplar Forest too), he correctly read the spirit of his fellow Americans. Being content with the basics for existence, with a few luxuries now and then, has characterized immigrants to these shores.

By the time he had reached a position of leadership, Jefferson saw:

Those who labor in the earth are the chosen people of God, if ever He had a chosen people, whose breasts He has made His peculiar deposit for substantial and genuine virtue. It is the focus in which he keeps alive that sacred fire, which otherwise might escape from the face of the earth. Corruption of morals in the mass of cultivators in a phenomenon of which no age nor nation has furnished an example. It is the mark set on those, who, not looking up to heaven, to their own soil and industry, as does the husbandman, for their subsistence, depend for it on casualties and caprice of customers. Dependence begets subservience and venality, suffocates the germ of virtue, and prepares fit tools for the designs of ambition.[1]

He expanded these thoughts in a letter to John Jay in 1785: "Cultivators of the earth are the most valuable citizens. They are the most vigorous, the most independent, the most virtuous, and they are tied to their country, and wedded to its liberty and interests, by the most lasting bonds. As long, therefore, as they can find employment in this line, I would not convert them into mariners, artisans or anything else."

Yet he was prophetic about the limitations of an agrarian economy. In the letter to Jay that one day the number and productivity of farmers would exceed demand for their products. "This is not the case as yet, and probably will not be for a considerable time. As soon as it is, the surplus of hands must be turned to something else. I should then, perhaps, wish to turn them to the sea in preference to manufactures; because, comparing the characters of the two classes, I find the former the most valuable citizens. I consider the class of artificers as the panderers of vice, and the instruments by which the liberties of a country are generally overturned."[2]

This philosophical ideal certainly formed the basis for many of Jefferson's actions. When policies promoting a regenerative sustainable agriculture on a new continent ran afoul of the political scene, whenever he felt he had a choice, agriculture always won.

In conjunction with this land-based ideal was Jefferson's sincere attachment to the world of nature, a passion he shared while growing up with his oldest sister, Jane. Thus Jefferson had a genuine love of the land on a personal level. His precise observations of the first blooms, the first migratory birds to arrive, the harvest dates of his fruits and vegetables—all indicate his life-long fascination with the outdoors. This alone would have motivated him to center his life on farming.

He wrote to Samuel Vaughan in 1790 that "my present situation and occupations are not friendly to Agricultural experiments, however strongly I am led to them by inclination."[3] He explained in 1809 to Philip Tabb: "In agriculture I am only an amateur, having only that knolege which may be got from books. In the field I am entirely ignorant, & am now too old to learn. Still it amuses my hours of exercise, & tempts to the

taking due exercise."[4] Even then, as a sixty-six-year-old-man, he would surely have repeated what he had said after serving as secretary of state: "I am but a learner; an eager one indeed but yet desperate and occupied with it as if I was the greatest adept."[5]

This characteristic, coupled with his natural genius, is the key to his mastery of so many fields. It led his granddaughter, Sarah N. Randolph, to say that her grandfather's "thirst for knowledge was insatiable, and he seized eagerly all means of obtaining it." She added that was it was his habit, "in his intercourse with all classes of men—the mechanic as well as the man of science—to turn the conversation upon that subject with which the man was best acquainted, whether it was the construction of a wheel or the anatomy of an extinct species of animals; and after having drawn from him all the information which he possessed, on returning home or retiring to his private apartments, it was all set down by him in writing—thus arranging it methodically and fixing it in his mind."[6]

In 1795, after leaving the office of secretary of state, Jefferson wrote about his feelings about agriculture. He asked General Henry Knox...

> Have you become a farmer? Is it not pleasanter than to be shut up within 4. walls and delving eternally with the pen? I am become the most ardent farmer in the state. I live on my horse from morning to night almost. Intervals are filled up with attentions to a nailery I carry on. I rarely look into a book, and more rarely take up a pen. I have proscribed newspapers. Not taking a single one, nor scarcely ever looking into one. My next reformation will be to allow neither pen, ink, nor paper to be kept on the farm. When I have accomplished this I shall be in a fair way of indemnifying myself for the drudgery in which I have passed my life. If you are half as much delighted with the farm as I am, you bless your stars at your riddance from public cares.[7]

That same year Jefferson wrote James Madison, "the little spice of ambition which I had in my younger days has long since evaporated, and I set still less store by posthumous than present name.... I am proceeding in my agricultural plans with a slow but sure step. To get under full way will require four or five years. But patience and perseverance will accomplish it."[8]

In 1795 Jefferson was fifty-two and no doubt thinking of the years during which he had actively practiced law and, as a young prodigy amongst men many years his senior, had first tasted political power on various governmental committees. Time spent as governor of Virginia (1779–81) no doubt spelled the end of any illusions he may have had that he was well suited to political office. Indeed, he wrote while secretary of state that "when I first entered on the stage of public life (now twenty-four years ago) I came to a resolution never . . . to wear any other character than that of a farmer."[9]

But ever the man of principle and imbued with the conviction that he owed the country his service when no one else could provide the talent required, he put aside his own preferences. His 1792 letter to George Washington, urging Washington to serve a second term as President, is indicative of his concept of *noblesse oblige:* "I am perfectly aware of the oppression under which your present office lays your mind, and of the ardor with which you pant for domestic life. But there is sometimes an eminence of character on which society have such peculiar claims as to control the predilections of the individual for a particular walk of happiness, and restrain him to that alone arising from the present and future benedictions of mankind. This seems to be your condition."[10] This was in line with his own earlier sacrifice and for those yet to come. He wrote Washington in December of 1789, in response to Washington's request that he assume the position of secretary of state, "It is not for an individual to choose his post. You are to marshal us as may be best for the public good. . . . If you think it better to transfer me to another post, my inclination must be no obstacle."[11]

Although he made no effort to obtain it, Jefferson told James Madison in 1797 that the vice-presidency was "the only office in the world about which I am unable to decide in my own mind whether I had rather have it or not have it."[12] The office, he told others, gave the incumbent a high position, good salary, and ample leisure—in his case to pursue his farming and building interests.

It was fortunate for America that when the chips were down the public interest came first in both Washington's and Jefferson's lives. Once committed to the task, each exerted his respective formidable abilities to get the job done. If their innate talents had not been enough, their roles as plantation masters were the best possible recommendation for high public office in that day. A large plantation was a self-sufficient colony, incorporating numerous tasks requiring detailed planning and intelligent supervision. The large number of people totally dependent on the owner's abilities also required a long-term commitment.

Even though technically well suited, Jefferson never enjoyed his political service, except for his sojourn abroad. Several statements abundantly show how he felt:

To a Mr. Donald, 1788: "I had rather be shut up in a very modest cottage with my books, my family, and a few old friends, dining on simple bacon, and letting the world roll on as it liked, than to occupy the most splendid post that any human power can give."[13]

To Randolph Jefferson, 1789: "The very short period of my life which I have passed unconnected with public business suffices to convince me it

is the happiest of all situations, and that no society is so precious as that of one's own family."[14]

To Martha Randolph, 1792: "The ensuing year will be the longest of my life, and the last of such hateful labors; the next we will sow our cabbages to-gether."[15]

To Nicholas Lewis, 1792: "I am never a day without wishing myself with you, and more and more as the fine sunshine comes on, which seems made for all the world but me."[16]

To a Mrs. Church, 1793: "I am then to be liberated from the hated occupations of politics, and to remain in the bosom of my family, my farm and my books."[17]

To Thomas Mann Randolph, 1793: "You see how much my mind is gone over to the business of a farmer, for I never know when to finish, if once I begin on the subject."[18]

To Henry Remsen, 1794: "I am so much immersed in farming & nail making . . . that politics are entirely banished from my mind."[19]

To James Madison, 1794: "I would not give up my own retirement for the empire of the universe."[20]

To General Horatio Gates, 1794: "The length of my tether is now fixed from Monticello to Richmond. My private business can never call me elsewhere and certainly politics will not, which I have ever hated both in theory and practice. I thought myself conscientiously called from those studies which were my delight by the political crises of my country. . . . In storms like those all hands must be aloft. But calm is now restored, and I leave the bark with joy to those who live the sea. I am but a landsman, forced from my element by accident, rejoining it with transport, and wishing to recollect nothing of what I have seen but my friendships."[21]

To Ferdinando Fairfax, 1794: "I have returned to farming with an ardour which I scarcely knew in my youth, and which has entirely taken the lead of my love of study. I indulge it because I think it will be more productive of health, profit, & the happiness depending on these, and perhaps of some utility to my neighbors."[22]

To Monsieur D. Ivernois, 1795: "I have returned, with infinite appetite, to the enjoyment of my farm, my family and my books, and had determined to meddle in nothing beyond their limits."[23]

To Edward Rutledge, 1795: "[Your son] found me in a retirement I doat on, living like an antediluvian patriarch among my children and grandchildren, and tilling my soil."[24]

To John Adams, 1796: "In the retired canton where I am, I learn little of what is passing: pamphlets I see never; papers but a few; and the fewer the happier. . . . I leave to others the sublime delights of riding in the storm, better pleased with sound sleep and a warm berth below, with the society of neighbors, friends and fellow-laborers of the earth, than of spies and sycophants. No one then will congratulate you with purer disinterestedness than myself. . . . I have no ambition to govern men. It is a painful and thankless office."[25]

To Martha Randolph, 1806: "My daily rides too are sickening for want of some interest in the scenes I pass over: and indeed I look over the two ensuing years as the most tedious of my life."[26]

To Augustin Francois Silvestre, 1807: "Attached to agriculture by inclination as well as by a conviction that it is the most useful of the occupations of man, my course of life has not permitted me to add to it's theories the lessons of practice."[27]

To Monsieur Le Comte Diodati, 1807: "I long for the enjoyments of rural life, among my books, my farms and my family."[28]

To Timothy Matlack, 1807: "I shall then begin to occupy myself according to my own natural inclinations, which have been so long kept down by the history of our times; and shall bid a joyful adieu to politics and all the odious passions & vices of which they make us the object in public life."[29]

To John Dickinson, 1807: "I am tired of an office where I can do no more good than many others, who would be glad to be employed in it. To myself, personally, it brings nothing but unceasing drudgery and daily loss of friends. . . . My only consolation is in the belief that my fellow citizens at large give me credit for good intentions. I will certainly endeavor to merit the continuance of that good-will which follows well-intended actions, and their approbation will be the dearest reward I can carry into retirement."[30]

To Robert R. Livingston, 1808: "It is now among my most fervent longings to be on my farm, which, with a garden and fruitery, will constitute my principal occupation in retirement."[31]

To Charles Willson Peale, 1809: "I begin already to be much occupied in preparation for my departure to those scenes of rural retirement after which my soul is panting."[32]

To Pierre Samuel Dupont de Nemours, 1809: "Nature intended me for the tranquil pursuits of science, by rendering them my supreme delight. But the enormities of the times in which I have lived, have forced me to take part in resisting them, and to commit myself on the boisterous ocean of political passions."[33]

1

Jefferson in the Context
of His Times

I have often thought that if heaven had given me choice of my position
and calling, it should have been on a rich spot of earth, well-watered, and near
a good market for the productions of the garden. No occupation is so delightful
to me as the culture of the earth, and no culture comparable to that of the
garden. Such a variety of subjects, some one always coming to perfection, the
failure of one thing repaired by the success of another, and instead of one
harvest a continued one through the year. Under a total want of demand except
for our family table, I am still devoted to the garden. But though an old man, I
am but a young gardener . . .

–Letter to Charles W. Peale, 1881[1]

The first Thomas Jefferson in America was the future President's
great-grandfather. By 1679 the first Thomas Jefferson farmed within the
boundaries of the old Henrico County, south and east of present-day
Richmond on the level lowland inhabited by the bulk of Virginia's population of that era. His son, the second Thomas Jefferson, also lived in
Henrico County but west of his father's stake. He was a modest planter of
tobacco, yet a cut above most. His son, Peter, following in his father's
footsteps, went even farther west. Peter Jefferson's earliest known grant in
the region is dated June 14, 1734. Before he married Jane Randolph in 1739
he had staked out the claim which would become the heart of his son's
Albemarle land. Within a year after surveying it he received a patent for
1000 acres, which included the later site of Monticello. Peter eventually
acquired additional land in the vicinity. According to Thomas' autobiography, his father moved to what became known as Shadwell in about 1737,
the third or fourth settler of that area.

1

Peter Jefferson was a planter of modest means compared to the gentry of the Tidewater, yet he was successful at growing tobacco, maize, and wheat. Considering the fact that he came from an agricultural background, he might have chosen a richer tract. But Virginia at this period could best be described as one vast forest, its agricultural capabilities untested. It would be a long time before the colony was more than a discontinuous string of plantations along its rivers. Perhaps Peter, like his son Thomas, saw Virginia as a potential Eden, endowed with all necessary prerequisites for producing untold wealth if men only managed their affairs well.

Peter played a part of some importance in setting up the county of Albemarle. Unlike most pioneers he was not without financial resources, and his marriage connecting him to the wealthy Randolphs eased the way. In addition, Peter was intelligent and diligent. Nevertheless, none of this could compensate for a lack of rich, deep topsoil. Thus, as a future farmer, Thomas Jefferson (the third to bear that name) had his lot in farming cast by his father's unfortunate selection of land.[2]

Upon his father's death in 1757, Thomas Jefferson inherited some 2650 acres on the Rivanna River and a similar tract elsewhere, mostly in Albemarle. The holdings along the Rivanna included Monticello, Shadwell, Portobello, Pantops, Tufton, and Pouncy's. Peter gained the first three of these tracts before Thomas was born in 1743. At that time this area was considered remote for it was far from the Tidewater region where Virginia history had begun, where the first Thomas Jefferson had settled, and where most Virginians still lived.

Thomas Jefferson's other major holding, at the foot of the Blue Ridge Mountains, was similarly chosen for him. Jefferson's future father-in-law, John Wayles, was not the first white owner of the 4000-acre tract in Bedford County; Reverend William Stith, a resident of Charles City County, Virginia, on October 23, 1749, was granted the property he called Poplar Forest. Wayles, also a resident of Charles City County, bought Poplar Forest in 1764.

What, if anything, Stith did with the property is not known. Wayles planted tobacco. Wayles (and maybe Stith) probably sent an overseer and a gang of slaves to pioneer the raw wilderness. This was frequently done by planters of means, as Peter Jefferson did while still living at Tuckahoe and after patenting the Monticello site. While Wayles had selected property well suited to the lucrative leaf, transporting the product to market must have caused considerable problems in the earliest years. Nevertheless, these were reasonably resolved by the time of his death, when Poplar Forest went to his daughter, Martha Wayles Jefferson. The number of hogsheads of tobacco grown there annually by Thomas Jefferson dropped in 1774, the year he acquired the property, and then remained fairly constant for the remainder of his life. At least in Bedford County he had been fortunate in his inheritance; he at this time referred to it as his "little fortune."[3]

Since Jefferson is best known for his political contributions, it is easy to assume that the events he influenced and the offices he held dominated his interests. As already seen, though, his writings strongly indicate that, except for his family, his chief passion was growing plants and observing nature. Engaging in politics was his duty to his country, not a role he sought. Although he proclaimed that building and renovating was one of his favorite amusements, even architecture is not given the loving lyrical words agriculture and horticulture repeatedly commanded.[4]

Because Jefferson was a man of heroic proportions, it is easy to assume that in all of his ventures he was exceptional. He never considered his gifts extraordinary, however, and remained throughout his long life a humble man, surprising many by his lack of pretension. For example, although he had long been recognized as an authority in agriculture, after concluding service as secretary of state in 1793, he wrote to Judge Archibald Stuart, a Staunton, Virginia, friend: "But I am again a new beginner in the world, & it is usual for *old* settlers to help *young* ones."[5]

It is necessary to put Jefferson's contributions in the field of agriculture into the perspective of his times. Living in an age of supermarkets well stocked from around the world by an efficient transportation system, it is easy for us to forget that almost all people once were forced to grow their own food supply. How well they ate depended on where they were located. The closer people lived to the frontier, the more likely they attempted no garden at all; their livestock ran wild in woods and meadows. Hence the amenities of the table were few or nonexistent. Under these circumstances field corn was grown and possibly wheat. Menus were usually rounded out with salt pork, pigeons, and wild game.

Whether plants were grown in gardens or field, the colonial grower faced a considerable difference in weather conditions than his European relatives across the ocean, and the soils presented their own peculiarities. Americans had to learn how to handle both problems. Neither was there a clear consensus as to how, or even what, to grow on American shores. In truth, after centuries of neglect Europeans themselves were still experimenting with farming, fruit growing, and gardening, attempting to improve these most basic of human activities. Jefferson was part of the effort to improve food production on both sides of the Atlantic. His holdings may have been sizeable for the period and put him far from the class of small farmer, yet the differences between the two in planning, tools, and work were virtually nil except for the fact that Jefferson himself did very little of the physical labor. His social status, his public service, and his other varied interests left him little time to personally plant and harvest.

We are fortunate he chose to leave a legacy based on the products of his mind rather than of his hands, as he would have preferred, for there is no doubt he enjoyed hands-on gardening and farming. His slave Isaac, for example, recalled, "For amusement he [Jefferson] would work sometimes in the garden for half an hour at a time in right good earnest in the cool of the evening."[6]

How recently basic knowledge of agriculture and horticulture has been assembled; tools and procedures we take for granted would have astounded Jefferson, as would modern plant varieties and animal breeds. To understand the problems Jefferson faced it is necessary to review how the colonists and later pioneers set upon the task of feeding themselves. Without such a review it is impossible to grasp the significance of Jefferson's place in agricultural history and to appreciate the contributions he made as a farmer, horticulturist, and landscaper.

As Americans before him, Jefferson really had little information to help him. White settlers to this country for many years were faced with the same scene as the native Indian. It is said that in the colonial period a squirrel could travel from the Atlantic to the Mississippi without ever touching ground. This vast area was basically in virgin timber with natural meadows in the bottomlands. The Indians had created openings of up to 100 acres and more on occasion for their maize fields, but their ability to maintain the same plot year after year depended on young, fertile glacial soils or a flood plain which was periodically rejuvenated by water-borne topsoil. Their agricultural success was hampered because maize, their chief crop, is a heavy feeder and depletes fertility comparatively quickly.

Long after Jefferson's day farmers continued the Indian style of agriculture, the same method which had been used throughout the world since farming began 10,000 years ago and which is still used in some remote areas. The only possible courses of action for the farmer without fertilizers were to slash and burn the trees, reap, and move on, or to slash and burn, crop, and then allow the land to lie fallow (uncultivated) for several years.

The virgin forests pioneers encountered were formidable, especially because of the tools available to remove the trees. A typical settler could clear no more than three acres a year.[7] First the underbrush was cut down or grubbed out, then burned, the ashes adding to the soil's natural fertility. Larger trees were treated in one of several ways; the same community and even the same farmer might try them all. Trees might be girdled. A groove was cut around the trunk, severing the pipeline to the roots. By the following season girdled trees were dead, and the farmer could plant around the trunks, digging out brittle roots. If the trees were cut down, the trunks provided material for houses, fences, or firewood. Farmers who had enough lumber torched dead trees where they stood or cut them down before burning them. Moving the giants was a chore. Planters who expected to plow, felled trees in the direction of the furrow. Those who used only hoes, felled trees at right angles to the row.[8] For the man who intended to "reap and run," the logs were more likely burned in huge piles, with the ashes collected and sold for potash, a convenient source of money for pioneers who had few ways to obtain cash. Humus under the pile was, of course, destroyed, but this was of no concern since the reap-and-run planter was a transient farmer. He probably did not even know what humus was or that its rich organic matter contributed substantially to soil fertility.

Whether the farmer stayed or moved on, after the soil was depleted of nutrients, the tract was abandoned to recover as best it could. Depending on location, the field might become overgrown by weeds which not even cattle would touch; it might be covered with herbaceous vegetation of some use to pasture livestock, or trees and shrubs might reclaim the land. Each presented its own difficulties when the farmer decided to crop it again. Not until settlers reached west to Ohio and beyond, did they find glacial or deep prairie topsoil they could farm for many years without paying the price of reduced harvests due to depleted soil.

One European source of fertilizer—manure from large farm animals—was not available to the Indian because no large animal native to the western hemisphere was suitable for domestication. But collecting manure in one place was also difficult for the European immigrant, even when horses, mules, cattle, and oxen were brought across the ocean. These animals had no barns, stables, or feed lots on the frontier and were of necessity allowed to forage where they could in woods and natural meadows. Even in New England the animals were on their own nine or ten months of the year. South of New York they routinely foraged year round, even though in winter food was frequently insufficient. The northern farmer usually was handicapped by a lack of labor. He had himself and his family. It often was necessary to commercially fish or work at a craft to raise cash. Collecting manure dropped by wandering animals was not within his time budget, even if he understood its importance to his soil. A southern planter like Jefferson commonly owned thousands of acres and solved the labor problem with the use of slaves. Still, it is unlikely many plantation owners ever had sufficient help, slave or hired, to assign part of the work force to picking up dung.

Confining cows in pens was used as early as 1688 in the colonies and became a general practice by the end of the eighteenth century.[9] Temporary rail pens for cows were moved about the fields where manure was needed, a laborious practice.[10] Some tobacco planters followed a rule of keeping 100 cattle for every 1000 plants. Pens were moved weekly. Not surprisingly, this was an expensive procedure compared to producing on virgin land.[11] Only with the advent of barbed wire in 1873 could farm animals, large and small, be confined easily within a specific area. By that time the farm machinery and market were such that the farmer could afford to set aside fields where nothing but supplemental food for his animals was grown.

Much has been made of the Pilgrims' use of fish to fertilize maize fields. However, recent research indicates that the Indian Squanto, who is credited by tradition with showing the Plymouth farmers of 1621 how to add several fish to each hill of corn for fertilizer, learned this from the white man himself. Squanto had been in continuous contact with western Europeans long before 1621. He had been kidnapped in 1614 and taken to Spain. His travels thereafter took him to Newfoundland and England before he returned to Cape Cod as a pilot and guide for Captain Thomas Dermer. Plymouth was not even the earliest North American settlement where whites used fertilizer, and fertilizing had been done in Europe.[12]

The Indian came from a different cultural context. Men hunted and fished; women grew the crops and gathered them. The spring fish harvests of alewives sufficed only for food during the Indians' hungriest season and for drying and smoking for the following winter. Plymouth farmers are known to have used two to four fish per hill of corn, with 360 hills per acre. Each acre therefore required between 720 and 1440 fish. An Indian woman needed up to 3.3 acres of corn to feed her family. Just the logistics of transporting the required number of fish would have been formidable for a woman with no wagon or animal to haul it. Although the English male worked the fields, he could do little better except on fields next to the coast, and there only in years the quantities of fish exceeded food needs.

Whitefish were later used by farmers on Long Island. Around 1800 a single net reportedly took up to two hundred thousand fish a day in June and July. These were sold for a dollar a thousand and ten thousand were used per acre for a liberal application.[13] The American economy had differentiated sufficiently along the Seaboard so that farm products could be sold for cash. This meant farmers could farm and let fishermen catch the fish.

Rockweed was also used as an organic fertilizer with good results. As with fish, only farmers on the coast could benefit. Rockweed was spread ten loads to the acre, a considerable task except for the fact that its effects lasted for several years, by which time the weed was able to renew itself sufficiently to withstand another cropping.[14]

After the mid-1700s, limestone and marl deposits in New Jersey began to be used as soil amendments in a tentative fashion. On the Maine coast farmers burned lime but inexplicably exported it, perhaps because of the cash it brought. To the west of Philadelphia every farmer was said to have had a lime kiln. In New Jersey farmers putting limestone on their fields and gardens claimed it stifled weeds. Gypsum (used to make plaster of paris) was a more important soil additive. The idea of applying it was brought to America several years before the Revolutionary War by a Philadelphian. A decade or so later German immigrants who were accustomed to its benefits in Europe were applying it in America. Meanwhile men who were making their names in other fields experimented with gypsum on their own farms.[15] In Virginia gypsum was introduced as early as 1784, but Jefferson was not convinced of its merits until he read Loudon County farmer John A. Binn's "Treatis on practical farming," published in 1803.[16]

The loss of fertility associated with repeated cropping, especially with maize and tobacco, quickly became apparent to those with eyes to see. By the mid-1700s the failure of wheat crops in Connecticut along Long Island Sound was being attributed to depletion of soil fertility. Declining yields of grain soon were noted around Philadelphia and by the end of the century around New York and Boston.[17] Meanwhile the tobacco fields of the Tidewater region were rapidly becoming exhausted; soil destruction was increasingly evident inland as well. By the 1790s, a mere 60 years after it was first plowed, a new settler in Jefferson's Albemarle County described it as "a scene of desolation that baffles description — farm after farm worn out, washed and gullied, so that scarcely an acre could be found in a place fit for cultivating."[18]

Land prices went up as towns became cities. This effectively eliminated all but what might be called truck farmers at their outskirts. With a smaller amount of land to work, such farmers could take better care of it. At the turn of the nineteenth century in New York City, for example, manure was collected from city streets and private stables and carted to nearby farms. Potash hauled down the Hudson and whitefish from Long Island Sound were both spread liberally on the fields.[19] By the 1830s, if not before, men in New York and Boston were carting out slaughterhouse offal and human excrement.[20] Residents of villages and small towns, on the other hand, were typically farmers and also lawyers, doctors, store owners or those who worked at other needed occupations. Large farms typically abutted these small villages.

In less developed areas farmers repeated the mistakes of earlier pioneers, moving westward and southward with almost casual abandon. Maize or tobacco continued to be the typical first crop on new land, although in some places wheat, rye, or potatoes were planted. This was particularly true in the northernmost colonies where, by the time land was cleared, there were not enough growing season days left to bring maize to maturity. In the middle colonies, to compound the ravages of a perpetual maize planting, other grains were often sown between the rows.[21] Jefferson himself did this.

While white settlers had followed the Indians' lead and grown maize, tobacco, beans, and squashes, all of American origin, these were proven crops only when grown in the Indian manner. European oriented farmers, however, were too often determined to eventually plant in the European manner—cropping the same fields with the same crops year after year. England and western Europe had long since been denuded of most of their virgin forests, but farmers there had not grown maize and tobacco, both heavy feeders on soil fertility. Furthermore, better farmers had been reasonably conscientious about applying all available manure. On the other hand, native and foreign observers of America during the later 1700s commented on the careless management of farms they saw. Farmers whose families had been in America for generations were particularly apt to farm in a slovenly fashion, following in the ways of their forefathers, whose primary efforts had frequently revolved around defending their land against Indians who had previously lived there. It is not surprising that the raw frontier of America did not foster agricultural improvement.

Plowing was seldom done during the earliest colonial period. Plow animals were scarce, as were plows. Plows of the era were hardly worth the trouble anyway, as they could scarcely scratch the surface. The harrow, the only other farm implement drawn by animal power, was not much more efficient. In fact, farm tools in general were barely different from those used in biblical days. Tobacco was grown strictly with hand labor. Maize and potatoes were planted by hoe, while wheat and other grains were raked in by hand or by a harrow drawn over the field.[22]

Frequently two years of grain were followed by one year with a grass crop planted for fodder. Such a rotation was not sufficient to increase soil fertility.[23] Nevertheless, it was not as destructive as the common practice of allowing abandoned fields to revert to weeds until such time as the farmer thought they had recovered sufficiently to produce more grain.

Today when land lies "fallow" it is kept bare of vegetation by cultivation or herbicides to conserve soil moisture. In pioneer methods fallow land was planted with a pasture crop or grew up in weeds. This fallow period, which had typically lasted from seven to fifteen years, was shortened to one to two years after the Revolutionary War.[24] This shortened fallow was part of a modest transformation in the agriculture field caused by an upsurge of patriotic pride, demanding that the American farmer take control of his own destiny. More sophisticated crop rotation schemes also made their appearance. Not surprisingly, they were mostly confined to men like Thomas Jefferson and George Washington with education and resources. The typical pioneer was strapped keeping body and soul together. Small grain crops were alternated with each other and with maize, potatoes, peas and clover. The more knowledgeable farmers recognized that switching crops, each with its peculiar demands on soil fertility, permitted a much shortened fallow. The farmer could remain on his land indefinitely, while still managing to grow enough to supply the needs of those who depended on him, with perhaps something left over. Most farmers who practiced a rotation of crops did not choose them for their ability to save soil fertility, but because they were needed for grazing, hay or could be sold. Where crops were grown was a matter of chance, convenience or habit. Even men like Jefferson at times were dominated by these factors. At least they were willing to forgo traditional methods, crops, and tools if others seemed better; indeed they actively sought alternatives.

In addition to the problem of worn-out soils, almost all farmers were beset by factors largely beyond their control. Foremost was a lack of capital. At least unlike other under-capitalized businesses, farmers with a bit of luck could hold on because the farm family was able to grow or make virtually everything needed to survive. Only salt, molasses, sugar, and perhaps a few spices had to be purchased.[25] The slightly more affluent might include tea, tobacco, rum or other liquor, indigo, or a few yards of cloth on their shopping list. Other items found for sale at local stores were glassware, dishes, iron and steel bars, and powder and shot.[26] Farmers thus of necessity were jacks-of-all-trades, as was required to maintain a farm and a livelihood. Where there was a village store, farm products could be exchanged for the few non-farm items it carried. The storekeeper took farm products to urban areas too far away for the farmer to reach. This entrepreneur might even be a shipowner who exported to other colonies or to Europe. For most farmers there was no effective market and hence no opportunity to accumulate capital.

While colonial Americans continued to wrest a living from the land along the lines dictated by earlier generations, innovation in methods was afoot abroad. The turning point towards a new agriculture in England seems to be 1760, the year George III, "the farmer," ascended the throne. That gentleman was truly interested in farming. Fortunately during this period, men like Arthur Young, John Sinclair, and Robert Bakewell were involved with experiments to improve the farmer's lot. Their work was based to a large extent on that of the Englishman Jethro Tull (1674–1741), one of the greatest improvers of English agriculture. In about 1701 he invented a seed drill which sowed seeds in rows where formerly seeds had been broadcast in a random pattern. Planting in rows permitted cultivation between the rows. Tull went on to invent a horse hoe, a horse-drawn tillage implement, to benefit more from the drill. Tull thereby solved three former problems: He saved seed; he kept down the weeds; and land between rows was in effect fallowed, thereby reducing the overall fallow period for a field.

Tull was probably not the first to design a seed drill, but was likely the first to actually build and operate one successfully. His design was the prototype of later designs. By the end of the eighteenth century, the use of drills and clean farming through frequent cultivation was widely adopted in England and the Continent by better farmers.[27]

Such men were instrumental in making Jefferson a better farmer. The vast majority of gardening and farming books in his library were by English and European authors. Most were written during Jefferson's lifetime, although his library included those earliest professionals: Cato, Varro, Columella, and Palladius.[28] American farmers who did not read or did not have free access to books were thus deprived of the benefits of this foreign thinking. But European technology still needed to be translated for climate and soil conditions in America. Jefferson, Washington, and a few other forward-looking contemporaries were quick to pick up these new ideas and try them out. It is understandable that the man tied mentally and physically to his land, with a wife and family to support, would not take such chances. Even men of wealth and intellectual curiosity had a bottom line to meet and were inclined to stray from the accepted. Rural conservatism won out most of the time, even when better ways were clearly demonstrated in the neighborhood.

The center of America's pursuit of agricultural improvement was Philadelphia, the center of so much other history. Leaders gravitated to the city for a variety of reasons. In an age when almost all Americans engaged in agriculture for at least part of their income, it is not surprising that Philadelphian farms should be among the very best, especially because the land and climate were more amenable to farming than in many other parts of the colonies.

William Penn whose home, Pennsbury, is not far from Philadelphia, can probably be considered the first important horticulturist of the region. By 1685 he was at work on his estate. From England he got numerous seeds and plants, some rare, plus grasses for his lawn. He transplanted trees from Maryland, and wildflowers from the forest were domesticated. While the result was magnificent, Penn's time and interest were not of a true scientific nature, nor did he deliberately educate others about the best way to grow domestic or foreign plants. Yet, as the founder of a major colony, his interest in horticulture could not go unnoticed, especially because he planned for every lot in his new city to have a house in the middle, with a garden on one side and an orchard on the other.[29]

John Bartram (1699–1777) is more appropriately titled the founder of American botany. Bartram was a Quaker farmer whose parents and grandparents came to Penn's new colony in 1682. While Bartram did not establish the first botanic garden in America, the one he began in about 1729 outside Philadelphia is first by merit of its profound influence on Americans even to this day. The five- or six-acre garden was part of a tract of some three hundred acres owned by this good farmer. In it he had probably the finest collection of native plants in America. Bartram was a keen observer, careful, accurate, and an indefatigable collector who frequently went far afield in search of new prizes. His reputation soon spread abroad, where King George III appointed him royal botanist. For half a century Bartram was the largest and most dependable exporter and importer of plant material in the colonies. Linnaeus called him "the greatest natural botanist in the world." Jefferson, Washington, and Benjamin Franklin all were involved with seed, root, and information exchanges with Bartram or his son, William.[30]

Franklin's botanical contributions are largely forgotten. Begun in 1732, the year of Washington's birth, *Poor Richard's Almanac* continued for 25 years. In its later editions Franklin, who believed agriculture was the chief source of a nation's wealth, used articles on all phases of that subject, including growing fruits and vegetables. A practical man, Franklin is credited with being an experimenter and demonstrator in the use of fertilizers. He traded ideas and knowledge regarding agriculture with farmers and the scientifically minded both in America and abroad, establishing relationships across the sea with like-minded people who traded seeds, plants, and observations. He personally sent apples abroad to promote American varieties. He founded the American Philosophical Society in 1743 to "promote useful knowledge," and the Society disseminated information in a variety of fields. Bartram was among its original members. Although a first order of business under Franklin's presidency of the Society was the establishment of a botanic garden, this project never fulfilled its potential. Whether it was this or some other facet of the group's endeavors that first attracted Jefferson, we do not know, but he was elected a member in 1780 and president from 1797 to 1814. Undoubtedly he found stimulation from men involved in many fields.[31]

With Jefferson, however, the written word was most important. Unfortunately, few gardening books and pamphlets were published. Almost no farmers stopped to analyze what they were doing and why. In the colonies the first agricultural publication had consisted of a series of six essays written between 1749 and 1759 by Jared Eliot (1685–1763), a Connecticut doctor and minister. Titled *Essays upon Field Husbandry in New England*, the preface stated the work was not "an account of what we do in our present Husbandry, but rather what we might do to our advantage."[32] Apparently Jefferson did not own a copy, perhaps because he felt New England's farming problems were too dissimilar to those of Virginia.

Eliot's interests were wide ranging. He asked Franklin for his observations on the cause of storms, a long-standing interest of that future founding father. Eliot corresponded for many years with Bartram. Both demonstrated an appreciation for the problems of erosion. Eliot, who recognized that much of Connecticut's grazing land was already exhausted, carried out many experiments his neighbors must have wondered about. For example, he was a fervent advocate of deep plowing. Most farmers settled for furrows between four and six inches deep, if only because plows of the era could not be coaxed to dig more deeply.

The next agricultural publication may have been John Randolph, Jr.'s *A Treatise on Gardening*. Jefferson had two copies of it. Randolph (1727–1784) was the last attorney general of Virginia under the crown. A resident of Williamsburg, his job and his affiliation with the great Randolph family perhaps induced him to publish his work unsigned as well as undated. The small book treats separately each of the vegetables and herbs commonly grown and concludes in typical English fashion with a calendar of garden chores month by month. Whether intended for friends or the *Virginia Gazette*, or perhaps both, is uncertain.

In 1790 the Reverend Samuel Dean (1733–1814) of Maine published *The New England and Farmer or Geological Dictionary*. Planting by the moon, Dean kept a detailed account of his various experiences growing fruits and vegetables. He performed many agricultural experiments, advocating contour plowing, terracing, and strip cropping. Jefferson did not have this New England work in his library either.

The American Gardener by John Gardiner and David Hepburn was published in 1804. Jefferson had the 1818 edition. This book was probably written by Hepburn, who had working experience with plants in both England and America. It followed the English month-by-month format of practical suggestions.

Jefferson had several volumes by John Beale Bordley, including *Sketches on Rotations of Crops and other Rural Matters*, published in 1796, and *Essays and Notes on Husbandry and Rural Affairs*, published three years later. Bordley of Maryland, a lawyer as well as farmer, had a 1600-acre tract on the Chesapeake which he ran as an experiment station. His books are basically concerned with the results of his experiments. His was the first real American attempt at a scientific approach, something which was bound to appeal to Jefferson. Bordley also spread knowledge of the new English agriculture. One of his recommendations was to pen livestock in a permanent central lot for ease in collecting manure for compost. By supplying ample litter, he told his readers, the liquid manure could also be saved.

The Englishman William Forsyth's *A Treatis on the Culture and Management of Fruit Trees*, also in Jefferson's library, was the first book published in America devoted wholly to fruits. Forsyth was the superintendent of royal gardens at St. James and Kensington. Although his credentials were impeccable, the book demonstrated the necessity for a man like Bordley when it came to applications for American fruit growers. The editor attempted an introductory chapter and notes to translate English experiences into American conditions, but he was not overly successful. Nevertheless, Jefferson may have found the directions on planting, pruning and harvesting fruits of some use. Certainly the discussion on diseases of fruit trees was unusual, if not accurate, in an age when little was known about such things. Forsyth's discussion on the planting and care of forest trees would have been the most beneficial to Jefferson. While others were cutting them down en masse, Jefferson planted trees and conserved those still standing.

In 1806 Jefferson was literally presented with the first really useful and adequate book on horticulture published in America: Bernard McMahon's *The American Gardener's Calender*. McMahon was a Philadelphia nurseryman with whom he would transact business again and again. Jefferson, early in his second term as President of the United States, must have been delighted with the sixty-seven kinds of vegetables listed and the twenty-six aromatic, pot and sweet herbs, with the common ones coming in many varieties, and dreamed of his coming retirement when he could experiment with them at will. Of interest to today's gardeners is the fact that only sweet corn is missing from McMahon's inventory. Some included on McMahon's list, such as rampion, rocambole, and orach, are seldom, if ever, found now.

McMahon was more than a merchant of plants and seeds. He can be described as America's first landscape gardener. Although he relied heavily on Humphrey Repton, the English authority in the field, McMahon managed to translate the rage of naturalistic design then sweeping England to the American situation. When Jefferson first came to know this remarkable man is not known. Ever the gardener, it is hard to believe he did not make McMahon's acquaintance soon after the latter established his business, which he seems to have done soon after coming to this country in 1796.

McMahon abounds in advice. Gardeners should "consult the rural disposition in imitation of nature." He advised "abolishing long straight walks," recommended "rural open spaces of grass-ground" and suggested "winding walks, all bounded with plantations of trees, shrubs, and flowers in various clumps." Jefferson had already achieved some of this at Monticello, but it is of interest that the winding walks and flower beds behind the mansion were sketched out by him the year after McMahon gave him a copy of the book. It would serve many others for fifty years as the standard authority in various areas of gardening, going through eleven editions, the last in 1857.

John Taylor (1753–1824) at his Caroline, Virginia, home performed a similar service in the agricultural field. His series of essays assembled as a book entitled *Arator*, first appeared in 1813. Going through eight editions, it is judged to have been more widely read and to have had more influence on southern agriculture than any other book published before the Civil War. Taylor, who was recognized as an exceptionally good farmer, compared notes with Jefferson, who kept a copy of *Arator* in his library.

Taylor deplored the erosion which was proceeding apace on the new nation's farms and pointed out ways to control it. He advocated contour plowing, deep plowing, a four-field rotation system, restoration of worn-out lands by fencing out grazing animals, and replenishing soil with vegetable organic matter as well as manure. Unfortunately, the majority of farmers ignored his advice.

It is curious that Jefferson's library lacked a copy of Mrs. Martha Logan's *The Gardener's Kalender*, which was published in 1779 after her death at age 77. She was quoted for years as an authority on the subject. Jefferson, who did his best to convert his two daughters into gardeners and who succeeded with his oldest granddaughters, should have been delighted with Mrs. Logan's expertise, not to mention her general abilities. In addition to writing, she sold garden seeds and plants, managed a plantation, and boarded and taught children in her South Carolina home. Another surprising omission in the collection of a man so in love with fruit was William Cox's *A View of the Cultivation of Fruit Trees*, published in Philadelphia in 1817. The first American to write on pomology, the science of fruit cultivation, Cox's book remained unsurpassed for years due to its scope and general excellence.

In addition to books, Jefferson was helped greatly in his development as a horticulturist and farmer by personal friends. One of these was Judge Archibald Stuart, of Staunton, Virginia. Jefferson bought sheep, potatoes and seed for the fine hay-producing grass called timothy from him for years. Dr. George Logan of Philadelphia received favorable mention in a letter Jefferson wrote to his son-in-law, Thomas Mann Randolph, in 1793: "I am availing myself of the time I have to remain here [Philadelphia], to satisfy myself by enquiring from the best farmers of all the circumstances which may decide on the best rotation of crops; for I take that to be the most important of all the questions a farmer has to decide. I get more information on this subject from Dr. Logan than from all the others put together. He is the best farmer in Pensylv^a. both in theory & practice, having pursued it in many years experimentally & with great attention."[33]

Randolph was himself a very knowledgeable farmer and one of the most successful of his day. He was particularly valuable to Jefferson because his land lay adjacent to Monticello. Jefferson was especially impressed with his son-in-law's introduction to the region of horizontal contour plowing, so useful on the hilly land around the Monticello area. As early as 1789, Jefferson had discussed his ideas regarding his mouldboard plow with the young man. In 1808 Randolph invented a hillside plow which threw furrows downhill both coming and going, thereby stemming erosion. This design was probably influenced by Jefferson's thoughts on the subject.

While Jefferson was no doubt fascinated with Randolph's invention, his admiration for the younger man's ability is evident years earlier. It shines through in their correspondence, particularly as it relates to crop rotations and general care of the land. These letters show two equals who had thought long about the subjects and had experimented as well. Randolph was the more successful, mainly because he was usually in residence on his farm. Despite his agricultural and political accomplishments as a member of Congress, the Virginia House of Delegates, and governor of Virginia, Randolph was something of an eccentric. In his later years he became debt ridden because of poor management, causing Jefferson no end of consternation regarding the future of his daughter Martha and her children.[34]

Jefferson wrote to Randolph in 1793: "Judge Peters, an excellent farmer in this neighborhood [Philadelphia], tells me he has taken this method from the President . . ."[35] George Washington's "method" was the notion of growing corn and potatoes together. Richard Peters, a lawyer, Revolutionary War veteran, and owner and planter of Belmont (now part of Fairmount Park, Philadelphia), was one of the founders of the Philadelphia Society for the Promotion of Agriculture, and the organization's first president. Along with several other members of the society, Peters established several farms in various parts of Pennsylvania where "all foreign and domestic trees, shrubs, plants, seeds, or grains may be cultivated and, if approved as useful, disseminated." Peters' *Agricultural Enquiries on Plaster of Paris* was in Jefferson's library.

Washington was also an excellent and enthusiastic farmer and forward-looking horticulturist. Jefferson greatly valued the experience of the older man. The two must have exchanged ideas and information many times in person as well as by letter. The agricultural careers of the two men are remarkably similar perhaps because they shared an intense love for the land, particularly their own. As with Jefferson, no theme appears more frequently in Washington's writings.[36] Washington extolled the virtues of manure, (animal, marl, and green crops), and crop rotations. He delighted in experimenting with different plants and methods of growing them. Due to an increasing shortage of trees, Washington pursued the use of live hedges for fences. He also sought better farm machinery. In short, Jefferson found considerable inspiration from his President to challenge conventional farming practice.

Washington was more fortunate as a farmer than Jefferson. He lived during those years when wheat from America was essential to Europe's economy. Wheat exports dropped dramatically from the time of his death in 1799 to that of Jefferson's in 1826. Tobacco, upon which Jefferson was so dependent, experienced a similar decline.

Another founding father, James Madison, also served as a gardening and farming confidant. His correspondence with Jefferson covers a span of more than 30 years, and the two were frequent visitors to each other's estates. Madison's 5000-acre plantation at Montpelier, beautifully landscaped by its owner, was devoted to grains and tobacco. His agricultural practices were far ahead of his time and they won national attention. With his republican beliefs, Madison, like Jefferson, did not quite know how to deal with the delicate philosophical problem his slaves presented, especially because they were necessary to his plantation. Madison, however, stepped out ahead of his illustrious peers by warning that human life might be wiped out as humans upset the balance of nature by destroying even invisible organisms. Despite his agricultural and political skills, Madison endured financial disaster. Like Jefferson and Washington, his house was always full of guests. He too suffered through the chronic agricultural depression after Washington's death. The loss of $40,000 by a fickle stepson sealed Madison's financial collapse in his old age.

James Monroe, a political protégé of Jefferson's and fifteen years his junior, was also an enthusiastic farmer who depended on his lands. His 3500-acre plantation known as Ashlawn which he held for a time, was adjacent to Monticello. As a progressive farmer he followed the lead of his older friend, turning to grain when his soil fertility declined due to tobacco, and using clover and gypsum to rejuvenate his land. Madison reported that local farmers were amused by such a practice, but finally they had to admit the resulting improved yields were worth it.

Jefferson exchanged agricultural gossip with Monroe, but he did not engage in the serious give-and-take that he shared with men like Logan and Randolph. Monroe, unlike Jefferson, had a consuming interest in politics and was perhaps a comfort in the sense that he fell victim to the same economic and personal forces which destroyed his older friend's financial well-being.

On a more formal level, Jefferson found stimulation in groups such as Franklin's American Philosophical Society. Large landholders through the Revolutionary period seem to have counted it an honor and even a duty to be patrons of horticulture and agriculture. This was a reflection of the intellectual atmosphere of Englishmen and Europeans of the same period. Kings (for example, George III of England), Lords (for example, Lord Townshend) and Ladies (for example Jefferson's friend and La Fayette's aunt, the Comtesse Noailles de Tessé) were among them. Some, of course, were genuinely interested and led agricultural societies and experimentation on both sides of the Atlantic. The two most important of the European societies, at least for Jefferson, were the Board of Agriculture of London, to which he was named an associate in 1798, and the Agricultural Society of Paris, of which he was a member by 1808. Needless to say, membership in both societies was a great honor. This demonstrates that Jefferson was being overly modest when he claimed to be only an amateur and a neophyte in the field.

The American Philosophical Society set the tone for future organizations in the U.S. These societies were not designed for the working farmer, but for well-educated men in law, medicine, politics, commerce, and the clergy, and for whom farming was a secondary occupation and interest. These public spirited men could be expected to understand and appreciate new trends in the field and to promote useful inventions and methods. The English and European traditions of the period regarding agriculture were transferred to this country by such agricultural leaders as Jefferson.

The importance of encouraging such groups was recognized in 1776 by the Continental Congress, which urged each colony to establish "a society for the improvement of agriculture, arts, manufacturers, and commerce," with each group corresponding with the others.[37] The War years were too turbulent and demanding, however, and it was not until later when the first were established, including the Philadelphia Society for Promoting Agriculture and the South Carolina Society for Promoting Agriculture. By 1800 a number of other states had joined the list, while Massachusetts boasted two groups. Jefferson, due to his friendship with Logan and Peters, was in touch with, but apparently not a member of, the Philadelphia organization. Washington was made honorary president and Jefferson honorary vice-president of the South Carolina group. Jefferson provided a steady stream of plants, seeds, and encouragement to the society. By 1811 Jefferson set down on paper his own blueprint for a system of agricultural societies, detailing why they were needed, topics they should explore, and how they should be organized. His efforts in Albemarle County were realized in October 1817. Madison became the society's first president and continued in that role through the remainder of Jefferson's lifetime. [38]

Many of these early groups were short lived. Others were better organized, as can be seen in their publications. Material published by at least some of these societies was fairly extensive, running to five volumes over an eighteen-year span for the Philadelphia Society, ten volumes over thirty-four years for the Boston group, and four volumes over eighteen years for New York's society. Some of these papers were reprinted as pamphlets for wider circulation. There were also competitions with prize money for new and better farming methods and equipment. Jefferson sent an example of his son-in-law's hillside plow to the Philadelphia Society in 1817.

Farm papers did not make their appearance until 1810 with the *Agricultural Museum*, published in the District of Columbia by the Columbia Society. It lasted only two years. However, in 1819 the *American Farmer* began publication in Baltimore, and this survived, with name changes, for more than two decades. Others followed, but like the agricultural societies, they were not written for the typical rural farmer; yet they did serve to keep agricultural leaders informed and provided encouragement for the development of better agriculture.

The emphasis on agricultural education of the country's elite was not challenged until 1807 when Elkanah Watson, a wealthy New Englander, exhibited two Merino sheep at Pittsfield, Massachusetts. These highly bred animals were recent introductions from Spain. With an intense interest in improving all the animal stock of his country, Watson also bought a pair of improved swine and an English bull of note. These he promoted to the farmers of his community. By 1810, because of his instigation, his neighbors put on a livestock exhibition. As a result of this successful show, Watson formed the Berkshire Agricultural Society to produce annual fairs.

In the latter 1700s cattle shows had been a practice in England and France. At least one town in Massachusetts had held regular fairs before the Revolution, and others were held elsewhere. It was because of Watson, however, that large numbers of working farmers began to play an active role in improving their agricultural practices. Furthermore, he introduced the custom of including displays of other farm products.

Strangely, within a few years interest lagged in the Berkshire group, so Watson resigned as president. He then devoted his considerable energies to setting up similar groups elsewhere. These emerging organizations were aided by funds allocated by the various states. Unfortunately the concepts and dispersal of information on farming and agricultural competition were ahead of their time. By the Civil War, after tax monies were withdrawn, these county societies collapsed under the reality that farm life was still much the same as it had been for centuries. The idea of formal agricultural schools suffered from a similar conflict between high expectations and what was practical. The first professorship which included agricultural instruction, was established at Columbia University in 1792. Not until 1822 in Maine was a school opened exclusively for this purpose. Jefferson's efforts at the University of Virginia were at the forefront of a movement which culminated in state agricultural schools in the 1850s.

The post–Civil War years became another revolutionary period, during which major inventions of farm equipment began to transform rural life. The other major agricultural problem of how to translate crops and livestock into a cash market would in time be resolved as well. Until they could actually profit from what they raised, few farmers could be expected to be interested in how to improve the plants and animals they grew.

Jefferson was not alone in recognizing what was wrong with American agriculture, but he was certainly one of only a handful who saw that the final answer was not to reap and run. Rather the answer lay in using agricultural methods which repaired the extensive damage already done to fields and maintained soils at a productive level. To this end Jefferson devoted his adult life.

2
Farming for a Living

Jefferson told his friend John Adams in 1796 that he had no ambition to be in government. Even to the office of President of the United States he was indifferent, doing little more than what he had done in the campaign after Washington's retirement. He did not leave home during the entire time and wrote only one political letter. The Jefferson correspondence demonstrates beyond dispute that he served in a political capacity only because he strongly believed he owed such service to his country if he were asked. He himself admitted his temperament required peace and quiet, something politics has never provided. It is a tribute to his abilities that the career in which he took so little interest should be the one for which he is primarily honored. It is also a tribute to his abilities that, despite many years spent in public service, he should accomplish so much in the totally unrelated field of agriculture.

Interest in agriculture was natural; as was the case with most of his peers, Jefferson to survive financially needed the income from his land.[1] This same concern made him an observer of others at home and abroad, especially on his trip through the rural areas of France and Italy.

Of Jefferson's more than 5000 acres of Albemarle land, only about 1200 were in cultivation.[2] The land he inherited from his father and that he purchased was contiguous with the exception of two minor parcels. The main portion was divided by the small Rivanna River with about equal cultivated acreage on either side of the river. Below the river was Monticello and Tufton, which was somewhat more extensive a tract than the section above, which included Lego and Shadwell. As there were no bridges, the river was crossed at the Shadwell ford or Secretary's ford upstream.

The location of his land was not good. The surface soil of this property, although fertile in the beginning, was shallow and underlaid with a clay which plows of the period were unable to break. Rain frequently came in downpours, causing erosion in addition to excessive leaching of nutrients. Jefferson was well aware of the cost to himself. He wrote in 1795, "I imagine we never lost more soil than this summer. It is moderately estimated at a year's rent."[3]

At other times there were periods of drought when plowing could not even be attempted. By the 1790s, after 60 years of farming, Albemarle County was so full of gullies and so lacking in topsoil because of erosion, that the prerequisites for successful agriculture could hardly be found anywhere. Jefferson told Francis Willis in 1796 that "my hills are too rough ever to please the eye, and as yet unreclaimed from the barbarous state in which the slovenly business of tobacco making had left them."[4] To George Washington he added, "It will be the work of years before the eye will find any satisfaction in my fields."[5] Edmund Bacon, his long time and last overseer at Monticello, said of Jefferson's property, "It was not a profitable estate; it was too uneven and hard to work. Mr. Madison's plantation was much the most profitable."[6] Yet James Madison also died a poor man.

Such hilly land needed more careful tillage practices than did flat expanses, yet Jefferson had to work with what he had. Shadwell, his birthplace and the family home, is described as a weather-boarded house; Peter Jefferson was not living in the style for which his wife's family, the Randolphs, was known. This does not reflect on Peter's character or intelligence; indeed he was basically self-educated and dedicated to leading a worthy life. He may have decided to eshew debt, unlike the wealthy planters of his day. But he did not choose land wisely, though when he gained it, land in his area of the country was still fresh and fertility had not been depleted. Furthermore, nothing was known at that time about farming such terrain and soil. Even in Peter's son's and grandsons' days men found it advantageous to pack up, move elsewhere, and wear out yet another tract. Perhaps that is why Peter himself moved west. Perhaps he assumed Thomas would do the same.

The same situation assailed Thomas Jefferson in his holdings in Bedford County, lands his wife had inherited from her father, John Wayles. Once again Jefferson had not chosen the basic tract, which consisted of 4000 acres, 800 of which were cultivated.[7] What kind of planter Wayles was we do not know. His wealth may have been due to his law practice more than to his abilities as an agriculturist. Like so many other large planters, at his death he left an enormous debt, so his wealthy lifestyle had been based more on hope than reality. Jefferson's wife inherited her part of this debt along with the land, soon playing havoc with Jefferson's own finances.[8] Nevertheless, the Bedford property was better suited to farming than was the Albemarle land, especially for growing the tobacco on which Jefferson relied so heavily to pay off his debts. Still Bedford was not without its problems. The land lay a three-day's journey from Monticello. While Jefferson managed the trip with regularity after retiring from the Presidency (at age 66), it became increasingly a burden later.

With the large number of acres under his control and his lengthy absences from Monticello, not to mention Bedford, his abilities as a manager were sorely tried. One might suppose management would be his forte, but it was not. In fact it is not difficult to conclude he did not enjoy this facet of his life. A letter to Washington in June 1793 deals with the subject that plagued Jefferson all his life. Washington had passed along a query from the great English agricultural writer Arthur Young, to which Jefferson was asked to respond. "When I wrote the notes of last year (for Young), I had never before thought of calculating what were the profits of Capital invested in Virginia agriculture,"[9] said Jefferson, who was meticulous in recording the most minute expenditures in his account books, but now saw that something more was necessary to his financial well-being.

"Penny wise, pound foolish." There no doubt are other aphorisms as well to describe farmers who prefer working their fields to keeping their books. Too many neglect to consider whether all the expenditures, the hard work and the most excellent of plans have actually created a profit of sufficient proportions to live beyond a hand-to-mouth existence.

Two other times Jefferson admitted what was the reality of farming. In a 1798 letter to his newly married daughter, Maria, he discusses the need for economy in maintaining a harmonious relationship: "The unprofitable condition of Virginia estates in general, leaves it now next to impossible for the holder of one to avoid ruin. And this condition will continue until some change takes place in the mode of working them. In the meantime, nothing can save us and our children from beggary, but a determination to get a year beforehand, and restrain ourselves vigorously this year to the clear profits of the last. If a debt is once contracted by a farmer, it is never paid but by a sale."[10] Shortly before his death Jefferson wrote to James Monroe that "a Virginia estate managed rigorously well yields a comfortable subsistence to its owner living on it, but nothing more."[11]

In a year (1815) in which he was pursuing new inventions and investigations, he added, "I have found it necessary to put my affairs under the direction of my grandson Jefferson Randolph, my activity being too much declined to take care of them myself."[12] His attention was focused on the completion of Poplar Forest, his Bedford retreat, and plans for the University of Virginia. Fortunately Jeff proved a more capable and interested manager at Monticello than his grandfather and assumed this duty in 1821 for Poplar Forest as well.

The mansion at Poplar Forest in particular points out Jefferson's deficiencies as a manager of his own affairs. Begun in 1806, it served as a sanctuary from the hordes of visitors who descended upon Monticello. It also steadily drained Jefferson's finances and time which could, from a dispassionate view, have been much better applied to the management of his land.

In his early years, Jefferson gained about as much income from his law practice as from his lands. However, when he began his round of public service, his legal income dropped and then disappeared. His overseers often proved incapable, creating disasters on his farms. His income from the various posts he held typically was less than what he spent representing his constituents and his country. His ability to remain unruffled almost to the end, despite his perpetual inability to pay off his debts, can only be attributed to his faith in himself and the favorable response of the land to good practices. In the last years of his life, on the edge of total bankruptcy, he told James Monroe, "To keep a Virginia estate together requires in the owner skill and attention; skill I never had and attention I could not have, and really when I reflect on all circumstances my wonder is that I should have been so long as sixty years in reaching the result to which I am now reduced."[13]

Despite the anxieties he and his family experienced at the end of his long life, we can only applaud his decisions and debate whether he truly lacked skill. Skill in what? Jefferson, of course, meant that he had not made enough money. He had never truly come to grips with the prospects he was leaving to Martha, his surviving daughter, and his numerous grandchildren—he who had inherited so much by way of land and slaves from both his father and his father-in-law.

He had given his plantation of Pantops adjacent to Monticello to his youngest daughter, Maria, at her marriage. She left but one child, Francis, who in Jefferson's will was given the Poplar Forest mansion plus 1074 acres in lieu of Pantops. While he provided 1000 acres of Poplar Forest land to Martha, his older daughter, at her marriage and land to his grandchildren, Anne and Jeff, at their marriages, in the end Martha and her children received only what was left after the patriarch's considerable debts were paid. At least Jefferson died knowing his affairs were in Jeff's dedicated hands. While that young man could not rectify overnight a problem years in the making, he managed to hold the family's fortunes together sufficiently to allow his grandfather to die at Monticello in the bosom of his family and to keep afloat his mother and brothers and sisters who still remained at home.

Jefferson's skills were manifest in a different area than actively managing his plantations and his money. He recognized very clearly that no matter how affluent a society became, its stability still rested on agriculture, on its ability to feed its own people. This, proclaimed Jefferson, could best be achieved with a foundation of small farmers, each attuned to the land and its needs. Because he was more fortunate than most to hold a large acreage, it thereby became his responsibility to experiment, leading the way. He told Madison in 1810, "No sentiment is more acknowledged in the family of Agriculturists than that the few who can afford it should incur the risk and expense of all new improvements and give the benefit freely to the many of more restricted circumstances."[14] To this end he applied his many talents and demonstrated the skills which any farmer, in the final analysis, must practice.

Jefferson mourned his fellow citizens' habit of wearing out a piece of land and moving to "Aliabama." Profit, of course, was the motive for some; merely keeping body and soul together drove the rest to reap and run. Only a handful managed to get rich by farming. Because Jefferson chose to stay instead of run, he paid an enormous penalty. Had his lands been better for agriculture, had he been able to reside at Monticello full time, had he not paid the price of a generous heart by dedicating himself to furthering knowledge in this field, he would still have had to contend with a fundamental fact: Few men in history have managed to live well solely from the soil while at the same time leaving their capital of soil and water intact for generations to come. Only the Chinese and certain other select East Asians have ever managed to maintain their soil and water for significant periods of time, let alone managed to get rich.

Americans and Europeans knew nothing of these Asian successes, only of the achievements of certain people of the Eastern Mediterranean during pre–Christian times through the Roman period and that only because of books. By the 1700s a few Englishmen and Europeans practiced some reasonably good agriculture, but their results were little known and seldom copied. Farmers have always been conservative and until recent years, loath to try new equipment and procedures.

Jefferson's understanding of the necessary requirements for a truly regenerative agriculture failed in only one respect. During his life, had he managed more prudently what income he gained from the law, public service, and farming, his financial plight would have been eased. As it was, he asked of his land to do more than it was capable of. Not to mention the problems of debts incurred through his wife's inheritance plus his own public service, too many people (numerous family members, visitors, hired help, and slaves) were dependent on the capacity of the number of acres he could clear and maintain. Furthermore, he never economized on his lifestyle as a perceived wealthy Southern planter. In preserving the potential of his holdings as much as he could for the benefit of future years and future owners, he paid the penalty of bankrupting himself.

Jefferson was twenty-seven when he moved to Monticello in 1770, after his family home, Shadwell, burned. He had some gardening experience, but until 1767 his life had been that of a student, first at William and Mary and then with George Wythe, studying law. He had married in 1772 and immediately began fathering—and losing—children. After ten years he was a widower who was father and mother to his two surviving daughters, Martha and Maria. At first he was busy building his new house and making some semblance of order on his little mountain top, including establishing his orchards and vegetable garden. From 1775 to the end of 1793 he was in constant public service. From 1784 to 1789 he was out of the country entirely. These absences from home were not helpful to furthering his career as a farmer. Yet Jefferson was well aware that a significant portion of his income came from his land and that it behooved him to learn as much as he could so he could manage it as intelligently as possible.

The turning point came upon his return to America.[15] In September 1790, he explained to President Washington that he was planting his crops in the following sequence: "1. wheat, followed by winter vetch. 2. corn followed by winter vetch. 3. a fallow pease. 4. wheat. 5. 6. 7. three years of clover. A very decisive experiment has banished rye from my rotation. I mix potatoes with my corn, on your plan."[16]

Corn and potatoes were planted in alternate drills four feet apart. The use of field peas or some other legumes along with corn continues among organic gardeners if not farmers. This practice, of course, started with Indians who grew maize precursors and beans in the Mexican highlands. The idea of using clover as a fallow came from Young, who saw that merely allowing the land to be idle and covered by weeds was not enough. It had been recognized for centuries that clover, in some unknown fashion, helped the soil in addition to producing a valuable crop and forming a thick mat important in Virginia where trees and shrubs are quick to reclaim newly abandoned fields.

What motivated Jefferson to plan for crop rotation on his own lands is not clear. Before the great agricultural revolution in England, farmers there relied on a three-year crop rotation of winter grain, a spring crop and a year of fallow. Jethro Tull had pioneered an entirely different system, incorporating forage crops, roots, and non-native grasses. His premise, later shown to be incorrect, was that plants received necessary nutrients from tiny particles of soil. In order to achieve well pulverized soil he devised a system of deep plowing with crops drilled in rows so that cultivators could pass between them.[17] Jefferson was familiar with the latter approach although he never tried it. He did incorporate Tull's thinking about crop rotations and deep plowing. He may have seen both practices while abroad.

Young began his experiments in about 1763, but Jefferson apparently learned of them only through correspondence and Young's books. Young had been an unknown even to Washington until 1785, when the latter had written George William Fairfax to help him find a farm manager in England whose talents must include creating green manures. Young, who read the letter, then began a correspondence with Washington which lasted many years and would deeply influence both Washington and Jefferson.[18]

Edmund Ruffin (1794–1865) gives a description of the methods Jefferson would have seen at home:

> If not rich enough for tobacco when first cleared, (or as soon as it ceased to be so,) land of its kind was planted in corn two or three years in succession, and afterwards every second year. The intermediate year between the crops of corn, the field was "rested" under a crop of wheat, if it would produce four or five bushels to the acre. If the sandiness or exhausted condition of the soil, denied even this small product of wheat, that crop was probably not attempted — and instead of it, the field was exposed to close grazing, from the time of gathering one crop of corn, to that of preparing to plant another. No manure was applied, except on the tobacco lots; and this rotation of a grain crop every year, and afterwards every second year, was kept up as long as the field would produce five bushels of corn to the acre. When reduced below that product, and to less than the necessary expense of cultivation, the land was turned out to recover under a new growth of pines. After twenty or thirty years, according to the convenience of the owner, the same land would be again cleared, and put under similar scourging tillage.[19]

The Washington connection seems to be the real key to Jefferson's conversion to a more scientific crop rotation, for he followed his 1790 letter with a visit to Mount Vernon in 1792 to discuss the matter in person with the President. In June 1973 he wrote Washington, answering further queries of Arthur Young about farming in Virginia:

> My object was to state the produce of a *good* farm, under *good* husbandry as practiced in my part of the country. Manure does not enter into this, because we can buy an acre of new land cheaper than we can manure an old acre. Good husbandry with us consists in abandoning Indian corn and tobacco, tending small grain, some red clover following, and endeavoring to have, while the lands are at rest, a spontaneous cover of white clover. I do not present this as a culture judicious in itself, but as *good* in comparison with what most people there pursue. Mr. Young has never had an opportunity of seeing how slowly the

fertility of the *original soil* is exhausted. With moderate management of it, I can affirm that the James river lowgrounds with the cultivation of small grain, will never be exhausted; because we known that under the cultivation we must now and then take them down with Indian corn, or they become, as they were originally, too rich to bring wheat. The highlands, where I live have been cultivated about sixty years. The culture was tobacco and Indian corn as long as they would bring enough to pay labor. Then they were turned out. After four or five years rest they would bring good corn again, and in double that time perhaps good tobacco. Then they would be exhausted by a second series of tobacco and corn. Latterly we have begun to cultivate small grain; and excluding Indian corn, and following, such of them as were originally good, soon rise up fifteen or twenty bushels the acre.[20]

The day following this letter he wrote Madison, providing in an elegant chart an eight-year rotation for eight fields. His plan: year one, wheat with a fall fallow; year two, peas and corn, the peas in the sections of the row not strong enough for corn; year three, wheat with a fall fallow; year four, potatoes with corn; year five, rye with a fall fallow; year six, seven, and eight, clover. By staggering the sequence in the fields he expected to get each year two of wheat, one of peas and corn, one of rye, one of potatoes and corn plus three cuttings from the clover. He concluded, "As you are now immersed in farming & among farming people, pray consider this plan for me, well, and give me your observations fully & freely as soon as you can. I mean to ask the same from the President and also from my son in law. Cattle to be raised in proportion to the provision made for them. Also what number of labourers & horses will be necessary? Errors are so much more easy to avoid than to correct afterwards that I am anxious to be well advised before I begin."[21] There is no record of Madison's response.

Jefferson wrote Thomas Mann Randolph outlining the same plans the day Jefferson made this disclaimer to his son-in-law: "I am too little familiar with the practice of farming to rely with confidence on my own judgement."[22] As he explained to his daughter Martha several days earlier: "My head has been so full of farming since I have found it necessary to prepare a place for my manager, that I could not resist the addressing my last weekly letters to Mr. randolph and boring him with my plans."[23] He got a detailed response from his son-in-law which undoubtedly gratified him.

To George Logan he wrote in the same year, "Having engaged a good farmer to go and put one of his plantations in Virginia into a regular course of farming & being about to give him his plans, he takes the liberty of submitting it to Dr. Logan, in whose experience & judgement he has great confidence. He begs him to favor him with his observations on it, freely &

as fully in writing as his leisure will permit. He is himself but a tyro in agriculture, and it being of great importance to set out right in plans *de longue haleine*, he hopes it will be his excuse with Dr. Logan for the trouble he gives him."[24]

Jefferson pondered the results to his requests for information and with his usual panache began to tackle the problems of the practical farmer, resolved to break once and for all the long cycle of destroying the soil.

Jefferson had long been looking forward to retirement from public office. He had spent almost seven years abroad prior to assuming the position as Washington's secretary of state, a post he held from 1790 to 1793. Despite Washington's protests, by the end of 1793 Jefferson was determined to return to private life. Although he had not fought on the battlefield during the Revolutionary War, he had hardly shirked his duty to the fledgling nation. His expertise as a lawyer, a political theorist, a writer and a leader among men who in their own right were leaders, would have been wasted against British soldiers since he had no soldiering skills. More importantly, he had no private fortune to fall back on. He needed the income from his estates for current expenses and payment on past debts. Fortunately for his happiness he was addicted to growing plants.

After resigning as secretary of state, he hurried home to repair the increasing evidence of neglect at Monticello. As he wrote Washington in May 1794: "I find on a more minute examination of my lands than the short visits heretofore made to them permitted, that a ten years' abandonment of them to the ravages of overseers, has brought on them a degree of degradation far beyond what I had expected."[25]

His long pondered paper plan for crop rotation became a casualty to reality. His letter to Washington continued: "As this obliges me to adopt a milder course of cropping, so I find that they have enabled me to do it, by having opened a great deal of lands during my absence. I have therefore determined a division of my farm into six fields, to be put under this rotation: first year, wheat; second, corn, potatoes, peas; third, rye or wheat, according to circumstances; fourth & fifth, clover where the fields will bring it, and buckwheat dressings where they will not; sixth, folding, and buckwheat dressings. But it will take me from three to six years to get this plan underway."[26]

However, a plan outlined to John Taylor in December of the same year varies, as does one to James Monroe the spring of 1795. It is difficult to tell from Jefferson's writings which of the plans outlined were actually accomplished. In any event, it is obvious he recognized the necessity of abandoning a one-crop, tobacco or corn, culture even at Bedford, where he put in his first wheat crop by 1792.

It was fortunate his spirits were high. He wrote Ferdinando Fairfax in April 1794: "I have returned to farming with an ardour which I scarcely knew in my youth, and which has entirely taken the lead of my love of study. I indulge it because I think it will be more productive of health, profit, & the happiness depending on these, and perhaps of some utility to my neighbors, by taking on myself the risk of a first experiment of that sort of reformation in our system of farming, which surcharges the progressive depredation of our lands calls for imperiously."[27]

Still he had always to keep in mind his own need to keep his short-term solvency. Most of the products of his farms were used by his family, hired help and slaves. Prices of wheat and tobacco, his two cash crops, varied. His only other cash came from rent from his leased farms, his mill and his nailery. None of them were reliable sources. In fact, he wrote in 1809 that his nails had never commanded money, although this is perhaps an overstatement. The mill, which cost Jefferson over $10,000, proved a financial liability in the long run, nor was he able to make a tenant system work to his financial advantage.

During 1794 Jefferson kept a detailed dairy in his *Farm Book* about his agricultural activities. From its entries one must wonder how he found time for his other major projects. In 1794 he had begun remodeling his house (a project which was not completed for many years). He was busy rebuilding his vegetable garden and orchards and improving his landscaping. He had also begun his nailery. He notes to several correspondents with evident glee, "I live on my horse from an early breakfast to a late dinner & very often after that till dark."[28]

Obstacles to his success as a farmer remained, despite his enthusiasm and his presence at home. The first entry for 1795 in the *Farm Book* begins, "The fall of 1794. had been fine, yet little ploughing was done, partly from the want of horses, partly neglect in the overseers, & a three months confinement by sickness in myself, vis from Sep. 1. to the latter end of Nov."[29]

This is typical; despite all of his careful calculations of what should occur, in real life something untoward frequently intervened. Any active farmer or gardener will recognize both Jefferson's hopes and his frustrations. Yet, despite all this activity in 1794, he found time to carry out scientific experiments with seed germination.

Jefferson was in fact thoroughly enjoying himself, as indicated in a 1795 letter to William B. Giles: "If you visit me as a farmer, it must be as a condisciple: for I am but a learner; an eager one indeed, but yet desperate, being too old now to learn a new art. However, I am as much delighted and occupied with it, as if I was the greatest adept. I shall talk with you about it from morning till night, and put you on a very short allowance as to political aliment. Now and then a pious ejaculation for the French and Dutch republicans, returning with due dispatch to clover, potatoes, wheat, etc."[30]

The year 1795 saw more letters between Jefferson and his correspondents regarding agriculture, especially crop rotation. There are several undated plans for crop rotations which seem to be from this period. Crop rotation was also considered a tenant responsibility. In the *Farm Book* under a section entitled "Tenants" he writes: "Tie them up to some rotation of crops which shall include ameliorating years to counterbalance at least the exhausting ones."[31] Records confirm that he followed that plan on at least two occasions.

He also had very specific ideas about overseers. As a largely absentee owner he depended on his overseers. As early as 1773 he drew up a set of guidelines for himself regarding duties of overseers, as well as his obligations to them. While he was abroad he had arranged with Nicholas Lewis, an Albemarle neighbor, and Francis Eppes, his brother-in-law who lived in Chesterfield County, to supervise his affairs, but this was of limited help.

Managing such a large number of acres designated for crops, plus the numbers of slaves, free laborers, and farm animals that went with them and the personal gardening ventures of the owner, required a level of intelligence, knowledge, and dedication rare in any age. This was especially true in a country where a competent enterprising man could so easily acquire land and position on his own, something Edmund Bacon, Jefferson's last overseer at Monticello, did with considerable success.

As with so many things agricultural, time is needed to see results. Jefferson, no doubt, started 1796 in high hopes. His situation was well described by a visitor to Monticello, the Duke de la Rochefoucauld-Liancourt of France. The Frenchman describes in some detail the farming practices he saw and comments, "His system is entirely confined to himself; it is censured by some of his neighbors, who are also employed in improving their culture with ability and skill, but he adheres to it, and thinks it founded on just observations." He had found Jefferson "in the midst of the harvest, from which the scorching heat of the sun does not prevent his attendance."[32]

Jefferson was able to boast to James Monroe in July of 1796, "We have had the finest harvest ever known in this part of the country. Both the quantity and quality of wheat are extraordinary."[33] He was also able to take satisfaction with the performance at Monticello of his invention of a "mould-board of least resistance." Such farm tools were important for his success. Seeing the need, he added another venture to his crowded schedule. Using a threshing machine of Scottish invention as a model, he built one for his own requirements, first harvesting a crop successfully with it in 1796.

Then his happy world of rebuilding home, gardens, orchards, and farms fell apart. On November 4, 1796, he was elected vice-president of the United States. He had certainly not sought the job, but his countrymen had called him to duty. As an indication of how strongly he felt about putting the public's interest above his own, we need only know he made the journey to Philadelphia to be sworn in, a ceremony which could have been performed at Monticello. That was no small sacrifice, for travel conditions could be rough in February. He left February 20. The weather did not cooperate, and it took ten days of hard travel. Under the best of conditions the trip took a week.

As vice-president and then President from 1797 to early 1809, Jefferson was able to get home occasionally. It became easier when the government seat moved from Philadelphia to Washington, D.C., in 1800. Needless to say, Jefferson rejoiced in not wasting extra days on the road. Even so, what time he could spend at Monticello, was not conducive to a sustained effort of keeping to his plans for the improvement of his fields, particularly when his attention was diverted by other projects. These included renovations to his house, a constant process, the expansion of his vegetable gardens and orchards, landscaping, and later the laying out of flower beds and building the new house in Bedford County. As vice-president he was able to be at Monticello for some six months of the year for three years and over nine months the fourth. However, in two of these years he missed the spring deluge of activities completely and during the other two years he could not be home for all of this busiest of seasons. During his eight years as President, he was at Monticello for only a month in spring and two months in late summer and early fall. Thus in many respects he may as well have been an absentee owner.

Despite these long periods from home and under the press of governmental activities, Jefferson remained concerned about the status of his fields. With the constant drain on his finances that public service caused, he could not afford to forget the land's health. After 1796, however, due to the pressures on his time, his records are sparse. From notations made it is impossible to pinpoint what was going on at each plantation. Furthermore, as in 1798 for example, in an effort to help his sagging finances, he resorted periodically to growing tobacco because of the high price it was currently bringing. Also to help himself, he sought tenants for some of his lands, especially before he assumed the presidency.

Upon his retirement in early 1809 he found his plantations were not in as deplorable a state as they had been after previous absences, and he was able to proceed without agonizing over the relative virtues of various options. Experience had come to the rescue. His entry for 1809 in the *Farm Book* is a model of brevity.

His experience with crop rotation had been in line with other progressive farmers of the era. Most agreed that different plants placed different demands on soil fertility and that the soil needed to rest before small grain was planted. Northerners more often used bare fallows while Southerners favored planting fallow fields in tillage crops. The specific crop combinations often chosen appear naive today: Broad-leaved and narrow-leaved crops were considered complimentary as were tap-rooted and fibrous-rooted plants.[34] Prominent farmers were often at odds with each other. The eminent John Taylor favored maize over peas, turnips, and potatoes. Jefferson and Washington were equally adamant that maize exhausted the soil. Men were also divided in their opinions about the number of years that should be involved in a rotation. Some farmers considered it enough to plant cowpeas with maize; others alternated this combination with oats or wheat in the odd year. At the other extreme, Washington by 1792 had devised a seven-year rotation at Mount Vernon, while Jefferson and his son-in-law Thomas Mann Randolph went to an eight-year plan. Some gave up on the idea all together. After he had devised a rotation for his brother's land, Jefferson received this response: "[I] am a fraid it will be two great an undertakeng for Me."[35] Even his European colleagues astonished him. In an 1808 letter regarding the proceedings of the Agricultural Society of Paris he said: "I have been surprised to find that the rotation of crops and substitution of some profitable growth preparatory for grain, instead of the useless and expensive fallow, is yet only dawning among them."[36]

From correspondence and entries into the *Account Book*, the *Farm Book* and the *Garden Book*, it is apparent Jefferson's interests shifted or changed emphases over the years. As in the career of any long-time horticulturist and agriculturist, knowledge increases, and certain practices and results become so commonplace they are no longer worthy of recording. In addition, he had no doubt long concluded that being a leader in experimenting with new practices and crops, even demonstrating their superiority did not necessarily mean others would follow his example.

With his own land Jefferson would do his best. He told Martha in 1793, "We will try this winter to cover our garden with a heavy coating of manure. When earth is rich it bids defiance to droughts, yields in abundance, and of the best quality. I suspect that the insects which have harassed you have been encouraged by the feebleness of your plants; and that has been produced by the lean state of the soil. We will attack them another year with joint efforts."[37]

Not only does Jefferson speak in the best organic gardening tradition, but he recognized that his soils needed something more than crop rotation to repair the damage caused by perpetually planting crops of corn and tobacco. Manure, as Jefferson indicated, might be the obvious answer; to an organic gardener today it is. But as has been noted, fences were difficult to build and maintain, and fodder hard to provide, so animals were commonly allowed to graze in fields and woods where the manure was lost for farming. The farmer who wanted manure could help himself most easily by herding in and enclosing his animals for the night or allowing them to graze in crop fields, something Jefferson shunned. A moveable cow house put in the field which needed the dung was another method Jefferson spoke of, a plan apparently never followed.

Thus he had to be content with spot applications of manure in his fields where it was most needed. He seems, however, to have used it unsparingly in his gardens per these instructions to his overseer Edmund Bacon in 1808: "6. waggon loads are first to be laid on the old asparagus bed below the wall, which Wormley must immediately spread even & then fork it in with the three pronged garden fork, taking care not to fork so deep as to reach the crown of the Asparagus roots. Then begin at the S. W. end of the garden, and drop a good waggon load of dung every five yeards along a strait line through the middle of the garden from the S. W. to the N. E. end. This will take between 60. & 70. loads in the whole, which will do for the first year."[38]

Jefferson used manure in all stages of decomposition, from fresh to well rotted. Considering his penchant for noting down everything of interest to him and his love of experimentation, it is surprising that he left no indication of which method he found best. He did, however, note in his *Account Book 1775*: "27 head of cattle convert 65 loads of straw & haulm (besides what they eat of it) into about 300. loads of dung. Horses well littered yeild from 12. to 17. loads of dung per horse. 88. fat hogs converted 5. loads of straw and 4 of stubble into 90 loads of very rotten dung. But they had not litter enough. They would have made 12. or 15. loads into manure. This is much the best of dungs. The above from Young's *rural aeconomy*."[39] His *Farm Book* quotes Arthur Young's experiments regarding the amount of dung produced by folding or fencing in cattle and sheep.

Dr. George Logan, whose skills Jefferson so admired, showed that it took 150 cattle to manure 60 acres a year, a fact Jefferson carefully noted. He proposed for himself in his *Farm Book* an experiment comparing the virtues of dung folded vs. dung spread.

Jefferson was well aware that he grew only enough livestock to supply meat, milk, butter and wool for his plantations. The Duke de la Rouche-foucauld-Liancourt wrote after visiting Monticello in 1796:

> But his land will never be dunged as much as in Europe. Black cattle and pigs, which in our country are either constantly kept on the farm, or at least return thither every evening, and whose dung is carefully gathered and preserved either separate or mixed, according to circumstances, are here left grazing in the woods the whole year round. . . . The quantity of his dung is therefore in proportion to the number of cattle which he can keep with his own fodder, and which he intends to buy at the beginning of winter to sell them again in spring; and the cattle kept in the vicinity of the barns where the forage is housed, will furnish manure only for the adjacent fields.[40]

Jefferson must also have been aware of the debate concerning the best method of applying manure. Should it be plowed under or used as a top dressing? If the latter, should it be applied just at the base of plants or over the entire field? A similar debate centered on compost. In addition to cornstalks, the better farmers used the same materials organic gardeners use today.

Green manures, however, were the most practical method of return-ing fertility to the soil. For centuries plants like clover, alfalfa, beans and peas had been known to improve the soil in some way, although such men as Jefferson and John Taylor who advocated the practice were still consid-ered advanced. Nitrogen itself was not discovered until 1772. Only within the last century have the mechanisms of nitrogen fixation been discovered, involving bacteria contained in root nodules. A knowledge of non-symbiotic fixation of atmospheric nitrogen is similarly recent. Taylor also advanced the idea that rain was the best fertilizer of all and recommended the plowing under of vegetable manures to retain surface moisture. It has since been shown that approximately five pounds of nitrogen per acre enters the soil each year from precipitation. This is in a form readily available to plants, so it is a definite aid in maintaining good plant health.

Englishman William Strickland visited Monticello in 1795. A first-class farmer, he was a member of the Board of Agriculture of London. Jefferson said he had concluded:

> But it is well known here that a space of rest greater or less in spontaneous herbage, will restore the exhaustion of a single crop. This then is a rotation; and as it is not to be believed that spontaneous herbage is the only or best covering during rest, so we may expect that a substitute for it may be found which will yield profitable crops. Such perhaps are clover, peas, vetchs, etc. A rotation then may be found, which by giving time for the slow influence of the atmosphere, will keep the soil in a constant and equal state of fertility. But the advantage of manuring, is that it will do more in one than the atmosphere

would require several years to do, and consequently enables you so much the oftener to take exhausting crops from the soil, a circumstance of importance where there is more labor than land.[41]

While rotation of crops was a fairly straightforward idea, the quality and needs of the soil was more difficult to ascertain. Today farmers rely on soil tests to determine nutrient levels and pH readings. In Jefferson's day observation of plant response was the only indication of soil quality. Unfortunately, factors such as light intensity, temperature, precipitation, diseases, and cultural practices also entered into the equation, masking soil characteristics. This explains the extent of the fumbling shown so well during Jefferson's lifetime to develop a rational approach to agriculture.

Jefferson had grown clover since 1768. That year he bought seed; the following year he was pleased to gather his own. In later years he gathered seed wherever the clover did not grow tall enough for hay, but he always had to buy some seed. How he used the small amounts of clover in the earliest years is not clear, although he must have recognized its value as food for his stock. When he started making hay from it is not clear either. The practice of growing a crop specifically for feeding livestock was still in its infancy.

He got the idea of substituting clover for an unproductive weed fallow from Logan, who, in turn was indebted to Young, who was at the center of the agricultural revolution in England. A clover fallow was planned by Jefferson in 1793. His enthusiasm ran high for this legume from then on, although he recognized its limitations and had found some of his fields too poor to support any variety of it. By 1790 he was planting the English field pea as fallow in the poorest spots. Washington reported at Mount Vernon that where he could manure his land sufficiently he got good crops, but could not make clover succeed by itself as part of a rotation.

Jefferson wrote his son-in-law in 1793: "I had first declined the introduction of red clover into my rotation because it lengthens it so much: but I have determined now to take it in, because I see it the source of such wonderful richness around this place, and for a Virginia table it will certainly give unbounded plenty of meats, milk, butter, horse-food, instead of being eternally on the scramble for them as we are in Virginia for want of winter & summer food"[42] He was also very concerned about keeping his lands covered at all times so the red clay would not be baked by Virginia's hot summer sun. Clover provided such cover.

Jefferson included clover in all his crop rotations, sometimes three years running, other times two years, followed by a fallow. When he later leased land, use of clover was written into the contract with his tenants. In addition to clover, he also experimented with peas, buckwheat, and winter vetch, while Washington tried Eastern Shore bean and buckwheat. Others used lower grades of tobacco as a green manure. It was obviously not clear what made certain plants better than others for improving the soil. Animal manure was long known to be beneficial. Somewhat later bones, blood, and other animal parts were all tried as fertilizers. The use of salt to nourish plants indicates beyond doubt the prevailing uncertainties of the chemistry involved.[43]

Taylor extended the concept of manures to include such minerals as gypsum, lime, and marl, which he advocated in combination with animal manures. Without the manure, he said, they were only stimulants. How much he was influenced by John A. Binns of Loudon County is hard to say. Jefferson credited Binns for his own enthusiasm for gypsum in his earliest correspondence on the subject. Strangely, by 1816 he was giving his friend, Judge Peters, credit, saying "we are indebted to you for much of our knowledge as to the use of the plaister, which is become a principal article of our improvements, no soil profiting more from it than that of the country around this place. The return of peace will enable us now to resume its use."[44]

Binns first used gypsum in 1784 and after nineteen years of testing on his own farm he published a *Treatise on Practical Farming* in 1803 promoting gypsum, clover, and deep plowing. Jefferson was an immediate convert, sending copies of the publication to both his sons-in-law and to John Sinclair and William Strickland in England.

Binns was a most unusual farmer. Unlike others, Jefferson wrote Sinclair, the "very unlettered" man ". . . began poor, and has made himself tolerably rich by his farming alone. . . . The county of Loudon, in which he lives, had been so exhausted and wasted by bad husbandry that it began to depopulate, the inhabitants going southwardly in quest of better lands. Binns' success has stopped that emigration. It is now becoming one of the most productive counties of the State of Virginia, and the price given for the lands is multiplied manifold."[45] Sinclair responded that gypsum was not efficacious everywhere for, "it is singular, that whilst it proves such a source of fertility with you, it is of little avail, in any part of the British Islands, Kent alone excepted. I am thence inclined to conjecture, that its great advantage must arise from its attracting moisture from the atmosphere, of which we have in general abundance in these Kingdoms, without the intervention of that agent; and the benefit which has been found from the use of this article in Kent, (one of the dryest Counties in England) tends to countenance this hypothesis."[46]

Unlike manure, gypsum had to be hauled some distance. Until 1815 it had been secured primarily from Nova Scotia. Demand, however, was sufficient to encourage the opening of mines in western New York and along the Hudson River. Farmers were willing to haul sleigh loads from the quarries up to eighty miles in the winter. Gypsum was also shipped down the Hudson and Susquehanna Rivers. Jefferson's first order was in 1810 for six tons from a dealer in Baltimore. He had tried Richmond, but none was to be had there. His last order was made just months before he died.

Jefferson bought gypsum in lumps and ground it at Monticello in his own mills. He ground for neighbors as well, but as he used the same mill stones to grind grain, his bread customers, as he called them, eventually refused his services for that purpose because of the alleged damage the gypsum did to the stones. Perhaps these complaints were what prompted him in 1811 to request advice from a mill owner he had visited outside of Washington on the best method of grinding small amounts of gypsum for toll. He may also have been prompted by a desire to increase the use of gypsum among his neighbors. Always on the lookout for sources of cash income, he undoubtedly considered such a mill worthy of his attention for that reason alone. By 1818 he managed to begin a canal to carry water from the river to the proposed site, and he began construction of the mill itself, but there is no record that either was ever completed.

Getting gypsum to Bedford was even more costly. In 1815 Jefferson asked his Bedford overseer, Joel Yancy, to see if there was a local mill to grind the lumps, because to grind and barrel the gypsum at Monticello added to transportation costs. The following year he wrote the overseer that the cost of transportation was too high to consider buying the mineral for Bedford. By 1819, in yet another letter to Yancy, he proposed that the overseer begin building a dam and canal for a mill. This apparently was never done. However, the determination of a seventy-four-year-old man to pursue the right course of action must be admired. He told Yancy that "straw will do something, good manure more, but nothing short of plaister and clover can recruit our extensive fields. The miracles this is working in this neighborhood can be believed only by those who see them."[47]

Gypsum, for all of Jefferson's enthusiasm for it, was not the entire answer to the problem, as Sinclair's letter indicates. Some American farmers complained that on sandy and gravel soils its effects seemed to diminish after several years of good results. Farmers who were disappointed were apt to apply gypsum to crops other than clover. Nonetheless it is easy to understand why these men were confused. Much later it was found that gypsum's sulphur content tends to make soil acid. As most eastern soils are naturally on the acid end of the pH scale, the use of gypsum was self-defeating in this respect. However, when soils are sufficiently neutral, gypsum helps liberate potash for plant use and conserves the nitrogen in rapidly decaying organic matter. Jefferson would have been fascinated with the results of recent research. Two University of Georgia agronomists have found that, especially in the Southeast, gypsum supplies calcium to lower soil levels, detoxifies aluminum, seems to soften hardpan, and dramatically increases water absorption.

Lime soon supplanted gypsum before Jefferson died. Lime had been tried before the Revolution and was introduced to lower Virginia as early as 1794. It was not until Edmund Ruffin championed it, though, that lime was found to do what Jefferson had foreseen was necessary. Ruffin, after serving in the War of 1812, set out to repair his worn-out lands on the James River with vegetable manures as recommended by Taylor. Confronted with disappointing results, he explored an idea he found in the English chemist Sir Humphrey Davy's *Agricultural Chemistry* that soil acidity was the reason for his poor results and that lime was the answer. His careful analysis of the lime content of different marl deposits, of the effects of marl applied alone and in conjunction with various manures, and the cost effectiveness of its use were unusual for his time. In 1821 Ruffin reported the results of his experiments to the Prince George County Agriculture Society and in the *American Farmer*. As a tireless advocate of lime, along with other beneficial practices, he soon became the most influential leader in Southern agriculture and one of the greatest America has produced.

It is strange that his fellow Virginian, Jefferson, with his extensive grapevine of informants, does not seem to have considered switching from gypsum to lime. It is ironic that he should have missed this opportunity to experiment with it as he owned a plantation called Limestone on the Hardware River in Albemarle County, from which he quarried limestone for building purposes.

3

Crops Jefferson Grew

During the Colonial period in Virginia and Maryland there was really only one agricultural crop: tobacco. The men who settled the Tidewater quickly found the leaf not only grew well there but brought large profits abroad. It was a way to wealth which simply could not be duplicated by any other cultivated plant.

In these colonies the typical plantation was extensive and not infrequently included land in more than one location. Total acreage ran into the thousands (and even to 100,000 acres), which worked against the development of towns and cities. Many estates south of Virginia's Rappahannock River ranged from 8000 to 20,000 acres in the early 1700s. Soon grants of 2000 to 40,000 became common, most sought by men who were merely adding to their home plantation. Thomas Jefferson's father, Peter, his father-in-law John Wayles, and he himself all owned more than one tract each.

Land was acquired by headrights (government grants to settlers), by other types of government grants, and by outright purchase.[1] As tobacco culture was so labor intensive and profitable per acre, a planter needed comparatively little land under cultivation in any one year to produce a living. However, tobacco is also very destructive of soil fertility.[2] Given the scanty knowledge of soils and fertilizers available to remedy this situation and the cheapness of land, it was easier to open fresh plots than to find the answers to continued production on the same tract.

In the earlier years of the colonies it was considered ideal to have one overseer for every twenty slaves with each slave farming forty to fifty acres. While each worker could tend only five acres per year, the excess acreage took into consideration that each tract could be cultivated only three to four years before exhaustion. After a twenty-year cycle the slave could return to the first plot, which was now considered "rested." But such extravagance of alluvial land in the Tidewater could be indulged in only until the mid-1700s when a mere ten or twenty acres was commonly available for each worker. Production also declined since the soil could not fully regain its former fertility. Thus each planter held the bulk of his plantation acreage in reserve for future crops. Such slash and burn agriculture in time had to come to an end under increased population pressure. Ultimately, the tobacco market plunged, partly because fresh lands were being opened in the West.

Jefferson understood the value of his land. He wrote in 1787, while abroad, "I am decided against selling my lands. They are the only sure provision for my children, and I have sold too much of them already."[3] In 1796 he said that "for of all things it [land] is that of which I am most tenacious."[4]

Considering the nature of the work involved, the frequently scattered locations of the tobacco fields, and the fact the plantation owner was likely to also serve in politics or the professions, the use of overseers became inevitable. These men usually worked for a share of the crop. This would seem to encourage use of good conservation and cultural methods. Unfortunately, overseers were seldom among the most responsible and intelligent of farmers, and few stayed with any one planter for more than one year. Jefferson was not immune to the problems associated with using overseers. Inevitably they sought to extract immediate wealth. Meanwhile, before the Revolution the planter himself was able to enrich himself well beyond all expectations had he remained in England.[5]

Tobacco planters in the Colonial period also labored under subservience to British needs. England, after all, did not go through the exercise of setting up colonies out of the altruistic desire to form new nations which would compete with herself. Regulations by both the English and colonial governments changed over the years. When restrictions were particularly burdensome, planters retaliated by opening only their best fields. Increased competition from European growers complicated the efforts of English and Americans. While we may not be too concerned over the financial fortunes of these individuals, we must, like Jefferson, be very much concerned with the consequences to the soil. Even before his death, between the devastating effects of growing tobacco, maize, and soon cotton as well, the South would become forever the poorest region of the U.S.

English merchant traders exploited the new opportunities presented by the colonies. Colonists, whose role in life was to provide raw materials for British manufacture, were forced to buy finished goods from England because American production was confined to the individual home. The farmer was caught between his legitimate expenses and prices that were set by someone who cared nothing about the costs involved to the producer. Although as a group the English merchants were unfairly characterized as villains for the misdeeds of a few, Jefferson followed the custom of his peers by blaming these traders for much of his financial trouble.

The following scene from Maryland was repeated in Virginia as well. The English traveler Isaac Weld in the later 1790s reported:

> The country is flat and sandy, and wears a most dreary aspect. Nothing is to be seen for miles together, but extensive plains, that have been worn out by the culture of tobacco, overgrown with yellow sedge, and interspersed with groves of pine and cedar trees. . . . In the midst of these plains are the remains of several good houses which shew that the country was once very different from what it is now. These houses . . . have now been suffered to go to decay, as the land around them is worn out, and the people find it more to their interest to remove to another part of the country, and clear a piece of rich land, than to attempt to reclaim these exhausted plains. In consequence of this, the country in many of the lower parts of Maryland appears as if it had been deserted by one half of its inhabitants.[6]

The Englishman William Strickland, after his tour in the same period, concluded Virginia had reached "the lowest state of degredation" agriculturally, and Maryland was little better. Travelers in the first two decades of the 1800s were equally uncomplimentary. Only in a few counties in Virginia and Maryland were farms less damaged. Wheat, clover, gypsum, and deeper plowing coupled with a serviceable transportation system were responsible for these rare counties, but even there not all land was fertile. Jefferson's Albemarle, to a large extent due to his efforts, was one of these fortunate areas. Even there Monticello was an oasis.

As population increased and shifted ever westward and southward, to a great extent in response to worn out soils, especially in the Tidewater, both Virginia and Maryland suffered a severe drain of their youngest and hardiest men. As for the land itself, it was estimated at the Virginia Convention of 1829 that the land values of the state had declined from $206 million in 1817 to $90 million in 1829. Jefferson, who died in 1826, was sorely tried by this remarkable devaluation in the years prior to his death when he attempted to rescue his failing fortunes by selling property. His heirs were similarly thwarted when called upon to eliminate the family debts.

After the Revolution in the Piedmont where tobacco was grown, it became only one of two or more crops. Even such a man as Jefferson, who relied on the leaf from his Bedford County estate to pay off his debts, grew considerable quantities of wheat there as well. However, the vacillations of foreign markets for grain were an impediment to a more sensible agriculture. The pre–Independence tobacco marketing system, the only one which had developed in Virginia and Maryland was still available for all who needed quick cash. The profit on a hogshead might be lower than a planter needed to repay his debts, yet it was a source of cash in an era when cash was hard to come by. Not until urban areas grew larger, rivers were cleared, canals opened, and roads, bridges, and railroads built and maintained, could farm products efficiently and economically be united with people who had both the need and cash for them.

By 1781 Jefferson had already concluded that for Virginians wheat was the superior crop. Yet he was descended from tobacco growers and was one himself. As for his peers, in the days before the Revolutionary War, "tobacco planter" and "gentleman" were synonymous. Growing the leaf for sale identified a man's status in life, although it often locked that man into debt.

Jefferson's life-long financial predicament was due mainly to what he termed "the great Wayles debt." His father-in-law John Wayles had left a deficit of £4000, as well as land and slaves to his daughter. Her part of the debt, an indeterminate share of the whole, was one of the largest in Virginia at the time of Wayles' death.[7] This debt appears to have been the result of inconsistent profits on tobacco and a taste for high living based on British fashions and subsequent indebtedness to British claimants. The same deadly combination brought down many other Tidewater planters. To a French correspondent Jefferson explained in 1786, "These debts had become hereditary from father to son for many generations, so that the planters were a species of property annexed to certain merchanthouses in London."[8]

Tobacco was first planted by the white man in Santo Domingo in 1531, in Cuba in 1580, and in Brazil in 1600. This was *Nicotiana tobacum*, native to South America, Mexico and the West Indies. *N. rustica* was the species cultivated by Indians east of the Mississippi and some parts of southeastern United States and northern Mexico. It was a low plant, described as being of "byting taste." John Rolfe of Jamestown understood that the poor quality of this Virginia tobacco lay with the species, not its cultivation or curing. It was he who began experimenting in 1612 with seeds of tobacco from the West Indies and Venezuela, the Oronoco and sweet-scented varieties of *N. tobacum*. In two years time he exported four barrels of his crop to England, the first tobacco from the colony, saying that "after a little more triall and expense in the curing thereof, it will compare with the best in the West Indies."[9]

Once the cultivation procedure was learned and demand abroad was established, tobacco quickly became the Virginia crop of choice. To raise cash the dirt poor farmer not infrequently planted it to the exclusion of crops which could feed his family. The owner of a large plantation devoted to nothing but the leaf could live in luxury or at least appear rich, for indebtedness remained a perpetual problem. In Virginia today tobacco is still the state's largest cash crop, accounting for 10 percent of the state's total agricultural income.

When wars disrupted the trade, Americans suffered accordingly. In the early years there was also concern by purchasers about the physiological effects of tobacco consumption. Tobacco had been used by the Indians for its medicinal qualities in addition to ceremonial purposes. While it had been introduced to Europeans as a curiosity soon after the discovery of America, it was soon touted for its alleged curative powers. Until the 1800s it was used as a cure-all for everything from blood poisoning to rheumatism, from toothache to indigestion. In an era when medicines came out of the kitchen garden, tobacco was a welcome addition to a slender arsenal. Snuff, cigar, and pipe tobacco only gradually came to consume a larger part of the crop.

By 1790 tobacco ranked first in American exports, with a value in excess of $4 million. This was possible at this late date only because of the new lands brought into production to the west and south of Tidewater Virginia and Maryland.

In a social environment in which a man was measured by the quality of the tobacco he grew, even though plantations were being ruined by the mid-1700s, it took courage to switch to another crop. The years after the French and Indian War (1758–59) saw a few Tidewater planters attempt without enthusiasm to break the dependency on tobacco. Hemp and indigo were tried, but without the success needed to pay for a lavish lifestyle. Tidewater planters mostly remained with tobacco until mounting debts compelled a switch to wheat. Edmund Ruffin wrote some years after the fact that it was not until after the War of 1812 that tobacco was no longer grown in the Tidewater.

This tug of war between conflicting needs on both sides of the Atlantic would go on for years. Ultimately domestic consumption of tobacco took an ever larger share of the American crop. At the same time European growers supplied more and more European demands.

As inroads into the wilderness were made, it was found tobacco could not be grown in all soils. Some, like those in Bedford County, supported it better than did those, for example, of Albemarle. Only trial and error determined which soils would support the precious crop.

Colonists had recognized two major types of tobacco varieties as mentioned, and by Jefferson's day no others had been added to the roster.

The Oronoko (a corruption of the South American name "Orinoko") grew best in the rich, heavy soils of low-lying alluvial land adjacent to rivers, and the sweet-scented variety preferred sandy loams.[10] Jefferson apparently grew both kinds. The dissimilarities of soil were considered partly responsible for the differences between the two. The differences were not great; the Oronoko had a longer, more pointed leaf, while the sweet-scented had a milder flavor. Although Jefferson thought the two types were very distinct from each other, by the end of the 1700s tobacco inspectors, who found such classification beyond their capabilities, were apt to label all tobacco as Oronoko.[11]

Growing tobacco on a large scale was not an easy task. No less a determined person than George Washington failed to master the technique, much to his everlasting embarrassment. However, an 1801 letter from Jefferson to Thomas Mann Randolph indicates that Jefferson grew tobacco better than he modestly admitted:

> I promised to procure for the Chevalier de Freire minister of Portugal an account of our manner of cultivating tobacco so detailed as that a person might, by it's instruction, puruse the culture with exactness. I always intended to have got two or three judicious planters to state to me their methods, which I should have noted down, and out of the whole have made out one. I now see that it will not be in my power to do this; and yet if I fail it will be ascribed to jealously or illiberality. I must therefore pray you to pay this debt for me. It will be more easy for you as you possess the subject within yourself which I did not. The principal division of the kinds into Sweet scented & Oroonoke, with only a partial specification of the principal varieties & their qualities will be sufficient.[12]

This request is particularly strange because Jefferson provided detailed instructions regarding tobacco culture for the Dutchman G. K. van Hogendorp in 1784.[13] Deep in the first years of his Presidency, Jefferson may not have had time. He was more likely attempting to boost the ever fragile self-esteem of his son-in-law.

John Taylor of Caroline in his *Arator* provides this mini-sketch of what was involved in growing this crop: "It would startle even an older planter to see an exact account of the labour devoured by an acre of tobacco, and the preparation of the crop for market. . . . He would be astonished to discover how often he had passed over the land, and the tobacco through his hands, in fallowing, hilling, cutting off hills, planting and replanting, toppings, succerings, weedings, cuttings, picking up, removing out of the ground by hand, hanging, striking, stripping, stemming, and prizing."[14]

Planters, not surprisingly, talked tobacco whenever they met. As much of the process of growing the crop was dependent on intuition based on experience, each gentleman had his own point-of-view. Jefferson could hardly have been unaware of this. Thus it is difficult to believe he really felt incompetent regarding a crop upon which his lifestyle literally depended. One wonders if his father felt knowledgeable when he gambled his fortunes in Albemarle. Peter's luck held, however, for by the mid-1700s Albemarle joined the counties of Goochland, Orange, Hanover, and Culpepper in sending large numbers of hogsheads to Richmond. Thomas in his turn, while plagued with Albemarle soils long worn out because of tobacco, was favored by the Bedford soils even more suited to the leaf. However, with this estate ninety miles from Monticello, he had to rely heavily on his overseers.[15] The record of his visits to his Goochland and Cumberland County properties is so sketchy it is obvious Jefferson was dependent on his overseers there even more than at Poplar Forest.

Jefferson began growing tobacco in 1768, when 9787 pounds were harvested at Monticello. As the crop was made on shares, he realized only 8060 pounds. He would work on shares in the future. At Albemarle he never got totally away from tobacco except briefly, though it was the crop from Poplar Forest that rescued him from his debts. At Poplar Forest he recorded thirty-five hogsheads in 1774, his first crop from his new Bedford property. The following year the number dropped to twenty-six. From 1799 to 1824 the figures varied from twenty to twenty-nine, all clearly identified as Bedford tobacco. Its quality fluctuated, as did the market price, causing the owner endless anxiety.

Even at Poplar Forest, trying to track the number of hogsheads produced is difficult. The size and weight of the barrels changed over the years. Also, a crop was not necessarily sold the year it was grown or it might be sold to more than one person. When the British invaded his properties in 1781 the harvest was lost altogether. Elk Island on the James River, Goochland County, Virginia, apparently was particularly valuable. Jefferson's *Account Book 1775* shows twenty hogsheads harvested there. In 1781, due to the British, an estimated seven hogsheads were lost from his Cumberland property because the slaves were taken away by the enemy and were not there to cultivate it. The British demolished tobacco houses and barns at Elk Island and Elk Hill across the river in Goochland County. The tobacco was burned, and crops in the field destroyed. The disaster must have put a severe crimp in Jefferson's finances. The experience apparently caused him to reconsider the wisdom of holding such far-flung properties. By 1788, while he served in Europe, he began trying to sell his land in both counties. The Cumberland property was sold in 1791, Elk Hill in 1793. Elk Island was not listed on his 1794 land roll.

Records indicate he made an effort to grow his tobacco on first-year land. No mention is made of growing longer than two years on any one plot. As on other plantations which had supported the leaf for years, he used only a small portion of his estates to this crop, devoting the remainder to grains and livestock. In 1810, between twelve and fifteen acres of new land was devoted to tobacco at Lego in Albemarle. In 1811 at Poplar Forest Jefferson instructed his new overseer, Jeremiah A. Goodman, to prepare four acres of meadow ground for growing tobacco for one year and eight to ten acres of high ground for growing the crop two years in a row. He then indicated he expected from twenty to twenty-four acres of tobacco per year, this probably being the average for the years of his ownership of the estate. One worker was expected to take care of two to three acres and sixteen hands are mentioned in Goodman's contract, so at least one-half of the force supported this one purpose.

This emphasis on growing tobacco on new land only was based both on the crop's ability to quickly impoverish the soil and on the belief by many that using manure on older ground adversely affected its flavor. For whatever reason, Jefferson told van Hogendorp in 1784 that virgin soil was better than that which had been manured. This and other misconceptions are indications of the inevitable uncertainties encountered when exploring the possibilities of a new crop or a crop new to an area. Compared to wheat and barley, tobacco culture was still in its infancy in Jefferson's day.

Unlike many others, he was always mindful of what tobacco did to the soil. He was a conscientious farmer who worried about his responsibilities to the land. In his *Notes on the State of Virginia*, written in 1781, he said tobacco "is a culture productive of infinite wretchedness. Those employed in it are in a continual state of exertion beyond the powers of nature to support. Little food of any kind is raised by them; so that the men and animals on these farms are badly fed, and the earth is rapidly impoverished."[16] To his steward, Nicholas Lewis, he wrote in 1790 to plant wheat on as many acres as practicable. "In Albemarle, I presume we may lay aside tobacco entirely; and in Bedford, the more we can lay it aside the happier I shall be. . . . It is vastly desirable to be getting under way with our domestic cultivation & manufacture of hemp, flax, cotton & Wool for the negroes."[17]

And yet the weed would win out in the battles with his budget. In 1791 he made 13 hogsheads at Monticello in addition to his Bedford crop. Mention of tobacco at Monticello is repeated throughout the remainder of his life. In 1797, when the wheat crop was badly damaged, he was forced to plant tobacco "to make some [cash] for taxes and clothes." The following year he wrote frankly to John Taylor: "The high price of tobacco, which is likely to continue for some short time, has tempted me to go entirely into that culture, and in the meantime, my farming schemes are in abeyance, and my farming fields at nurse against the time of my resuming them."[18] In 1810 he wrote from Monticello he expected to increase his tobacco land from forty to sixty acres, for by doing this and increasing his wheat acreage from four hundred fifty to six hundred acres "In a couple of years more I shall be able to clear out all the difficulties I brought on myself in Washington."[19]

Jefferson's love-hate relationship with tobacco was based on more than its grave tendency to exhaust soil fertility. The weather was seldom fully cooperative. His records are littered with references to the forces conspiring against him. Spring could be "backward," as he once described a lingering cold spell. After leaving office as President he complained in March 1809 to his successor, James Madison, "No oats sown, not much tobacco seed, and little done in the gardens."[20] Spring might also be dry, as he told James Bowdin in 1806, when "not half a crop has been planted for want of rain; and even this half, with cotton and Indian corn, has yet many chances to run."[21] His fields also suffered midseason drought. He wrote his daughter Martha from Poplar Forest in 1815, "We are suffering from drought terribly at this place. Half a crop of wheat, and tobacco, and two thirds a crop of corn are the most we can expect."[22] Spring or fall frost could do extensive damage. Jefferson told Bernard Peyton in 1823: "I have lost here 10. M. plants of tobo. out of a crop of 80,000 plants and in Bedford 45,000 out of 300. M. but they were the latest and most indifferent, the best having been cut & secured before the frost . . ."[23]

Jefferson was not even assured of sufficient plants started from seed. His Bedford overseer, Joel Yancy, told him in 1820: "Our crop of tobo will be short, owing to the scarcity of plants, the first time I ever fail'd in plants, some of my most industrious neighbors fail'd intirely, and I am satisfied, there will not be more than ½ crops Tobo. in this part of the country."[24] However, he assured his anxious employer that his was as promising as any.

Insects, severe winds, and hail were other hazards. To van Hogendorp Jefferson mentions a fly which eats the plant; a ground worm which cuts off the stem; a webworm which eats the tender buds and covers the leaves with a spider-like web, killing them, and a horn worm which eats all but the fibrous parts of the leaf. Jefferson indicated he had found turkeys did a good job of searching out the horn worms. He also mentions occasions when his tobacco "fired" or dried before it had matured. Overseers might attempt to get fired tobacco through the inspection system, but this did nothing for a planter's reputation or his pocket book as the leaf was practically worthless.

After the tobacco was cut, usually in September, it was partially cured in the open field or in barns over fires. Great care was needed when the fires were set as the tobacco became very flammable. Someone had devised a system of flues, but Jefferson apparently never tried this innovation. Equally strange, considering his penchant for observing details, Jefferson claimed in 1801 that in his life he had never seen a leaf of tobacco picked.

Free laborers made the wooden barrels for hogsheads. The tobacco, usually unstemmed, was then packed by slaves who were often careless, causing considerable monetary losses at market.

The crop whose care had begun as early as January when the plant beds were made now faced the hazards of going to market. The trip began via wagon from Monticello to Shadwell Mills or the town of Milton. There the barrels were floated down the Rivanna River to the James River and on to Richmond. From Poplar Forest the wagons wound their way to Lynchburg, and the tobacco was usually floated down the James to Richmond, although some times it was sold in Lynchburg. Many tobacco warehouses lined Lynchburg's streets by this time. Jefferson himself owned at least one warehouse (presumably in town) for his Bedford tobacco. The warehouse burned with all its contents in 1823 or 1824.

A letter to his Poplar Forest overseer in 1811 reveals Jefferson's constant efforts to do routine tasks in a more efficient manner. He noted that "the day I left Poplar Forest I met many carts with a pr of oxen & a horse carrying a hhds of tobo. to Lychbg and with great ease. It occurred to me that instead of making another wagon as I hinted to you, we had much better adopt this mode of carrying our tobo. to market, & wheat also. Each plantation might equip 2. such carts, so as with the waggon they might send 5. hhs of tobo. or 160. bushels of wheat a day to market. If you see no difficulty in this you had better engage the wheels, to be made as strong as those I saw there, to be ready as soon as may be."[25]

Lynch's Ferry, the focal point for transport in the region, was begun in 1757 by seventeen-year-old John Lynch on land originally bought by his father. It was established initially to transport miscellaneous goods and passengers across the James River, but the town of Lynchburg, chartered by 1786, soon came to be dominated by tobacco and quickly became preeminent as a tobacco center.[26]

Jefferson first patronized Lynch's Ferry in 1773 on his first trip to his Bedford holdings. How to get his tobacco to market was certainly on his mind. The Rev. William Stith had patented Poplar Forest a full eight years before the ferry was established, so, there is a question as to whether he actually grew tobacco in Bedford County. Was he perhaps one of those who motivated Lynch to think he could make a living from a ferry? Stith sold the property to John Wayles, Jefferson's future father-in-law in 1764, so he surely dealt with the enterprising young man.

Transporting tobacco down river was not an easy task. Jefferson, according to tradition, was present at the launching of the first flat-bottomed riverboat on the James River, called a bateau, which was designed by Anthony Rucker of Amherst County after a disastrous flood in 1771. Jefferson made this note in his *Account Book 1775*: "Rucker's battoe is 50.f. long. 4. f. wide in the bottom & 6. f. at top. She carries 11. hhs & draws 13½ I. water." The entry preceding this says: "Bought of Norris two tobacco canoes for £8. to be paid for in corn or wheat of this year at the market price."[27] Tobacco canoes were Indian canoes, doubled for stability. When lashed together side by side, eight or nine hogsheads could be straddled between them. A wedge of wood against the hogsheads at each end prevented them from shifting. They drew only a few inches of water. Continued use of canoes was doomed by the recognition that Virginia's river system was the key to opening up the interior of the state. The James River Company was chartered in 1784 with Washington as its first president. The river was gradually cleared of obstructions past the falls at Richmond, ultimately providing planters with a better flat boat transportation system.

However, even bateaux were not free of problems. When the river was low they might be delayed. Without adequate protection rain might leak into poorly-made hogsheads, wetting the contents. Occasionally a boat would run aground and sink, submerging hogsheads. Jefferson in 1801 told his agent in Philadelphia that there was always a risk of some injury on the bateaux. Jefferson used both tobacco canoes and bateaux to float his crops from Shadwell mills to Milton where they were transferred to larger boats. At Bedford he had to rely on boats owned by others for the entire journey.

Before the actual shipping came a tug-of-war over prices. Richmond generally won out although some of the crop was sold in Lynchburg, Philadelphia, New York, London, and other European cities. Prices varied according to the quality of the tobacco. In a shipment in 1824 Jefferson got $8.35 a hogshead for his choicest leaf and $2.45 a hogshead for the poorest, for a net of $1523.21. Whether to sell at once or hold off for the prospects of a better price later was always an agonizing decision. His was a never ending struggle to get as much as he could for his crop.

Export prices fluctuated widely. From 1800 to Jefferson's death in 1826 tobacco usually sold for from eight cents a pound to a low of six cents a pound (a reflection of the uncertainties leading up to the roadblocks caused by the War of 1812). After the war the price shot up to nineteen cents in 1816 but plummeted back to six cents by the mid-1820s. Jefferson called the 1816 price "tobacco fever," but noted in 1817 that little was being planted. The high was due in large part to the fact that American tobacco farmers had cut acreage drastically during the interruption of commerce in the War of 1812. War-time prices had gone to less than two cents a pound for common tobacco, which constituted a large portion of the crop. When prices rebounded there was an increase in planting, pushing the price downward until the Panic of 1819. After that the industry suffered for years. To James Maury Jefferson wrote in 1815: "Our tobacco trade is strangely changed. We no longer know how to fit the plant to the market. Differences of from 4. to 21. D. the hundred are now made on qualities appearing to us entirely whimsical."[28]

Competition also came from Europe. In 1801 Jefferson received a letter from a friend traveling in Germany who reported the leaf was planted "very generally" there.[29] Some farmers abroad were encouraged to grow the crop because of restrictions against importation imposed by their governments. Britain, on the other hand, was a notable example of a country which preferred the revenues of tobacco duties to local production, thereby continuing its colonial policy. It continued to tax American tobacco for many years. However, once tobacco growing was firmly established on the Continent, it caused serious impediments to American sales.

Domestic consumption came to the rescue as the American population grew. A Virginia merchant of the era estimated that Americans used ten thousand to twelve thousand hogsheads by 1809 and fifteen thousand by 1817. Part of the increase was due to the fact that only the best of the crop was exported. American users also were more willing to buy tobacco which had been poorly cured or injured by water.

While Jefferson had some damaged hogsheads or hogsheads filled with poor quality leaf, his crops appear to have been remarkably good. In 1792 he reported to Randolph from Philadelphia that his Bedford tobacco of the year had arrived in miserable condition, but "the purchaser admitted my Albemarle tobo. of the last year to have been equal to any he ever saw, and that the good and uninjured part of this was as good as that."[30] He pointed out to a correspondent in 1799:

> It [tobacco] is made on the red mountain lands. My tobaccos have always been considered here in Philadelphia, London & Glasgow as of the first quality, & both here and in Philadelphia I have always been able to command for them from half a dollar to a dollar a hundred more than the market price of the best James river. In Philadelphia I have sold it several times for manufacture & have always had a dollar more than any body else: and the quality of the last crop is so extraordinary that I may safely say if there ever was a better hogshead of tobacco bought or sold in New York I may give it to the purchaser.[31]

He told his factor (agent) in Richmond in 1801 that "the crop from this place is declared by the Milton inspectors to be the *very best* crop ever passed at that inspection"[32] His factor in Philadelphia in 1801 after complaining about a recent shipment of Bedford tobacco urged Jefferson to take his overseer to task or "you will soon lose your Character of raising fine Tobacco."[33] While Jefferson no doubt was pleased with these accolades of his tobacco, it is certain he would have been happier if the crop concerned had more redeeming values.

Wheat was Jefferson's second cash crop. Fortunately for him he found his Albemarle soils receptive and he himself judged his crops to be of high quality. He was fortunate indeed to have so profitable a crop. It served him well even in Bedford, where he devoted acreage to this grain.

He told Randolph in 1791 "I am happy to hear the crop of wheat is likely to turn out well. 3000 bushels of wheat will be of double the value of tobo. made by the same hands at the same places the last year, which was a favorable year too: and when we consider that the first year of transition from one species of culture to another is subject to disadvantages, it gives favorable hopes of the change in future. It is an additional proof that 100 bushels of wheat are as easily made as 1000 lb of tobo."[34]

His son-in-law concurred with Jefferson's evaluation of the virtues of wheat and urged the then–Secretary of State to concentrate on wheat upon his return to Monticello. Randolph wrote:

> There are advantages in the culture of wheat; to which moisture is unfriendly, and the more equal exposure to the air from the inclination of the plain on which it grows, beneficial. Some of the worst diseases to which this plant is liable are produced by fogs and heavy dews. The nature of the soil and the elevation of the ground in the Southwest Mountains is so peculiarly favorable to the growth of wheat, that from two years' observation I have found the most slovenly agriculture to produce here a more abundant crop of a heavier grain than the most laborious cultivation with the best instruments can force from the lowlands of Virginia. From these considerations I have determined to drop immediately the culture of Indian corn on my lands and am convinced that you will find it advisable to do the same.[35]

The crop rotation plans Jefferson worked on in 1793 includes two years of wheat in an eight-year rotation. Randolph independently made the same decision for his own eight-year rotation.

Wheat and other small grains were tried in all of the colonies as immigrants arrived. The first mill in Virginia was constructed as early as 1621. As people moved inland they found soils and climate more conducive to growing small grains. Now the wheat belt is considerably to the west.

Wheat was seldom grown as a first crop, for before planting it was necessary to free the land of tree stumps, a laborious job. Plows and animals to draw them were in short supply, which forced most pioneers to forego wheat in favor of maize. Yet a heritage of grain was an inducement for many to work hard on their wheat patch, if only to vary their diet.[36] In the 1600s and early 1700s small grains were increasingly planted but basically for home consumption. In Virginia, where tobacco yields were declining by 1755 to 1760, wheat began to take over. If crops were abundant, then small amounts were exported, primarily to the West Indies and to England where populations were increasing. Later the French Revolution created opportunities in France. Tens of thousands of barrels of wheat and flour were exported yearly from Virginia when harvests were good.

Trade in wheat between colonies also increased. In some parts of New England where wheat had begun to fail before 1700, farmers who wished to grow the crop moved north and west. The northern Seaboard came increasingly to depend on Pennsylvania, New York, and even Virginia for wheat. By the time of the Revolutionary War there was an increased demand for grain in urban areas and on American plantations, which grew mainly the profitable cash crops of tobacco. When crops were poor, grain was imported from colonies which had an excess or people did without. Colonial governments were careful to prohibit exports when grain was in short supply within their borders.

Jefferson was himself turned into a farmer midway in life. He wrote in his *Notes* in 1781: "Besides clothing the earth with herbage, and preserving its fertility, it [wheat] feeds the laborers plentifully, requires from them only a moderate toil, except in the season of harvest, raises great numbers of animals for food and service, and difuses plenty and happiness among the whole."[37] John Beale Boardley, the American author of agricultural books, added that as wheat farming moved southward, people became happier for they were no longer dependent on British storekeepers who had kept them submissive through indebtedness. Unfortunately it became common practice in the South to inter-crop maize with wheat as in the middle and northern colonies. This only hastened the destruction of the soil. This appears to have been the method used by Peter Jefferson and by Thomas prior to 1793.

Even so, it was well this agricultural transformation kept up with the political transformation of the 1770s and 1780s. Without it the new American nation could hardly have maintained its independence from Britain. Some planters made the transition gracefully and successfully. At least one, William Byrd III, solved his debt dilemma by killing himself. Others, including Jefferson's father-in-law, died a natural death but left their enormous debts for heirs to resolve as best they could.

Thus at a time when the tobacco market began fluctuating in prices and demand and Tidewater soils were becoming increasingly exhausted,

Virginia and some other colonies were fortunate to have a wheat market open. Permanent substitution of wheat for tobacco in the Tidewater began as early as the decade of 1720s while maize was grown on higher ground, but it would take more decades before the last of the great plantations were converted. Neither wheat nor corn grown there could compete with inland regions.

Jefferson's comments on this transformation are found in his *Notes* of 1781:

In the year 1758 we exported seventy thousand hogsheads of tobacco, which was the greatest quantity ever produced in this country in one year. But its culture was fast declining at the commencement of this [Revolutionary] war and that of wheat taken its place; and it must continue to decline on the return of peace. I suspect that the change in the temperature of our climate has become sensible to that plant, which to be good, requires an extraordinary degree of heat. But it requires still more indispensably an uncommon fertility of soil; and the price which it commands at market will not enable the planter to produce this by manure. Was the supply still to depend on Virginia and Maryland alone as its culture becomes more difficult, the price would rise so as to enable the planter to surmount those difficulties and to live. But the western country on the Mississippi, and the midlands of Georgia, having fresh and fertile lands in abundance, and a hotter sun, will be able to under sell these two States, and will oblige them to abandon the raising of tobacco altogether.[38]

Wheat was being grown increasingly along both sides of the Blue Ridge Mountains by the last decade of the eighteenth century. Jefferson reported in 1793, "In 4 years the 3 little Counties of Augusta, Rockbridge, and Rockingham . . . from having but one Manufacturing Mill only has upwards of 100 Merchant Mills in great perfection . . . and our adventuring farmers are coming with their Batteaus loaded down James River through the Blue Ridge within 3 and 4 miles of Lexington."[39] Roanoke, just to the southeast of Bedford, was still predominantly in tobacco as late as 1791.

When Peter Jefferson began growing wheat on his Albemarle lands is not known, but on his death in 1757 a mill at Shadwell is recorded in his will.[40] Thus Peter was an early convert to grain. While the mill conceivably could have been built to grind corn, Peter had long been growing that crop; His sudden interest in a mill suggests he had recently gone into wheat. His wheat crop was probably small, only enough for his own consumption.

In his *Account Book* 1767 to 1770 Thomas Jefferson notes he was obligated to give 180 bushels of wheat and 24 of corn to have his mountain top at Monticello leveled. Not until 1774 does he record wheat again and then only to mention an early May frost had killed it, along with many other plants. As with his father, Thomas's early plantings were probably for his own use. By 1790, though, he urged Nicholas Lewis, a neighbor who was looking out for Monticello in the owner's absence, "to press, for myself, the going into that culture [of wheat] as much as you think practicable."[41] He wrote a friend the same year that his crops of wheat were good in quantity and quality, indicating his acreage had probably increased. Three years later he was feeling very comfortable with the idea of growing wheat, as he shows in the crop rotation schemes he was putting on paper and beginning to implement. He wrote that year his own Albemarle County was switching entirely to the culture of wheat, despite the lack of mills and distance from market.

Jefferson had 350 acres of wheat at Monticello and Shadwell in 1795, the following year, only 300. In 1810 he noted he was increasing his wheat acreage from 450 acres to 600 acres in an attempt to get out of debt. He was growing wheat at Bedford by 1792, probably one of the first farmers in that area to do so. By 1811 in a memorandum to his overseer there he specified which fields were to be planted in wheat and oats, for a total of 209 acres. As Jefferson considered oats a by-article until about 1815 when he included them in his rotation schemes, the percentage of acres devoted to oats would have been small. As for his crop he told a friend in 1815, "Our best farmers (such as Mr. Randolph, my son-in-law) get from ten to twenty bushels of wheat to the acre; our worst (such as myself) from six to eighteen, with little or more manuring."[42]

Although wheat had been grown on this side of the Atlantic since the earliest colonial days, much still needed to be learned about varieties to use. By 1674 both winter wheat (planted in the fall) and spring-planted wheat were grown in Virginia, but for years farmers debated the pros and cons between the two and the merits of the numerous varieties within each group. When the crop was indifferent after months of work and waiting, the farmer didn't know whether it was due to improper soils, sowing at the wrong time, the climate, or the variety.

It is not clear whether the wheat grown in Jefferson's day or earlier had similar characteristics to that grown today. With better control of information now, wheats are more reliably sorted out into winter wheats particularly well suited to the southern part of the wheat belt, and spring wheats to the north.

Almost all of Jefferson's wheat was of the winter type, allowing him to sow between August and December as the work load and the weather dictated. For Jefferson, soil conservationist, having his fields covered by even the minimal growth of the crop during the colder months was far preferable to leaving them bare and open to wind and water erosion. As the harvest did not begin until late June and into August, the soil was covered with vegetation most of the year. Other men were merely pleased that winter wheat was not as subject to the infection known as rust.

In his lifetime Jefferson tried several varieties in addition to the wheat he identified only as "common." Various people sent him sample seed. In 1790 he got from Washington a wheat with his friend's glowing recommendations. Jefferson wrote from Georgetown to Randolph:

> I inclose you some wheat which the President assures me from many years experience to be the best kind he has ever seen. He spread it through the Eastern shore of Maryland several years ago, and it has ever been considered the best of the white wheat of that state so much celebrated. It is said to weigh 62. 63. 64. lb to the bushel. The grain, tho' small, is always plump. The President is so excellent a farmer that I place full confidence in his recommendations. Will you be so good as to make George (under your directions & eye) set it out in distinct holes at proper distances so as to make the most seed from it possible? The richest ground in the garden will be best, and the partition fence they are to make will guard it. After harvest we will divide the produce. I imagine the rows should be far enough apart to admit them to go between them with the hoes for the purpose of weeding.[43]

Randolph reported the following year that the wheat had done poorly. Such were the hazards of trying a new crop or an old crop in a new location.

In 1797 a friend sent Jefferson two wheats new to him. He wrote in his thank you letter, "I received safely your favor of Aug. 9, with the two packets of Smyrna & Sicilian wheat. The latter I shall value as well because it lengthens our fall sowing, as because it may be sown in the spring, and in a soil that does not suit oats (as in the case of ours) we want a good spring grain. The May wheat has been sufficiently tried to prove that it will not answer for general culture in this part of the country. In the lower country it does better."[44] He was still growing May wheat in 1806. What results he had with the Sicilian are not recorded, but is was being grown by other Virginians after the war. It was a welcome addition to a farmer's resources. It tended to escape smut and rust, and made excellent super-fine flour.

Wheat rust first appeared in the Colonies around 1660 and spread rapidly. Its connection to barberries was appreciated quite early by farmers. Eradication, however, was difficult to achieve, especially because most educated individuals within the agricultural field were not convinced of the relationship between the plant and the disease until 1870 when European botanists showed conclusively that barberry is a host to this wheat parasite in some stages of its growth. Jefferson leaves no clue as to where he stood on the matter, nor does he provide information on the smut other than to note that his wheat was afflicted.

He seems to have been more plagued by the Hessian fly, which came to the colonies in straw bedding used by Hessian troops during the Revolutionary War. Damage was first noted on Long Island in 1779. Farmers in some areas suffered so much destruction they thought of giving up the crop. Jefferson showed a different spirit. He wrote Randolph in 1791: "A committee of the Philosophical Society is charged with collecting materials for the natural history of the Hessian fly." Jefferson was a member of this committee. Unfortunately no record remains to inform us if anything came of this proposed inquiry. Society members, after all, were busy men, earning a living in non-entomological fields. Nevertheless, it is apparent Jefferson had the interest to examine such an academic subject to get the problems resolved. His letter to Randolph continues:

> I do not think that of the weavil of Virginia has been yet sufficiently detailed. What do you think of beginning to turn your attention to this insect, in order to give its history to the Phil. society? It would require some summer's observations. — Bartram here tells me that it is one & the same insect which by depositing it's egg in the young plumbs, apricots, nectarines & peaches renders them gummy & good for nothing. He promises to shew me the insect this summer. I long to be free for pursuits of this kind instead of the detestable ones in which I am now laboring without pleasure to myself, or profit to others. In short I long to be with you at Monticello. [45]

The following year Jefferson was able to personally play the entomologist. He wrote Randolph after noting that Philadelphia, where he was currently serving his government, abounded with Hessian flies: "I have several of them now hatching. The examination of a single one which hatched a week ago gives me reason to suspect they are non-descript, and consequently aboriginal here."[46] He noted a particularly vigorous species of bearded wheat and good husbandry seemed to prevail against the fly.

Jefferson's interest in the subject had probably been spurred by a letter from Randolph earlier in 1792. His son-in-law told him, "I am sorry to inform you that you have lost considerably by the Weevil both in Albemarle & Bedford. I do not know exactly the damage at Poplar Forest but at this place except 500 bushels which were ground early in Autumn the wheat has been so injured as to be unfit for flour & has been purchased by Colo. Lewis for his distillery at ½ Dollar per bushel. In disposing of it thus you have been fortunate. I have now 816 bushels at Varina which is so injured that a person who engaged the purchase of it in September refuses to take it off my hands at any price."[47]

Jefferson had written in his *Notes* of 1781 that the solution to controlling the weevil lay in killing its eggs. He had concluded sadly: "But all these methods abridge too much the quantity which the farmer can manage, and enable other countries to undersell him, which are not infested with this insect."[48]

Two boons were to save America from the worst of weevil damage. One was the Scottish threshing machine which Jefferson introduced to Virginia and which quickly spread there and elsewhere. The second was that the best planting dates to avoid the weevil were worked out for the various areas where wheat was grown. Farmers were also trying new varieties, applying greater quantities of manure and cultivating the ground more thoroughly. Other factors soon bedeviled the farmer. Wheat became increasingly afflicted with rust and the grain worm which crossed from Canada to northern New York and Vermont between 1825 and 1830. Utopia is still in the future. Rust and the fly continue to plague farmers.

Weather was also a consideration. Drought, excessive rain, hail, wind and cold temperatures all took their toll. When the fly, rust, and weather all conspired against him in the same year, even this devoted farmer must have blanched at the odds against success with wheat. If his correspondence is taken at face value, he lost much or all of his wheat crop about once every three years. Without access to the actual yearly harvest totals it is impossible to determine whether his analysis during the season is justified. A particularly brutal blow to his financial well-being is well documented for 1814. The weather produced a short crop of wheat and then the British blockade prevented him and his neighbors from marketing what they had. The price later fell so low that he gave wheat to his workmen and horses instead of corn. The correspondence is valuable in determining his state of mind. Only a perpetual optimist could withstand such frequent discouragement. Only a dedicated farmer would not have thought of returning to the law as his chief occupation if he, as Jefferson, had such an option available.

In the early years, after the wheat was harvested and threshed at Monticello, it was sent down the river, subject to the same hazards as tobacco. When Jefferson completed his flour mill at Shadwell in 1806, he could grind his own flour, as much as 600 barrels or as little as 200, depending on the crop. It was more advantageous for the farmer to ship flour rather than the unground grain. However, he had to hire millers, who seldom paid their rent of flour on time, adding to Jefferson's constant financial woes. As the rent came to 200 barrels a year, it was a significant amount. Yet having flour made at someone else's mills, as in Bedford where he had none of his own, was not without its hazards. He wrote Martha in February of 1811 that "my wheat is in an embarrassing situation. The dam of the mill in which it is has now broke a second time, and the Miller refuses to deliver my wheat altho he had promised in that event to redeliver it. It will take another month to mend his dam, by which time the price and the river both may fail us. I propose to make another formal demand of it, & if he refuses, I may have parted with my crop for a lawsuit instead of money. Besides that he is not able to pay all who are in my situation with him."[49] Some 1400 bushels were involved. The flour was sometimes sold in Lynchburg, but Richmond usually paid more so the flour or the grain itself was floated downstream.

The price Jefferson got from his wheat fluctuated considerably, ranging from $15 a barrel to less than $3. Each crop was graded as to quality and priced accordingly. Even a year of good prices was of no help to a farmer whose crop was only middling or perhaps even unsalable.

By 1819 Jefferson was no longer personally involved with growing wheat at Monticello. He received flour as rent for his mill and from his grandson Jeff for the hire of two of Jefferson's Albemarle holdings. Only at Bedford was wheat grown under his auspices. By 1821 Jeff was responsible for Bedford as well.

Maize, along with tobacco, proved the scourge of American farmland.[50] Under Indian management destruction of soil had been minimal because of low population pressures, but with the arrival of Europeans after 1600 populations began to increase rapidly. Coupled with sheer numbers was the expectations among whites that they would make a higher standard of living than they had had in the old country. In America everything seemed possible, and hard work paid off. With fresh land easily available there was a great incentive to make an easy profit.

Maize was an excellent candidate to achieve this goal. Like the Indians before them, the newest arrivals found corn peculiarly well suited to freshly cleared land and to its cultivators, whose tools were few and primitive.[51] Maize could be easily planted around stumps of newly burned and cut virgin timber. Nothing more was needed than a sharp pointed planting stick. As the white man's weeds had yet to become omnipresent and few native American plants to this day have shown themselves to be agricultural pests, the maize crop could be left largely untended if necessary until the harvest. Virginian Robert Beverley in 1705 remarked that corn was weeded by the Indians only once or twice.[52] Cobs were easily husked, and the kernels dried well for storage. Yields were much higher for maize than for wheat, and a smaller proportion of the seed was required for the next year's crop. When not eaten right off the cob, preparation required only a simple pestle and mortar or a small hand mill, while wheat required a large mill justifiable only for considerable quantities of the grain. Best of all, maize was good food for man and livestock. Jefferson even enjoyed feeding corn to his deer out of his hand.

The most serious fault of maize (besides the fact it is a heavy feeder) lies in the necessary spacing between plants and rows, which leaves the ground subject to water erosion unless another crop is planted in between. The native fashion was to grow beans and squash with the corn, copying nature's example. Whites tried small grains, peas or other legumes, and potatoes. When wheat or hardy legumes were planted, the soil was at least covered over winter. Otherwise when corn plants are young, and especially over the winter when the land is bare, wind erosion becomes a factor as well. The greater the gradient, the greater the erosion. Most white farmers took to running their rows uphill and down, a practice pursued into the mid-1900s, which exacerbated the problem.

Of the varieties of maize grown in Virginia before and after the Revolution, some had white kernels while others were red, yellow, blue, or streaked. Jefferson's records show he tried well over a dozen different kinds in his own garden. Whether they were for table or field use is not clear. His earliest references are only to "Indian corn" which was eaten by both man and farm animals. The type is unknown. Later references to the grain are named after their donor, place of origin or innate characteristics as they were, of course, all "Indian corn." As usual, Jefferson sought out new types and was the recipient of interesting examples from acquaintances and total strangers. A special prize for him was the variety grown by the Mandan Indians of the Missouri River valley, given him by Meriwether Lewis.

The earliest colonists had modified only slightly the Indian method of growing maize in which five to six seeds were planted in hills four feet to five feet apart with the ground between hills not broken up unless beans, squash, pumpkins or melons were planted. Hills were thinned to two to three stalks. After the stalk was half grown it was hilled up further. Suckering the corn (pulling off nonproducing shoots) once or twice was common. Before the ears were harvested and while the leaves were still green and tender suckers were customarily pulled, wrapped in bundles and used for winter fodder for the livestock. The top just above the highest ear was likewise cut and cured for fodder. Despite the damage this did to the development of the ears, Jefferson used both practices. He also at times fed chopped corn stalks to his livestock.

White farmers soon began sowing small grain among the standing corn. The theory was that the sprouting grain would benefit from the shade. The farmer benefited (until the soil wore out) by having to prepare the land just once for two crops.[53] Sometimes nature caused more work, as Jefferson complained in 1795 when a terrible storm in August knocked down the mature corn crop, and the wheat had to be put in by hoe.

Washington took an entirely different approach, planting potatoes between or within rows of maize. The idea was not original with him. He wrote to Jefferson, "But of all the improving and ameliorating crops, none in my opinion, is equal to Potatoes on stiff, & hard bound land as mine."[54]

Presumably the corn used in payment to get his mountain top leveled in 1768 was grown on Jefferson's own land. His father had grown maize as well as tobacco, and Thomas was then only twenty-five. The transaction was recorded in his new *Account Book*. By 1775 he had been married three years, his house was well under way, and the grounds were being laid out. Although he had been absent from Monticello for long periods attending to governmental business, by then he could not have failed to understand the reasons why it was necessary for him to grow maize despite its destructiveness.

The questions regarding the ecological morality of continuing with maize came to a head in 1792 when Randolph put it this way to his father-in-law:

> I am convinced that the step we have taken for the preservation of our lands in the abolition of the culture of tobacco is of no importance compared with the one we have to make with regard to Indian corn. That crop whatever precautions are taken must always be ruinous to lands, which lie so unequally as ours in a climate subject to such excessive droughts and where the rain falls for the most part in torrents. By constant tillage the surface is reduced in dry weather to an impalpable powder which is swept off in the first shower by the force of the water rushing down the declivities. Besides, the want of dew and fog, occasioned by the elevation of the ground, must render it an unproductive crop in dry summers.[55]

Jefferson's response provides his rationale for continuing with it:

> I concur with you in opinion that it is a very hurtful culture to such lands as ours. I have been hesitating between it's total abolition, and the tolerating just as much as would feed my negroes. Two motives occasion this hesitation. 1. their attachment to it as a food, an attachment which, under existing circumstances, must have weight. 2. the multiplying the chances of a crop, because years are often such that your small grain fails, while the Indian corn flourishes. I believe in general it may be adviseable to cultivate several species of food, as wheat, rye, Indian corn, potatoes, peas &c. in order that if the season occasions some of them to fail entirely, we may find a resource in the others.[56]

Jefferson could have added that after the kernels were removed, all parts of the maize plant were useful as stock feed, as litter for the barnyard or plowed under as a green manure.

Thus while fully aware of the disadvantages of maize, both men were nonetheless forced to grow at least some. To minimize the damage Randolph began his new rotational scheme for corn in 1793, and, undoubtedly spurred on by the above letter, Jefferson made plans for doing so that same year. He wrote the Englishman William Strickland in 1798, after describing the crop rotation scheme worked out five years before, "Under this easy course of culture, aided with some manure, I hope my fields will recover their pristine fertility, which had in some of them been completely exhausted by perpetual crops of Indian corn and wheat alternately."[57]

It seems clear that Jefferson and Randolph were leaders in this type of crop rotation. The Duke de la Rouchefoucauld-Liancourt of France, who visited Monticello for several days, observed upon his return home in 1796: "The culture of tobacco being now almost entirely relinquished in this part of Virginia, the common rotation begins with wheat, followed by Indian corn, and then again wheat, until the exhausted soil loses every productive power; the field is then abandoned, and the cultivator proceeds to another, which he treats and abandons in the same manner, until he returns to the first, which has in the meantime recovered some of its productive faculties."[58]

The extent of the damage to the land can be imagined. In 1792, not including in-state consumption, Virginia exported 684,627 bushels of corn, Pennsylvania 414,262, Maryland 232,142—with lesser but still significant amounts from North Carolina, South Carolina, and Georgia.

The first plan devised by both Jefferson and Randolph allotted two years for growing maize out of an eight-year rotation, one year in conjunction with potatoes, one year with peas, in an attempt to decrease soil damage. As Jefferson had told Randolph of Washington's scheme of growing corn and potatoes together at the time he learned of it in 1792, the young man presumably was influenced to follow suit. Washington claimed he made "as much corn as if there were no potatoes, and much more potatoes than corn."[59] Where the idea came from of substituting peas for potatoes is unclear, but the Indian practice of growing beans with maize would have been known. The following year, 1794, Jefferson was planning for one year of corn in six. The outline appears in a letter to John Taylor written May 1. By December 29 of that year he wrote Taylor again, this time assigning corn once in seven years. What his final decision was is unknown. On at least two occasions leases of his land to tenants allowed for corn only once in five years. Jefferson was trying to do what was right.

Jefferson was less aggressive in dealing with the ravages of intermixing wheat and corn partly because he was away so much in service to his country, and partly because of Taylor, who was considered the foremost agriculturist of his day. Taylor was as much concerned as Jefferson and Randolph with restoring fertility to the land, but he believed maize would actually help achieve that. His theory was that the atmosphere was the

ultimate source of fertility, which only plants could trap. Maize could do
this trapping and provided great use and market. He recommended that
livestock be kept out of arable fields and be confined instead to pastures
with tough grasses to protect the soil. Manure produced by the stock grazed
there could be easily collected and spread where it was most needed. As
Taylor wrote Jefferson, "We seek after a vegetable proper for poor ground it
is found in corn."[60] Taylor was quick to remind his peers that, while crop
rotation could help maintain soil fertility, it could not restore abused soil.
There was no substitute for manure.

Jefferson was still experimenting, trying to become a better farmer as
late as 1815, when he was 72. He wrote Charles Willson Peale:

> But we have had a method of planting corn suggested by a m͞r Hall which
> dispenses with the plough entirely. He marks the ground off in squares of 10 f. by
> a coulter, or an iron pin. At each crossing of the lines he digs 2 f 3 I. square
> (equal nearly to 5. square feet) as deep as the mattock will go. This little square
> is manured as you would have manured the whole ground, taking consequently
> but 1/20 of the manure; a grain of corn is planted within 6. I. of each corner, so
> as to produce 4. stalks about 15. I. apart. This is to be kept clean of weeds either
> by the hoe, or by covering it with straw so deep as to smother weeds, when the
> plant is 12. I. high. He asks but 2. laborers to make 2500 bushels of corn. He has
> taken a patent for his process, and has given me a right to use it, for I certainly
> should not have thought the right worth 50. D. the price of a licence. I am
> about trying one acre.[61]

Jefferson must have thought it strange any man should think to patent a
method of such obvious value to his fellow farmers, particularly because the
enforcement of it would have been virtually impossible. The Duke de la
Rouchefoucauld-Liancourt reported that Jefferson told him he got 18
bushels of corn per acre on average. Today the record is 121 bushels.

Even with careful planning Jefferson was usually faced with buying
additional corn. His records for the 30 years of 1790 to 1820 show that in
eight years he had no significant crop at all. He mentions only three
sizeable crops. Unlike wheat, maize on his farms was not very susceptible to
crop pests and diseases; at least their maladies do not consume space in his
records. Maize was subject to frost, drought, hail, wind, and flooding and
consequently some years the crop was short not only at Monticello but
for the entire neighborhood. The same was true at Bedford. In that case—
or if the price was too dear—Jefferson substituted wheat for his workers. As
corn was paid for in cash, this cost had to be weighed against the worth of
his wheat.

The following correspondence shows some of the trials and tribula-
tions he experienced with maize. He wrote to Randolph in February 1796,

"There is vast alarm here about corn. The price at present from 15/ to 18/. but not to be had indeed at any price. My situation on that subject is threatening beyond any thing I ever experienced. We shall starve literally if I cannot buy 200 barrels, & as yet I have been able to find but 60."[62]

To his Bedford overseer Yancy in March 1817 he wrote, "The quantity of corn I have been obliged to buy here and it's high price will take all the money of the year nearly; for the June as well as August drought, of which you had only the latter reduces us below the third of an ordinary crop."[63]

Yancy wrote in May 1820: "We have hard times here also another such a year as the two last will produce a famine, I shall be much put to it to get bread untill Harvest."[64] After this failure Yancy was able to report the following year: "The corn turned out nearly what I expected, at Tomahawk 210 barrels and at B. creek 257 barrels, total 467 barrels and I think there was upwards 400. put in the houses, it was all accurately measured, and sorted besides there was about 30 barrels of lost corn as numbered which answers well for stock."[65]

Corn was frequently used in lieu of cash if the seller would accept it. Jefferson's *Account Book* for 1775 shows he bought two tobacco canoes "to be paid for in corn or wheat of this year at the market price."[66] Overseers were paid in shares. Of the 210 barrels of corn at Tomahawk at Bedford in 1821, the overseer got 16. Jefferson also received corn as payment on at least one occasion for leasing his land.

As he was always looking to the future, it is not surprising that Jefferson used a machine to shell his corn. Along with a drawing and information on its construction which he apparently made for his own use, he noted that two men could shell 100 bushels of corn a day with the machine by turning the handle by hand. As usual he continued to look for improved equipment. Five years later, in 1808, he found a large steel handmill for grinding his corn and in 1814 a machine capable of crushing the ear of corn, cob and all, for grinding in a mill. In 1819 he got another kind of corn shelling machine. Corn had won out in the end.

The minor grains—rye, barley, oats, and buckwheat—were not widely grown in the South during the Colonial period and then usually only for home consumption. This was the case with Jefferson, who grew all four.

His first attempts with rye apparently were not good. In 1790 he wrote Washington, "A very decisive experiment has banished rye from my rotation."[67] But by 1792, when he was seeking a new overseer at Monticello, he emphasized that his acreage was "remarkably friendly" to rye as well as wheat. He was certain, though, that it destroyed soil fertility. In his rotation rye was followed by a fallow or clover. Rye or barley constituted one year in at least one of his rotation plans. Rye was of importance to him as food for man and farm animals. In some years whiskey was made from it. The importance of rye to others is perhaps indicated by the fact that getting new seed from a friend was an unusual event. Jefferson mentions buying spring rye he had seen advertised in a Baltimore paper for which he paid only one dollar. Rye was perhaps most important in case he failed with wheat, as he told Randolph in 1792. It was, however, subject to the usual failings of small grains.

Barley soon followed the first planting of wheat in Virginia, but early enthusiasm for both wheat and barley waned as colonists discovered the virtues of maize. Farther north barley continued as a minor crop, with two thirds of the crop in the early 1800s being marketed in and around Albany, New York. Its use seems to have been primarily for malt, for feeding stock and as a backup for the wheat crop.

Jefferson grew barley only incidently in the earlier years and apparently gave it up by 1809 when there is a record that he purchased some. By 1815 he declared he did not grow it. He had used it as a substitute for rye in his rotations and for distilling into whiskey. He found the Hessian fly a greater pest on his barley than on wheat, but he noted to son-in-law John Wayles Eppes in 1803, after verifying that Eppes did indeed have the genuine insect, that "when they [the flies] drive us to this [wheat], they are a great blessing."[68]

Randolph had high hopes for barley. Jefferson told William Strickland that Randolph was eager to grow barley on a large scale. (Strickland had sent barley seed to Jefferson, which he turned over to Randolph.) Jefferson received seed from at least two other sources, one packet of which he noted as trying in his gardens. While he claimed to be impressed with the results, it did not convince him to return to barley production. Randolph's results with this crop are not recorded.

Oats were more prominent in Jefferson's planting scheme, but hardly rivaled wheat or corn. In 1801 he had over 80 acres in oats at Lego. This apparently was an exception, as he found oats did not really grow well in Albemarle. They were usually planted with clover. Oats were also grown in Bedford. Randolph, who like his father-in-law delighted in trying new crops and new methods, had oats in his rotation by 1793, while Jefferson did not until about 1815. Jefferson needed oats for his stock and so he bought from others when necessary. Oats had been grown in Virginia as early as 1649, but only Scottish settlers accepted oats as human food. The number of acres grown was determined by the needs of farm stock or urban horses.

Buckwheat suffered a similar image problem; it was eaten as buckwheat cakes by only a few farmers, Jefferson probably being one. Buckwheat was fed to poultry, horses, and swine and was used as a green manure. Washington was a convert to turning under buckwheat until he eventually decided that growing it destroyed as much soil fertility as it gave. Jefferson apparently came to the same conclusion after trying it in various crop rotation plans during the same period as did Washington. Both were probably spurred on by Logan's assessment that a green-dressing of buckwheat was equal to ten loads of manure to the acre. As Jefferson pointed out to Washington, he planted buckwheat where clover would not succeed. By 1808, however, buckwheat was mentioned by Jefferson only for an experimental garden and in 1812 in the vineyard.

4

Plants Introduced

Thomas Jefferson lived during a great transitional period in agriculture, the first since the days of the Romans. The Romans had finally solved some of the problems associated with the physical problems of growing crops. In the following centuries little changed until the last decades of the 1700s and the early decades of the 1800s when a new breed of man, the scientist, came upon the scene to study how plants function. What was the role of air? Soil? Fertilizers? Men such as Joseph Priestley discovered the purposes of oxygen and Jan Ingen-Housz uncovered plant physiological processes using carbon dioxide and sunlight. John Taylor was adamant that the great source of fertilizer was in the atmosphere. It was difficult for a man even of Jefferson's analytical mind to judge between the ideas of a Priestley (an English clergyman as well as a chemist), an Ingen-Housz (a Dutch physician as well as a plant pathologist) and a Taylor (an American political philosopher and agriculturist).[1] Confusion was inevitable as none of these men understood the related facts which would later be combined to create a whole model of plant biology.

In his harried life, due to his political duties and his wide range of interests, it is not surprising that Jefferson missed some of the pieces of agricultural riddles. While he read the views of others with great profit and exchanged ideas as a routine practice, his agricultural methods, especially as they pertain to specific plants, were very much his own thinking, based on his observations of how crops responded to various conditions. Even without the knowledge which is considered basic today in college agronomy courses, Jefferson was a very respectable farmer. By not becoming bedazzled by minutiae he was able to arrive at generally sensible conclusions. He was a keen observer and a meticulous record keeper, which permitted him a base of information few farmers possess even now.

Jefferson was a progressive experimental farmer, who helped transform agriculture from millennia-old dirt scratching methods, inferior seeds, and sheer luck, to a scientific determination of the best procedures to apply to specific soils with certain crops. Not until many other studies were applied to the wide variations in American soils and climates could farmers possess some semblance of certainty regarding the best practices to follow and what to plant. Meanwhile experimentation was imperative and, as usual, Jefferson was willing to be the leader.[2]

Concern for his fellow Americans show clearly in his efforts to introduce plants from which he himself could never benefit. He explained: "I have always thought that if in the experiments to introduce or to communicate new plants, one species in an hundred is found useful and succeeds, the ninety-nine found otherwise are more than paid for."[3]

Rice fell into that category, attempted by the South Carolina Society for Promoting Agriculture, established in 1785, of which Jefferson had been made an honorary vice president. His interest in rice was long standing. He had tried some in his meadow by 1774. He wrote in his *Notes*: "The climate suits rice well enough, wherever the lands do."[4] In 1808 he told Dr. Benjamin Waterhouse, "I cultivated it [rice] two or three years at Monticello, and had good crops, as did my neighbors, but not having conveniences for husking it, we declined it."[5]

Rice had been introduced into Virginia in 1647 by Sir William Berkely, the colonial governor. It reached into the Carolinas in about 1685 and later into Georgia. It was grown along the coast where malaria was prevalent. While understanding the dependence of South Carolina and Georgia on the crop, Jefferson also recognized the loss of health and even life which resulted from growing it there. Could some other rice be substituted for commercial production?

While in Paris he noted that the French used a lot of upland rice grown in Italy. The people preferred it for meat and oil-based cooking over the Carolina product imported via England. Carolina rice was only considered satisfactory when prepared with milk and sugar, a culinary method seldom used. Jefferson also noted that Italian rice came to market less broken than American rice and immediately wondered if there was a difference in the machine used to clean the grain. With his usual penchant for details, he found considerable confusion on the subject, which spurred his determination to learn the truth of the matter.

On a trip to southern France and northern Italy he discovered the reason for the difference in performance between Piedmont and Carolina rice was not cleaning methods, which were identical, but because two different varieties were involved. He also discovered that "Piemont" rice was not grown in that region of Italy but in neighboring Lombardy. Undeterred by an Italian ban on the exportation of rice seed (on penalty of death), Jefferson enticed a muleteer to smuggle several sacks across the border into France. Not sure of his man, he stuffed several pounds of seed into his own pockets. The two met according to plan and the ill-gotten gains arrived in South Carolina and Georgia.

Jefferson's efforts were not necessarily appreciated. Ralph Izard, in between jobs as a member of the South Carolina legislature and U.S. senator, wrote him from Charleston after he had received Jefferson's gift in 1787:

> We are much obliged to you for the trouble you have taken, & for the information you have given. When I was in Italy, the Rice of that Country appeared inferior to ours. I had been several years absent from America, & the difference did not then appear to me so great as it does now. The Seed which you have sent, & which you say is of the best kind, will bear no comparison with ours; & I am surprised to learn that the price is nearly equal. You say that our Rice dissolves when dressed with Meat: this must be owing to some mismanagement in dressing it. I have examined my cook on the subject, & find that as meat requies to be longer on the fire than Rice, they must be dressed separately, until each is nearly done, & then the combination is to be made. The water must boil before the Rice is put into it, or the grains will not be distinct from each other. The rice you have sent will be planted. I hope great care will be taken to keep it at a distance from the other Rice Fields; for if the Farina should blow on them, it may be the means of propagating an inferior species among us . . . As the quality of our rice is infinitely superior to that of Italy, I am persuaded it will annually gain ground in France, & finally exclude the other entirely. This is a considerable object to us, & will likewise be of service to the manufacturers of France. I believe Italy receives money from France in return for her Rice.[6]

Jefferson's primary motive to persuade American rice growers to switch to upland rice was to protect the health of American laborers from the mosquito-infested swamps. He also sought to encourage the cultivation of upland rice in Virginia, which had no suitable lowland areas. One must wonder if he knew that flooded rice produces more grains than dry land rice.

Undaunted by Izard's response, Jefferson continued promoting the grain. In a memorandum he wrote in about 1800 subtitled "Services to My Country" he lists this one:

> In 1790, I got a cask of heavy upland rice, from the river Denbigh, in Africa, about lat. 9° 30′ North, which I sent to Charleston, in hopes it might supersede the culture of the wet rice, which renders South Carolina and Georgia so pestilential through the summer. It was divided, and a part sent to Georgia. I

know not whether it has been attended to in South Carolina; but it has spread in the upper parts of Georgia, so as to have become almost general, and is highly prized. Perhaps it may answer in Tennessee and Kentucky. The greatest service which can be rendered any country is, to add an useful plant to its culture; especially, a bread grain; next in value to bread is oil.[7]

Interestingly he chose to commemorate the second batch, rather than the smuggled rice which involved so much derring-do.

Jefferson also got rice from other places. He was well aware there were various types. With his usual precision he noted that in Cochin-China six kinds of rice were cultivated, three requiring water and three growing in the highlands. He secured some of the dry rice for his South Carolina Society friends, as well as some Georgia men. He reported in 1808 to Waterhouse: "Nothing came of the trials in South Carolina, but being carried into the upper hilly parts of Georgia, it succeeded there perfectly, has spread over the country, and is now commonly cultivated; still however, for family use chiefly, as they cannot make it for sale in competition with the rice of the swamps."[8]

In 1809 Jefferson told his gardening friend, Governor John Milledge of South Carolina, of a particularly pleasing gift. "I have received from M. Thoüin, Director of the National garden of France, a collection of many different species of rice. Whether any of them possess, any properties which might render them preferable to those we possess, either generally or under particular circumstances of soil or climate I know not. But the scripture precept of 'prove all things & hold fast that which is good' is peculiarly wise in objects of agriculture."[9]

Naturally he shared his good fortune. Milledge's response must have gratified him: "The rice which you sent me, I distributed among some of our best rice planters near Savannah, one of the aquatic kind, is said to be equal if not superior, to the rice now generally Cultivated. The bearded rice grows well on high land, and requires only the usual seasons for bringing Indian Corn to perfection. I will have the result of the experiments published."[10]

After he left the office of President it is not surprising that Jefferson again sowed upland rice at Monticello. What kind he tried is not recorded. Dry land rice was again promoted. It had no serious insect or disease problems, yielded about five pounds of grain per 100 square feet, and grew from New York to Florida. The grain, however, had to be husked.

As noted, Jefferson was very much interested in providing a source of oil to his fellow citizens. He was not the first to hope an olive could be grown in America. Thomas Ashe wrote in 1682 of an olive tree growing in South Carolina which "prospered exceedingly," giving encouragement to grow several more. James Edward Ogelthorpe, who founded the English colony in Georgia in 1733, is said to have discovered abandoned plantations of olives, figs, oranges, and lemons. More olive trees were sent to Georgia in 1734. That year in North Carolina experiments with olive trees were being carried out. In 1755 more olive trees were brought to South Carolina and to Florida in 1760. In the West olives had been taken to the San Diego, California, mission by 1769 or perhaps as early as 1700.[11] Whether Jefferson knew of any of these attempts is not known.

This indefatigable promoter had been prompted initially to pursue the culture of the olive because of his travels in the south of France, during which he was consciously looking for plants which might succeed in what he felt was the similar climate in the American South. Jefferson had never traveled south of Virginia. If he had not previously known the importance of the olive to the small European farmer, he learned it on this trip. America too must grow this tree.

He wrote to William Drayton of the South Carolina agriculture society in 1787:

> The olive is a tree the least known in America, and yet the most worthy of being known. Of all the gifts of heaven to man, it is next to the most precious if not the most precious. . . . A pound of oil [olive], which can be bought for three or four pence sterling, is equivalent to many pounds of flesh, by the quantity of vegetables it will prepare, and render fit and comfortable food. . . . This is an article, the consumption of which will always keep pace with its production. Raise it, and it begets its own demand . . . cover the southern States with it, and every man will become a consumer of oil, within whose reach it can be brought in point of price.[12]

Two years later he wrote Ralph Izard from Paris that growing olives "should be the object of the Carolina patriot." Farmer to farmer, Jefferson provides all the reasons for growing the olives he has sent to Charleston. As early as 1774 he himself had planted some 1500 olive stones at Monticello but to no avail. He tried again in 1778 with a tree from Philip Mazzei, the Italian grape grower who had brought it to Monticello. By 1804 Jefferson knew his great plans and the many plants and olive stones he had sent home during his years abroad had not accomplished his goal. Yet he was determined this tree should succeed. Therefore, he wrote Stephen Cathalan,

> You remember how anxious I was, when with you at Marseilles, to get the admirable olive of your canton transferred to my own country, and how much trouble you were so kind as to take to effect it. It did not happen that any one of those among whom the plants were distributed took up the plan with the enthusiasm necessary to give it success, and it has failed. Mr. John Cowper of St. Simon's island in Georgia now proposes to undertake it, & being led to it by

inclination, and a gentleman of property, in the most favorable situation, he will give the culture a fair trial, and I trust it's favorable issue is beyond a doubt. He has been informed of the superior excellence of the olive of Marsilles, and knowing your friendly dispositions to our country I have taken the liberty of advising him to address himself to you to put his commission into faithful & careful hands.[13]

In 1810 James Ronaldson sent more olive stones from Paris, but Jefferson was forced to acknowledge to his friend three years later that 500 plants, "If any of them still exist, it is merely as a curiosity in their gardens; not a single orchard of them has been planted."[14]

Jefferson never gave up on the olive. He still was writing about it in 1817 to Judge William Johnson with whom he exchanged plants. Jefferson pointed out that "the olive, the Sesamus, the Cane & Coffee offer field enough for the efforts of your's and other states South & West of you. We, of this state, must make bread, and be contented with so much of that as a miserable insect will leave us."[15] As if to corroborate Jefferson's gloomy assessment to James Ronaldson, Samuel Maverick reported in 1822, "In So. Ca. at Charleston the olive tree looks healthy and well and some years produces fruit."[16]

Jefferson wrote plaintively to another correspondent in 1822, "I have long earnestly wished for the introduction of the Olive into S. Carolina & Georgia." Mentioning the trees still growing in South Carolina he added, "Cuttings from them grafted on seedling stocks would soon yield a plentiful supply of trees. Their culture is of little labor, as is that of silk also."[17] If someone would take the trouble to seriously pursue the growing of the olive, Jefferson was certain it would succeed in southeastern parts of the U.S. It is interesting that this otherwise astute botanist would not recognize that the olive requires a semiarid climate to thrive.

President Jefferson got sidetracked temporarily from promoting olives by an interest in sesamum oil. His New York friend Colonel William Few sent him a bottle in 1807. Jefferson proclaimed it an excellent substitute for olive oil and one of the most valuable acquisitions America had ever made. He was interested of course in Few's historical details about sesamum. As Columella and Palladius mention the culture of sesamum in Italy and both Romans were in Jefferson's library collection, it is surprising he was unaware of the quality of the oil before Few pointed it out to him. Senator Milledge (soon to become governor of South Carolina) had sent Few the seed of this marvelous plant. Seeds had been brought to the American South by blacks for their own use. Its virtues included the fact that benne, the blacks' name for sesamum, was easily harvested by hand by flailing the pods with a stick. Slaves ate the seed parched in broths and puddings. In addition to making salad oil, the white man used it for paint and lamps.

Jefferson naturally got seeds and instructions and tried growing sesamum, although never with unqualified success. His first efforts were in 1808 when he included sesamum in his instructions to his overseer Edmund Bacon as a farming article in the experimental garden. He apparently had second thoughts about who should be entrusted with this treasure, for the following month he sent the seeds to his oldest granddaughter, Anne, who was requested to supervise their planting in the nursery. His enthusiasm for the success of sesamum was due in part to the embargo he himself had ordered, which prevented importation of oil from abroad.

As usual he tried to convince others to try this newest wonder. Typically he shared seeds with such gardeners as nurseryman Bernard McMahon. He told the latter in 1811: "We now raise it and make from it our own sallad oil preferable to such olive oil as is usually to be bought."[18] But he admitted to Governor Milledge the same year, "Our cultivation of Benni has not yet had entire success." Frost was apt to catch it for one thing. After describing a press of his own invention, he explained to the Governor: "My greatest difficulty now is in separating the seed from the broken particles of the pod & leaf."[19] Although he was forced to conclude that, like cotton, benne could be grown in his part of the world only for home consumption, Jefferson continued to record planting it until his last entry in his *Garden Book* in 1824.

Because of its great value sesamum is still under consideration as an agricultural crop in the U.S. With mechanized agriculture sesamum yields more oil per acre than any other annual oil crop. In addition, it will keep for several years without turning rancid. In press cake form it is excellent as a livestock food. Jefferson's dream will become a reality when nonshattering cultivars necessary for mechanized agriculture are developed.

Curiously Jefferson overlooked the possibilities inherent in both maize and peanuts, both of which became major American sources of oil. Maize had been grown in American soil since the earliest colonial days. Peanuts evidently arrived with African slaves after the seeds had been brought to Africa from South America by early explorers. Jefferson in his *Notes* in 1781 lists peanuts as a crop cultivated in Virginia. Bernard McMahon included them among his 1806 list of kitchen garden plants. As they contain about 50 percent oil and were used for their oil during the colonial period, Jefferson obviously overlooked another excellent source that already being grown.

Cotton was first tried in Virginia in 1607 at Jamestown. Time showed it was not really suited to that state, but it became a staple farther south. Here too Jefferson missed a source of oil from a plant suited to American conditions. Huge quantities of cottonseed are a byproduct of the ginning of cotton fiber. Jefferson's neglect of cottonseed is particularly surprising considering his correspondence as secretary of state with Eli Whitney in 1793 concerning the patent issued for Whitney's cotton gin. Perhaps when he chose to promote the olive tree as a source of oil, he was lured by the historical role olives have played to overlook more unconventional oils.

Cotton for home manufacturing was another matter; Jefferson depended on it for his large family. His first record of buying cottonseed is found in his *Account Book* 1774 at which time he got three pounds. He told his Charlottesville neighbor Nicholas Lewis in 1790, "It is vastly desirable to be getting under way with our domestic cultivation & manufacture of hemp, flax, cotton & Wool for the negroes."[20]

Based on his personal experience Jefferson knew that cotton could not be grown easily in Virginia. He spelled out in an 1808 letter Virginia's limitation concerning this crop. Cotton could be cultivated satisfactorily only south of the Rappahannock River and east of the Blue Ridge Mountains. He observed that from the Rappahannock to the Roanoke River cotton could not compete with the yields farther south and therefore was grown there only for family use.

A letter in December 1808 to his Monticello overseer Edmund Bacon instructed: "As it will be necessary that we make preparation for clothing our people another year, we must plant a large cotton patch, say two acres at the least. A light sandy soil is best. I suppose therefore it should be in the low grounds at the mill dam. Seed can be procured from those who have cotton gins. The present method of cotton is very little laborious. It is done entirely with the plough."[21]

But seed was not that easy to come by. Jefferson wrote Bacon the following January, "I think you had better write to Gibson & Jefferson [his business representatives in Richmond] for cotton seed. Perhaps they would be able to get it & send it to you. But in the mean time omit no chance of getting some yourself if possible, it would be dreadful to have to pay for a year's clothing merely for want of seed."[22] Securing cotton seed would remain a problem. He complained in 1818 to Captain Bernard Peyton, "The impossibility of buying raw cotton obliges [me] to recur to the cultivating it myself. So much has it [got] out of practice that even the seed is lost in this part of the country. Could you possibly buy me a sack or barrel of about 5 bushels? It will be a great accommodation to me."[23]

The situation worsened because merchants were unhappy with home manufacturing that cut into their sales. Their money was made by selling the finished product, not the seed. Jefferson fought the resulting higher price by repeatedly attempting to grow his own cotton.

It is difficult to determine the extent of the harvest of this plant on his plantations. In 1781 he listed his losses to the British at his Cumberland

County plantation. He notes that because slaves went off with the enemy he lost, for want of cultivation, 130 pounds of cotton in addition to other crops and animals. His two acres at Monticello indicate that only a small amount was grown there. He promoted cotton to his friends farther south. From Paris in 1789 he wrote Edward Rutledge of South Carolina, "Cotton is a precious resource, and which cannot fail with you."[24]

While Jefferson was correct on both counts, it is hard to believe he foresaw that cotton growing would only temporarily enrich a few at the expense of the land of the region as a whole. As a result the South lagged behind the rest of the country for over a century. While Jefferson assigned cotton culture on his own land to the old and infirm, farther south where cotton could more profitably be grown, the crop revived the moribund institution of slavery. In his efforts to be self-sufficient and his advocacy of the virtues of the small farmer, the moral dilemma involved of using slaves to produce this cash crop seems to have escaped his attention. His death in 1826 precluded an awareness of the worst abuse of both humans and land.

Jefferson's efforts to promote useful crops and information about them did cause a contretemps of a different sort with cotton. The Agricultural Society of Paris in 1808 had informed the President of efforts there to grow several varieties of cotton and asked his assistance in providing seeds of cotton grown in the American South, both the green-seed short-staple variety and the longer-fibered sea-island strain, which had been introduced to America in 1786. Each had its virtues and liabilities. Separation of the seed from the lint of the green-seed was difficult. The fiber had to be cut or torn away which cost more to process. However, the soil and climate favored this variety. The seeds of the sea-island were easily removed and the fiber brought high prices. Unfortunately it could be grown successfully only on the lowlands of the southeastern coast.

Jefferson as a farmer could not refuse the request from Paris. The difficulty came when the Baltimore company to which a Jefferson friend sent the requested seed found it scandalous that the President ordered them to ship the seed thence to New York and from there to France. Jefferson explained to a Baltimore friend: "Their [the Baltimore company's] first object was to make a show of my letter, as something very criminal, and to carry the subject into the newspapers." Jefferson protested: "These societies are always in peace, however their nations may be at war."[25] To avoid offence, however, he asked the friend to get the cottonseed from the firm, pay the firm its expenses, send Jefferson the bill for reimbursement, then take the seed and use it for manure on his garden. The President's own embargo was in place and political hay would not be made of this gift. Governor Milledge offered to send more seed in 1811 when shipping to

France was less of a political liability, but with the impending War of 1812 it is doubtful any left American shores.

Jefferson did not overlook flax, which had been cultivated in Eurasia for millennia. This most useful plant provides fibers for linen cloth and seeds for oil, while the press-residue can be fed to cattle. It was grown in the earliest New England settlements. During the eighteenth century farmers increasingly planted small plots of flax for oil and linen fiber. Some of the seed was crushed in local mills, but large quantities were sent to Europe. In fact, in the eighteenth century flax seed was the most important agricultural export to Europe with wheat and some corn. Ireland imported ship loads, for in order to produce linen the plant was harvested before the seeds were ripe.

Jefferson thought flax was hard on the soil although he noted his friend, Dr. George Logan, believed otherwise. In his *Farm Book* Jefferson observed that nothing would grow immediately after flax except turnips and that a field would only produce flax one year in six or seven. He grew flax at Monticello as early as 1779. By 1790 he was seriously considering growing enough of it to clothe his slaves. Three years later he listed it as planted on a few acres. While he told his new overseer, Bacon, in 1809 that flax was quite as necessary as cotton and therefore to be sure to include it in his plans, and indicated to John Adams in 1812 that he raised some, in 1815 he claimed it produced so little he had never attempted it.

Ultimately flax as a crop designed for clothing people was totally replaced by cotton from the Deep South. Nevertheless, a suggestion in 1808 by William Bartram, son of John, should have piqued Jefferson's curiosity. Bartram sent a packet of mimosa seeds "tyed with a silky bark of a species of Asclepias, native to Pennsylvania, which should it prove a useful substitute for flax or cotton, in linnen manufacture, it can be cultivated in any quantities and with less expense, as it is a perennial plant, and thrives in almost any soil."[26] However, the letter came at the end of Jefferson's term as President and his thoughts were elsewhere. When he got home his enthusiasm was dominated by sheep.

Not surprisingly, Jefferson was interested in a local source of sugar. In 1809 he had to order at least nine hundred pounds of brown and white sugar from his Richmond factors. This was an expense he and his fellow farmers would be pleased to eliminate from their ever strained accounts. Jefferson explained to a French friend, C. P. de Lasteyrie, in 1808, "We have within the ancient limits of the United States, a great extent of country which brings the orange to advantage, but not a foot in which the sugar cane can be matured."[27] Although sugar cane had been introduced into Louisiana by Jesuits from Santo Domingo in 1751, it was not grown there commercially on a significant scale until the end of the century. Today only a small amount of cane, a crop of the humid tropical lowlands, is grown in the U.S., primarily in Louisiana and Florida.

As with molasses from the West Indies, cane was harvested with slave labor. *The Farmer's Almanac* in 1803 advised its readers to make their own sugar and not buy it from the Indies. The latter course would further degrade exploited workers. Was cane really a good sweetener to promote for America?

Jefferson does not seem to have considered the merits of honey. Honey bees had been imported from England to Virginia by 1621. Both the honey and beeswax were much prized, with small amounts of wax consistently among exports. Beekeeping was popular among the early settlers. There was minimal expense involved in insects and hives and the amount of labor by the farmer was negligible. In Virginia there were good natural sources of nectar, such as the tulip poplar, sourwood, and basswood. George Washington, Jefferson's agricultural mentor, kept bees, a fact which would not have escaped the younger man's attention, yet he turned to the sugar maple.

Jefferson explained to agriculturist, political economist, and diplomat Benjamin Vaughan in June of 1790 that "late difficulties in the sugar trade have excited attention to our sugar trees, and it seems fully believed by judicious persons, that we can not only supply our own demand, but make for exportation. I will send you a sample of it if I can find a conveyance without possessing it through the expensive one of the post. What a blessing to substitute a sugar which requires only the labour of children, for that which is said renders the slavery of blacks necessary."[28]

He found time to send maple seeds to Thomas Mann Randolph at the end of 1790. By May 1, 1791 he told William Drayton, president of South Carolina's agricultural society, "The attention now paying to the sugar-maple tree promises us an abundant supply of sugar at home."[29] The same day he wrote Washington, "A Mr. Nobel has been here, from the country where they are busied with the Sugar maple tree. He thinks Mr. Cooper will bring 3000 £'s worth to market this season, and gives the most flattering calculations of what may be done in that way. He informs me of another very satisfactory fact, that less profit is made by converting the juice into a spirit than into sugar. He gave me specimens of the spirit, which is exactly whiskey."[30]

Jefferson's interest in the possibilities of the sugar maple was fortified when he and James Madison made a month-long tour through the northern states in 1791. They left Philadelphia May 17. In Bennington, Vermont Jefferson saw the sugar maple industry first-hand.

With his new awareness of the virtues of maple sugar, he was no doubt unhappy when his son-in-law reported in July 1791 that only a few of the seeds Jefferson had sent him the year before had germinated and these died soon thereafter. However, he must have anticipated that result, for the day before Randolph wrote him Jefferson reminded William Prince, the Long Island nurseryman, "When I was at your house in June, I left you a note to furnish me with the following trees, to wit: Sugar maples. All you have."[31] Prince sold him sixty and sent them in November 1791. Jefferson also got maple buds for grafting from another source.

As usual he wanted to assure himself of a supply, not always easy considering the transportation of the times, so he wrote to Joseph Fay of Bennington, Vermont. Fay also saw the possibilities of the sugar maple and planned an orchard of them. Fay promised to forward seeds when they ripened. For some reason none were sent until the fall of 1792 when Fay wrote, "I have taken the earliest I can to collect a few of the maple seeds which you will receive herewith by the post; Should the soil of Virginia prove friendly you will soon be able to furnish the State, as they produce very spontaneously. . . . The seeds must be committed to the Earth as soon as convenient this fall in some place where they will not be exposed to be damaged by fowls & squirrels."[32]

Jefferson, who no doubt wondered when he would receive the seeds from Fay, could not have been too concerned. His tactic of multiple sources would pay off. He had written Randolph from Philadelphia the spring of 1792, "I am sorry to hear my sugar maples [those from Prince] have failed. I shall be able however to get here any number I may desire, as two nurserymen have promised to make provision for me. It is too hopeful an object to be abandoned."[33]

The climate and soils of Monticello proved a difficult matter. By 1794 Jefferson's records show only eight maples were still alive. He would try again. In 1798 he sent two more maples to Randolph. The fate of these trees is not recorded. His last proposal to establish this tree at Monticello, pending availability of plants, occurred in 1809. Today six sugar maples survive there. This persistence seems odd in view of the fact that Bacon, overseer from 1806, had by then more than forty hives of bees.

In Virginia sugar maples are native to the Piedmont where conditions permit but are common only at higher, cooler locations. This preference in temperature Jefferson did not take into account and even his determination could not make this maple respond on the consistent basis necessary for home manufacturing to succeed.

While unsuccessful himself, Jefferson did not hesitate to promote sugar maples in 1808 to C. P. de Lasteyrie in France: "I should think the maple-sugar more worthy of experiment [than sugar cane]. There is no part of France of which the climate would not admit this tree. I have never seen a reason why every farmer should not have a sugar orchard, as well as an apple orchard. The supply of sugar for his family would require as little ground, and the process of making it as easy as that of cider. Mr. Micheaux, your botanist here, could send you plants as well as seeds, in any quantity from the United States."[34]

Another early project to establish a domestic industry based on plants involved the grape. As a lover and connoisseur of fine wine, Jefferson naturally tried growing grapes. Cuttings from the Old World had been attempted on American shores almost from the earliest settlements. Two things were soon discovered. European grapes, which made fine wine, proved difficult to grow successfully in the Colonies, while native American grapes which had no trouble thriving generally made poor wine. Jefferson was not the first nor the last to attempt to overcome both problems.[35] In 1770 his old law mentor, George Wythe, sent him some vines, "the best I had." We are not told the variety. The following year Jefferson planted five cuttings from neighbor Nicholas Lewis on the southeast edge of his garden. Soon he and several other men subscribed £2000 sterling to bring the Italian Philip Mazzei to America to raise grape vines and make wine. Mazzei arrived in Virginia late in 1773. His search for good land on which to grow grapes ended at Monticello where Jefferson gave him some 2000 acres. The Italian stayed with his benefactor until a house could be built on his new farm. Mazzei had brought with him from Italy ten vignerons. Six more arrived the following year. The men planned a considerable vineyard on Mazzei's property, using vine cuttings from Europe.

Mazzei soon became acquainted with the numerous native grapes found around Monticello and chose six of the best from which to make wine. He saved one barrel for his own use and gave the other to his workers, who sold it for a shilling a bottle. He became much excited by the possibilities of American grapes, but political matters soon claimed his attention and he lost interest in the venture.

Jefferson's *Garden Book* for 1774 records that some of Mazzei's workmen planted thirty vines at Monticello, eight of which were identified as Spanish raisins, the others unidentified native sorts. Jefferson also provided a detailed account of how the workmen planted them.

What happened to these original vines is not recorded. When he was in France in 1785 Jefferson made arrangements for French vines good for wine and vines good for fresh table grapes to be sent home. The fate of these plants is not recorded either.

Jefferson wrote Anthony Giannini, one of Mazzei's vignerons, early in 1786: "How does my vineyard come on? Have there been grapes enough to make a trial of wine? If there should be, I should be glad to receive here a few bottles of the wine."[36] He did not truly expect Monticello wine to arrive at his doorstep; there is no evidence it was ever made there. Still, never one to admit defeat, he noted from Paris later in 1786, after comparing the quality of American pome and stone fruits with those of Europe: "I must add that tho' we have some grapes as good as in France, yet we have by no means such a variety, nor so perfect a succession of them."[37]

Despite his desire for his beloved country to excel in all areas, Jefferson seems to have developed second thoughts about his efforts to establish a wine industry. By 1787 he had seen first hand the southern part of France. He wrote from Paris to William Drayton in South Carolina:

> We should not wish for their wines, though they are good and abundant. The culture of the vine is not desirable in lands capable of producing anything else. It is a species of gambling, and of desperate gambling too, wherein, whether you make much or nothing, you are equally ruined. The middling crop alone is the saving point, and that the seasons seldom hit. Accordingly, we see much wretchedness among this class of cultivators. Wine, too, is so cheap in these countries, that a laborer with us, employed in the culture of any other article, may exchange it for wine, more and better than he could raise himself. It is a resource for a country, the whole of whose good soil is otherwise employed, and which still has some barren spots, and surplus of population to employ on them. There the vine is good, because it is something in the place of nothing. It may become a resource to us at a still earlier period; when the increase of population shall increase our productions beyond the demand for them, both at home and abroad. Instead of going on to make an useful surplus of them, we may employ our supernumerary hands on the vine. But that period is not yet arrived.[38]

Jefferson did nothing further about grapes until he came into contact with Peter Legaux, who lived near Philadelphia. Legaux was described by a later American botanist as being the smartest and most public-spirited grape grower America had yet produced. In 1801 Legaux offered the President some vines which Jefferson declined until the following year. He then planted thirty cuttings from Burgandy and Campagne, thirty from Bordeaux and ten from the Cape of Good Hope in the southwest vineyard.[39]

The big push with grapes, as with many of his activities, came in 1807 when he looked forward to retirement from the Presidency. From Timothy Matlack of Lancaster, Pennsylvania, he received cuttings of six purple Syrian grapes originally from Twickenham, an English estate he had visited while on his mission abroad. He wrote Matlack that he would be happy to receive more in 1809 when he returned home. A truly large group of grapes, both native and European, were ordered. Jefferson could significantly expand his collection. He had enlarged his vineyard once his garden wall and the terraces below it were in place. He was, typically, willing to try more; ultimately he had some 36 varieties.

In 1809, home from Washington, Jefferson began comparing grapes with his friend John Adlum of Maryland, who owned one of the best vineyards in America, collecting and growing numerous varieties for the commercial market. Jefferson wrote Adlum, "I think it would be well to push the culture of that grape [Fox grape], without losing our time & efforts in search of foreign vines, which it will take centuries to adapt to our soil & climate. The object of the present letter is so far to trespass on your kindness, & your disposition to promote a culture so useful, as to request you at the proper season to send some cuttings of that vine. Praying your pardon to a brother-amateur in these things."[40]

In the spring of 1810 Adlum sent 165 cuttings. Jefferson notes in his *Garden Book:* "Apr. 20. Planted in the 11. uppermost terrasses of the E. vineyard 165. cuttings of a native winegrape red^d. from Major Adlum of Maryland. This grape was first discovered by a gardener of Governor John Penn's & transplanted into his garden in or near Philadelphia. I have drank of the wine. It resembles the Comartin Burgundy."[41]

In 1811 Jefferson planted grapes at Poplar Forest, 11 of one variety, 21 of another, none identified as to type. In this year he also reverting to his earlier enthusiasm for the idea of establishing a domestic wine industry. He wrote, "Wine being among the earliest luxuries in which we indulge ourselves, it is desirable it should be made here and we have every soil, aspect & climate of the best wine countries . . . and abundance of lean & meagre spots of stony & red soil, without sand, resembling extremely the Cote of Burgundy from Chambertin to Monrachet where the finest wines of Burgundy are made."[42]

In 1812 Jefferson got a Cape of Good Hope grape, supplied by McMahon by way of Legaux who had gotten the variety from the Cape. McMahon commented: "This I am confident, from several years observation, is the variety of grape most to be depended on for giving wine to the United States, but particularly to be cultivated *for that purpose* in the middle and eastern states." McMahon also included "an improved variety of the Cape grape, somewhat earlier and better *for the table*, and equally good for making wine."[43]

But with this usual intense pride in his own country, Jefferson was happiest to discover and promote American grapes. This letter written on Christmas day 1815 to John David shows Jefferson in his role as facilitator:

In the earlier part of my life I have been ardent for the introduction of new objects of culture suited to our climate. But at the age of 72. it is too late. I must leave it to younger persons who have enough of life left to pursue the object and enjoy it's attainment. . . . There is in our woods a native grape which of my own knolege produces a wine so nearly of the quality of the Caumartin of Burgundy, that I have seen at my own table a large company acknolege they could not distinguish between them. I do not know myself how this particular grape could be known in our woods, altho' I believe it abounds: but there is a gentleman on Potomak who cultivates it. This may be worth your attention. Should you think it worthwhile to examine the aptitude of this part of the country for the wine, I shall be very happy to receive you at Monticello.[44]

Two weeks later he wrote to Major Adlum, "I am so convinced that our first success will be from a native grape, that I would try no other."[45]

It is surprising Jefferson waited so late to try scuppernong vines. He planted 15 of the muscadines in 1817. These grapes make a delicious wine which became a favorite with the master of Monticello. He wrote in 1817, "[North Carolina] Scuppernon wine, made on the Southside of the Sound, would be distinguished on the best tables of Europe, for it's fine aroma, and chrystalline transparence. Unhappily that aroma, in most of the samples I have seen, has been entirely submerged in brandy. This coarse taste and practice is the peculiarity of Englishmen, and their apes Americans. I hope it will be discontinued, and that this fortunate example will encourage our country to go forward in this culture."[46]

For a man who tried so hard to keep good records despite the pressures on his time, it must have pained him to admit to Samuel Maverick of South Carolina in 1822 that "age, debility and decay of memory have for some time withdrawn me from attention to matters without doors. The grape you inquire after as having gone from this place is not now recollected by me. As some in my vineyard have died, others have been substituted without noting which, so that at present all are unknown. That as good wines will be made in America as in Europe the Scuppernon of North Carolina furnishes sufficient proof. . . . The culture however is more desirable for domestic use than profitable as an occupation for market."[47] Jefferson wrote to Major Adlum that same year to make sure he knew of the merits of the scuppernong.

Maverick had told Jefferson about a large-scale effort to establish a wine industry which certainly caught the latter's interest. In 1816 a group of 150 French followers of Napoleon had come to America and was granted some 10,000 acres in Alabama by Congress. Mostly officers of the army and many far from young, they were taken under the wing of American sympathizers to begin an agricultural venture growing European grapes and olives with lemons and oranges as secondary crops. While the Frenchmen were not professional farmers, it became quickly apparent to them that neither olives nor European grapes were suited to Alabama any more than they were to points farther north. In 1822, when Maverick talked to several of the men, he reported they were still confident of the grapes but, after spending $150,000 on the project, the scheme eventually collapsed.

While Jefferson does not seem to actively have been involved in sending American grapes to Europe, others did—with devastating results. European grapes had failed in eastern America, primarily because they lacked winter hardiness and they were susceptible to fungus diseases and the American grape-root louse. About 150 years ago American grapes were imported into Europe, carrying the louse there too, which almost devastated European vineyards. Fortunately for America, nature came to the rescue with natural crosses between European and American species, giving the Concord, Catawba, Delaware and other grapes. Horticulturists did their bit by grafting European vinifera varieties onto American roots, which solved the European plight until resistant hybrid crosses were developed—the French-American varieties commonly sold today.

As for Virginia, at last it has a wine industry, centered appropriately in Charlottesville within eyesight of Monticello. With plantings first set out in 1974 the Albemarle County area quickly gained nine other licensed farm wineries. Some of the best wines in the East are made there.

Despite his desire to make America as self-sufficient as possible and his awareness of the benefits of promoting crops which would supply food and clothing, Jefferson always kept in mind the soil. He had tried clover and found some of his fields were too worn out even for this otherwise excellent soil ameliorator. He was therefore prompted to try sainfoin instead.[48] Sainfoin, a perennial legume was grown in southern Europe. It was one of the seeds he sent from Paris in 1786 to South Carolina's agriculture society, gathered from a luxuriant stand he had planted in his Paris garden. Long grown in Europe, Jefferson believed sainfoin also would grow well in America. It produced on the poorest land and was beneficial to the soil. It was a nutritious fodder, made good hay, and was liked by livestock, especially sheep. It was even a good honey producer.

Jefferson was not the only American interested in this legume. Washington asked for sainfoin seeds from the Englishman Arthur Young in 1786. Young sent only a small number the next year, saying he could not conceive that it would succeed for Washington. Although Washington continued to try, he was never successful in making it grow profitably at Mount Vernon.

Jefferson included it as a by-article in his 1793 plans and in his fermé ornée of 1808. He frequently mentioned it in his correspondence, but it never performed as well as he had hoped.

Sainfoin was still advertised for sale in Baltimore in the 1820 *American Farmer*. Although its use was then abandoned, both Jefferson and Washington were on the right track. While it has not achieved the status of a major American forage crop, there is renewed interest at U.S. experimental stations in this legume because of the threat to alfalfa by the alfalfa weevil.

Jefferson's letters show that he recognized that what worked on one man's soils did not necessarily work on another's. He was always open to new ideas and new plants to achieve his ends. For example, a friend had sent him roots of fiorin grass, which were of interest because of their reputation for satisfactorily covering ravaged soils. After giving them to Randolph to try on wet fields where the grass was subsequently winter damaged, Jefferson wrote that he would try it on a dry soil. "I suspect it to be a grass peculiarly adapted to the humid climate & the covered sky & mild winter of Ireland, but doubtful under our hot sun, cloudless skies & severe cold of winter, but yet it may possibly give us a good growth in spring before the summer heats set in, and another after they are over in autumn & before the severe cold comes on. I will give a careful trial in the hope that sufficient experiments may point out the situations in which we also may participate of it's benefits."[49]

Despite his enthusiasm for new plants for American farmers, he was mindful of the need for practicality. He explained to C. P. de Lasteyrie in 1808: "In general, it is a truth that if every nation will employ itself in what it is fittest to produce, a greater quantity will be raised of the things contributing to human happiness, than if every nation attempts to raise everything it wants within itself."[50]

But what if free commerce between nations was not possible? Jefferson wrote a New York friend in 1811 that "I am come over therefore to your opinion that, abandoning to a certain degree those agricultural pursuits, which best suited our situation, we must endeavor to make every thing we want within ourselves."[51] America was again about to be plunged into war. He held dearly to the idea that exchanges between academic societies should operate freely even in periods of hostility, but he was more realistic now about the inconstancies of trade.

5

Farm Implements

Colonial Americans could have had little inspiration from their farm implements. Their design had changed little for thousands of years. The pace of agricultural invention had been glacial since the initial discovery of domestication, cultivation, and of agriculture as a profession. The simple woodwork involved was done on the farm or plantation. Carts, sleds for winter use, plows, yokes, handles for various tools—all came from the farmer's woodlot. Blades for axes and hoes, prongs for pitchforks, iron edges for the wooden shovel, sickles—these and more were made by the village blacksmith in the North or a resident plantation or a neighboring plantation artisan in the South. Not until well after the Revolution were more promising tools in use on American farmlands. Jefferson did not live to see major advances.

The earliest colonists and even later pioneers would have been hard put without maize because this extraordinary crop could be conveniently grown using a digging stick. The seed was easily acquired and free as well, and harvesting involved a flick of the wrist without loss of a single precious kernel. Newly cleared land with its full complement of stumps and roots made plowing unfeasible, which was just as well since few farmers owned one. It is estimated that in 1649 there were no more than 150 plows in all of Virginia. A traveler in that state in 1686 reported astonishment upon finding that almost no planters used plows. A decade later other travelers made the same observation for Virginia and, several years later, for North Carolina.

Captain John Smith listed the following as necessary implements for the colonist: Hoes (narrow and broad), axes (broad and felling), saws (hand and whip), spades, shovels, and carpentry tools. These would be supplemented in time by a few additional items, usually heavy, crude, and clumsy. Plows, harrows and two-wheeled carts were the only animal drawn pieces of equipment available at the beginning of the nineteenth century. This was not necessarily an impediment; draft animals themselves were not owned by many farmers. As late as 1776 Colonel Landon Carter of Sabine-Hall, Virginia would deplore the idea that a plow was necessary even to raise wheat, commenting that his father and he managed to export large quantities using only a hoe. The Carters were probably exceptional in their method for their day.

Wooden plows left a lot to be desired. They were not necessarily heavy, but they were awkward. In fact it took considerable effort just to prevent a plow from being thrown out of the ground even though it barely scratched the earth. Harrows were not much better, with their wooden or iron teeth. Samuel Dean in his *New England Farmer* (1790) was of the opinion the wooden teeth on a harrow were virtually worthless except to cover seed with soil. Iron teeth, while more effective in pulverizing the soil, needed a keen edge to do the job effectively. Dean was surprised so few men steeled the points so they would remain sharp longer and pulverize the soil better, especially because the steeling was not costly. Jefferson at times dispensed with a man-made harrow in favor of a branch from a tree, sufficient for the task of covering clover seeds. He was not alone. Edmund Ruffin wrote that, even in the second decade of the 1800s, harrows were hardly known in Virginia. By 1840, however, they had become indispensable. Obviously their limitations, real or perceived, had been eliminated.

There were good reasons why few farm implements existed and why those that did were unsophisticated. Designs depended on the ingenuity of the individual farmer and the quality of the result depended on the skills he or someone in the community could bring to the task. Factories with standardized products were a thing of the future. Well into the 1800s a good idea could die soon after birth, especially if the reality took a talented blacksmith to make. Jefferson's efforts to change this situation were therefore in the vanguard. They are particularly impressive because with him, important as good agricultural implements were to his financial well-being, a role as inventor was only one of the many he engaged in. His mouldboard plow of least resistance might very well have brought him more fame if he had been known for nothing else and if it had not soon been eclipsed by devices built by men who devoted their energies primarily to invention.

Jefferson was well aware of the central role of the plow for the American future. He wrote to Charles Willson Peale in 1813: "The plough is to the farmer what the wand is to the sorcerer. Its effect is really like sorcery."[1] Plows date to the latter half of the fourth millennia B.C., by which time they were being used in the Middle East. Mankind had domesticated wheat and barley by 8000 B.C., so one must wonder what prompted the idea of a plow after 5000 years of farming without one. As the earliest representation of plows centers in Mesopotamia, the most probable explanation is that region's arid climate. During the hot season evaporation is excessive and a hard crust soon forms on the surface of disturbed soil. This must have become intolerable as populations increased. Animals had long been domesticated. Through selective breeding and the discovery that castration produced a more docile nature, oxen eventually assumed a more important role in human lives. Then some forgotten genius coupled a likely animal with a hoe and digging stick, both long in use, or simply used a tree limb with a branch at an appropriate angle for scratching the earth. Egyptians used similar plows for similar reasons by early dynastic times (ca. 3000 B.C.). Plows are mentioned in Pliny, Hesiod, Virgil, and the Old Testament.

Roman plows were probably superior to those generally used in Colonial America. Indeed, a crooked stick with an iron point attached served as a plow in Illinois as late as 1812. Only those who read or traveled widely were even aware of new models. Furthermore, most notable advances were still confined to Europe. The Dutch, hundreds of years after the Romans, are credited with a major improvement in plow performance: a mouldboard which turned a furrow instead of just loosening the soil. The mouldboard was made of wood. Its function was to carry the sod up to one side after it had been cut vertically by the plowshare and its cutting edge, or coulter. Then the soil was turned over. The less force needed to accomplish this task, the more efficient the plow. An improved version of the Dutch invention was patented as the Rotherham plow in England in 1730. George Washington ordered one in 1765 and preferred it to other plows. After this the pace of invention suddenly speeded up. By the end of his long life agriculture had been radically transformed from what it had been in his youth, at least among the more progressive farmers.

Jefferson had been aware of plows all of his life, having been the son and grandson of farmers and a farmer himself. As a keen observer of all that interested him, it is hardly surprising he would note the plows used in the countries he traveled in, despite the fact he had yet to become a real hands-on agriculturist at home. The year after he went to Paris he paid three francs to see a plow drawn by a windlass. Powered by four men instead of two horses or oxen, Jefferson decided this was not much of an improvement over traditional methods, but ever the innovator, he no doubt wondered about a better solution to this laborious job.

On his trip through the agricultural regions of northeast France in 1788 he took the trouble not only to observe the plows and the primitive mouldboards used, but to figure out a better design for the latter. (Most plows had no mouldboards at all.) Jefferson's plan for a "mouldboard of least resistance" was outlined in his travel journal dated April 19, 1788.[2] He probably had in mind the work of James Small, who standardized the shape and angle of the Scotch plowshare and the angle of the mouldboard. Whatever the source of inspiration, his design lay unfulfilled during his next years of public service.

After he returned to the U.S. late in 1789, Jefferson showed Thomas Mann Randolph a model of his proposed mouldboard. Randolph, pondering the idea, prodded his new father-in-law in April of 1790: "I must trouble you to communicate to me in your next letter the method of making the mouldboard which we admired so much at Monticello. The necessity I am under of turning my attention to the cultivation of my little farm, has inclined my thoughts of late toward agriculture."[3] Some months later Jefferson sent a model from New York.

Jefferson apparently did not find the time to oversee the construction of a mouldboard for himself until he left Washington's cabinet at the end of 1793. The delay caused him to be one-upped. In addition to Randolph he had confided his idea to James Madison and Dr. George Logan. Logan beat the inventor in constructing one. In July of 1793, Madison wrote Jefferson from Dr. Logan's, "You will see your theory of a mould-board more nearly realized than in any other instance, and with the advantage of having the iron wing, which in common bar shares or in great lies useless under the wood, turned up into the sweep of the board, and relieving it from the brunt of the friction."[4]

The following year Jefferson wrote John Taylor about his design: "I have imagined and executed a mould-board which may be mathematically demonstrated to be perfect, as far as perfection depends on mathematical principles, and one great circumstance in it's favor is that it may be made by the most bungling carpenter, & cannot possibly vary a hair's breath in it's form, but by gross negligence. . . . I will make a model of the mould-board & lodge it with Col? Harvie in Richmond for you."[5]

The degree of resistance of course affected the depth of the plowing as well as the amount of force needed to pull the implement. This was of great concern to Jefferson. He told Peale in 1813, "Ploughing deep, your recipe for killing weeds, is also the recipe for almost every good thing in farming."[6] And as Jefferson told Judge Harry Innes after discussing another mouldboard, "I can assure you that the same horses, in my farm, would make a furrow with this [Jefferson's own] mould board 2. I. deeper than they could with the common mould board, owing to the difference of resistance."[7]

By 1795 Jefferson had tested his invention at Monticello and found it fulfilled his expectations. Actual practice with it, however, turned up a new wrinkle. When the soil was damp the width of the toe tended to accumulate dirt. To such a habitual tinkerer this was no problem. By 1805 he had made another mouldboard, this one with a sharp toe. This alteration shortened the plow share some six or eight inches. His farming associates, he reported, preferred the latest design.

Jefferson went to considerable trouble to secure a dynamometer with which to test the amount of force needed to operate a plow with his mouldboard attached. In 1796 he complained to a friend, "I had some time ago conceived the principles of it [the mouldboard]. . . . I have since reduced the thing to practice and have reason to believe the theory fully confirmed. I only wish for one of those instruments used in England for measuring the force exerted in the drafts of different plows, etc., that I might compare the resistance of my mould-board with that of others. But these instruments are not to be had here."[8] After the elusive instrument was finally borrowed from Robert Fulton in 1810, Jefferson was able to make a scientific test.

He had long before received theoretical support from the great American mathematician, physicist and astronomer, David Rittenhouse. Before his death in 1796[9] Rittenhouse proclaimed it was indeed mathematically demonstrable that Jefferson's mouldboard provided the least possible resistance. By 1810 the inventor was using five plows fitted with the attachment on his own fields.

The final alteration Jefferson made to his mouldboard was to have it cast in iron. As early as 1798 he wrote Sir John Sinclair that he proposed to do this now that he was satisfied the dimensions were correct. James Small's mouldboard had been cast in iron while other early mouldboards, including his own, were wood, protected at times by iron plates. The iron plates concept came from Joseph Foljambe, who took out the first English patent in 1720. Plowshares and landsides made of iron had also been tried, but they all suffered from rough surfaces which increased drag.

The actual impetus for Jefferson's iron mouldboard apparently came when Dr. James Mease wrote him in 1804, asking for a pattern thin enough for casting. Dr. Mease had published a description of the mouldboard in his *Domestic Encyclopedia*. Mease had made a working mouldboard based on models owned by the American Philosophical Society and exhibited the resulting implement to Society members. They were not impressed, he had concluded, because these men were not practicing farmers. Mease apparently felt an iron mouldboard would improve acceptance.

Mease's letter came in the middle of Jefferson's Presidency, and it appears not to have been answered. It was not in fact until three years into his final retirement that he indicated he planned to order thirty mouldboards cast in iron. The pattern, however, was not sent to John Staples of Richmond until the spring of 1814. Jefferson told his old friend Peale the following year, "I have lately had my moldboard cast in iron, very thin, for a furrow of 9. I. wide & 6. I. deep, and fitted to a plow, so light that two small horses or mules draw it with less labor than I have ever before seen necessary. It does beautiful work and is approved by every one."[10]

Tireless promoter as he was, Jefferson sent models to various friends in addition to Taylor, including Chancellor Robert R. Livingston, and Philip Tabb in America and André Thoüin and Pierre Samuel Dupont de Nemours in Paris.[11] Englishman William Strickland visited Monticello in 1795 and was duly shown the invention. Upon his return home Strickland convinced the Board of Agriculture of England to request a model for their edification. On the eve of sending it Jefferson who had made the model himself, apparently had doubts about its design despite its many endorsements. In 1798 he asked the considered opinion of Robert Patterson[12] as to possible flaws. Upon being reassured as to its perfection, the model crossed the ocean in due course. A description was also sent to Sir John Sinclair, president of England's Board of Agriculture.[13] That year a description of the mouldboard was published in the *Transactions* of the American Philosophical Society. Jefferson presented his paper before the group in May 1798.

The Society of Agriculture of Paris considered the original model too. The members granted Jefferson a gold medal for it in 1807 and made him a foreign associate. He was no doubt gratified by a letter that informed him: "The Mould board, for which you obtained the Prize, has been pronounced by the Abbé Hauy, and others, to be mathematically exact, and incapable of further improvement."[14]

In return, the French society sent Jefferson a Guillaume plow which the President told Taylor the French thought was the best constructed plow ever known in the country. Jefferson reported:

> It is a wheel plough, as lightly made as we should have done it; and seeing no peculiar advantage in it's construction, I suspect it owes to it's lightness & shortness it's superiority over the ploughs with which it was tried; for the ploughs of Europe are barbarously heavy, & long, & therefore require great force. I believe Great Britain has lately begun to use lighter ploughs. I shall now not be afraid of sending to the society one of our best ploughs, according to their request, with my mouldboard to it. I shall previously try it's resistance to the draught, comparatively with theirs, by the same instrument they have used.[15]

A replica of Jefferson's plow at the Thomas Jefferson Visitors Center at Monticello shows it is a full ten feet long. Despite its apparent bulk one man could lift it fairly easily before the irons were added. As early as 1649 the Englishman Blythe in his *Improver Improved* was recommending plows light enough to be drawn by two horses or even one as opposed to the heavy clumsy machines which required four or more horses or oxen and still barely scratched the surface. In the eighteenth century it still took two men or a man and one boy with two to three horses or four to six oxen to pull a simple plow, and only one or two acres of land could be worked up per day. Jefferson's mouldboard, especially when cast in iron, made the task easier.

In the matter of agriculture Jefferson was very much the team player. His one goal was to improve farming, "the most useful of the occupations of man." He was not interested in getting credit for his efforts, and consequently they have been overlooked. The innate modesty of the man shows through no more clearly than when he promotes this invention so dear to his heart. He told Peale in 1815, after promising to send him a plow, "You will be at perfect liberty to use the form of the mouldboard, as all the world is, having never thought of monopolizing by patent any useful idea which happens to offer itself to me."[16]

How extensively his mouldboard was used is not known. While improved mouldboards had been made by others, they were too complicated for the majority of farmers to make. Jefferson's concept overcame this problem. It could be made to exact dimensions with just a saw and adze when not cast in iron and represented the peak of development of this part of the plow. Whatever the number eventually made, Jefferson should be honored as one of the first persons to attempt to standardize agriculture machinery.

The pace of plow invention suddenly picked up and others quickly upstaged Jefferson's achievement. His own son-in-law, Randolph, was one of the first to challenge the President as an innovator.

Having used plows of several designs, pulled by both single and pairs of draft animals, Jefferson was no doubt partially responsible for the pursuance by Randolph of the idea of a hillside plow. Jefferson was certainly the first distinguished American to promote contour plowing; but it was Randolph as early as 1793 at age 25 who began to experiment with a plow designed for horizontal plowing and his father-in-law credited him with introducing this method in their area. With an increasing number of children to support, he had good reason to apply his efforts to create money from his farm. His father-in-law no doubt envied the younger man for the long periods during which he was able to personally supervise his fields, thereby learning first hand the ins and outs of farming.

Like so many other Albemarle farms, Randolph's was hilly and, also like them, was worn out and gullied from past ruinous plowing and cropping practices. Fortunately for him, young Randolph shared Jefferson's intense interest in all phases of natural history. Furthermore, Randolph's education in Scotland provided a sound background in the classics as well as personal observation of Scottish farming practices. Thus he was aware of experimentation with contour plowing which dated to the early Roman empire. Pliny the Younger and Columella's works which describe it were both in Randolph's library.[17] Jethro Tull, the eighteenth century British agriculturist recommended such horizontal plowing in his *Horse-Hoeing Husbandry*, which was in Jefferson's library if not Randolph's. He may also have read of the method as presented by the English writer Francis Forbes in 1778.

By the end of the eighteenth century contour plowing was being both advocated and practiced abroad. There were isolated instances on this side of the Atlantic and Madison used horizontal drainage ditches on his hilly plantation in Orange County, Virginia. But it was Randolph who devised the plow used in Albemarle and the rest of Virginia's Piedmont region. Like his father-in-law he was always looking for the best way to improve farming. His own ideas about plowing evolved over a period of fifteen years before he was satisfied with his resulting implement.

As the thrust of hillside plowing is to, in effect, make a hill flat, Randolph first had to figure out a system of land preparation. With a rafter level, guidelines some thirty yards apart were laid across the hill to be plowed. This was followed by plowing along the lines. Then furrows were cut parallel to them. The virtue of Randolph's plow was that it threw the furrow downhill both going and coming. This was accomplished by a double share, welded together at right angles. Fixed to the plow on a movable bar, the vertical section acted as a mouldboard while the horizontal section cut the soil. With a single motion of the hand the plowman could pivot the unit depending on his direction across the hill. While the plow was necessarily heavier than usual, it could easily be pulled by two horses and could make furrows up to ten inches deep.

Although Randolph did not promote his accomplishment, Jefferson did. Taylor promoted Randolph's achievement in his *Arator*, and a few farmers began using the new invention, but most continued in the old method of plowing up and down hill (and would continue this practice into the mid-1900s). Edmund Ruffin pointed out the shortcomings of the hillside plow: It was more expensive, it was easily incapacitated, and the method itself required more care than most farmers were willing to give. When cut improperly the furrows could even trap water which in time caused the formation of the very gullies the system was designed to eliminate. While Jefferson wrote a friend in 1817 that Randolph's horizontal plowing would be the salvation of Albemarle as well as of Bedford County where the method was rapidly spreading, the fact remains that soon after Randolph's death in 1828 his plow was all but abandoned.

Yet he should be honored for the development of his plan for contour plowing which is the standard method of plowing hillsides today, albeit with different equipment. Certainly the high point in his agricultural life must have been the receipt in 1822 of a silver plate recognizing his achievement by the Agricultural Society of Albemarle he had helped found five years before. The Society at its founding had thirty members. Membership would include men who either had been or would become U.S. Presidents, governors of Virginia (of which Randolph would be one), a supreme court justice, a Virginia senator, a University of Virginia president and several state legislators. The men lived in Albemarle and four adjacent counties. The Society was based on Jefferson's scheme for a system of agricultural societies he had put forth in a paper in 1811.[18]

Randolph displayed his ability before his peers by pursuing an active roll in his society. Among other duties he presented several papers. Such efforts as determining the most efficient method of harnessing a horse to a threshing machine were dear to his heart. Recognition of his devotion to agriculture alone would have warranted his being elected president of the society in 1827, succeeding the seventy-five-year-old Madison.

It is ironic that so conscientious and technically capable a farmer, whose crops were correspondingly good, should have been a financial failure. While part of his monetary problems were due to a lack of expertise in marketing the products of his fields, like his father-in-law he too was encumbered by debts incurred by others and the general economic instability of the times. His political jobs as congressman and governor of Virginia were not helpful in getting out of debt either. Not surprisingly, especially with his volatile temper and a family to support which ultimately numbered eleven surviving children, Randolph became distant not only to his wife Martha and offspring but also to Jefferson.

Another type of innovation to the generic plow was made by Charles Newbold of New Jersey in 1797. He patented a plow in which the mouldboard, plowshare and landside were cast all in one piece, his solution to the question of how to most efficiently attach the mouldboard to the share, a technique which had proved elusive. Switching to a cast iron plow was prophetic of the metal plows of the future. They had been tried by this date at least in England. George Washington received two plows apparently made of iron from Arthur Young in England for Young wrote he could send wooden ones instead if Washington preferred. Young clearly saw the limitations of wooden plows: Alterations to them were virtually impossible, and once twisted out of the correct line they were useless. Considering Jefferson's close involvement with Washington in all matters pertaining to agriculture, it is strange that Jefferson did not carry his idea of a cast iron mouldboard to include the entire plow, especially because he had a competent man at his own blacksmith shop.

Newbold had his troubles promoting his plow, although he spent a great deal of money trying to convert farmers to his concept. Objections were multiple. The cost was considered beyond the budget of most farmers, and for many it probably was. Iron poisoned the soil, yet at the same time encouraged weed growth (which was true in that the weeds also benefited from improved cultivation). Beyond these notions the plow's most serious defect was that when the share became dull or was broken the entire plow had to be replaced.

Others also thought they had the solution to the perfect plow. Between 1800 and 1830 124 patents for plows were issued, plus plows of Scottish and English origin. The most noteworthy innovator was Jethro Wood of New York, who took out a patent in 1814 for a cast iron plow and one in 1819 for an improved version which incorporated Jefferson's mouldboard design. Wood's plow corrected a major flaw in Newbold's design. It was cast in several pieces which joined and were fastened together by lugs and interlocking pieces. When any piece required renewal or replacement, the task could be performed in the field—a great time and money saver. Use of such parts, standardized and interchangeable, would revolutionize farm equipment and Wood's plow became the standard of his day.

Wood had sent Jefferson one of his plows, which was received in March of 1817 (over five months after it was sent, an indication of the limitations of the era's transportation system). Jefferson was enthusiastic about the plow's possibilities and promised its inventor that he would promote it among his farming friends, noting though that nothing would come of it unless there was an outlet within Virginia, such as at Richmond, where the plows could be purchased.

By the 1820s newly designed plows using three to five oxen or horses overcame the ancient problem of furrowing deeper into the ground. Now a man could routinely cut into the earth eight or ten inches or more. Not until the 1830s did steel plows become common. John Lane in 1833 and John Deere in 1837 began their commercial manufacture. High-polished steel plows were especially desirable on the loamy soils in the Midwest, which stuck to the rougher iron plow. They were also better for cutting into the tough prairie sod. It is doubtful these western lands would have been expeditiously "won" without them. Where sod was tough, friction was so great with previous plows that three men and four to six oxen were needed to turn a furrow.

While Jefferson had been concerned with the ability of his plow to turn a furrow, the fact was that even his mouldboard design did not turn the furrow well or pulverize the soil satisfactorily. By 1839 Samuel Witherow and David Pierce had addressed these problems, creating a plow which bent the furrow-slice and twisted it slightly. These plows would all soon be superseded, and even the ideas behind plowing would change. Yet Americans had gone a long way in a comparatively short period of time.

Edmund Ruffin gives this concise description of plows as he knew them in Virginia prior to 1842: "Two-horse ploughs were rarely used, and only on the few richest and best cultivated farms. . . . On the far greater number of farms there was neither a two-horse plough, nor a mould-board plough for a single horse. Ninety-nine acres in the hundred were broken up by one-horse ploughs and half of the whole quantity with the trowel-hoe, or fluke-hoe plough, cutting wings to the share on both sides alike, and no mould-board. The ploughing was rarely deeper than three inches (often less)."[19]

Plows continued to be altered in design and later two or more were fastened together. To provide better hauling power tractors took over from horses, oxen, and mules. The pefect plow, though, may yet be invented. The latest, from England, is a "paraplow." Its knifelike vertical blades loosen soil, thereby letting water penetrate more easily. Crop residue is maintained on the surface, preventing the soil from crusting over. Runoff and erosion is minimized. Jefferson would have been impressed.[20]

Threshing, next to plowing, was the most serious operation for the farmer, for he could not rest until his crop was safely out of the fields and into storage. As threshing was always a very time-consuming enterprise, it is hardly surprising Jefferson would concentrate on its advancements as he had with the plow.

For millennia grain was flailed, either by a long pole or club or by a long wooden handle with a shorter, free-swinging stick attached at the end. With a flail a man averaged five to six bushels a day, and more if he were rewarded with part of the results.[21] When done indoors, the sound of the flail hitting the floor of a barn resounded like a drum and could be heard a good distance away.

Jefferson's wheat was treaded out, generally in the open air. In his 1795 diary he wrote for July 8: "Began to tread at Monticello with 7. horses. Were the harvest to go over again with the same force, the following arrangement should take place. The treading floor should be laid down before harvest."[22] After 1795 a threshing floor was not used to any extent at Monticello. When it was given up at Jefferson's other farms is not known.

There were other options. An Englishman, J. F. D. Smith, who toured America just prior to the Revolution and then bought land there soon thereafter, described his procedure. His platform was circular, 150 yards in circumference and twelve feet wide. It sloped gently to the outer edge. Both sides were fenced. The grain was put on the platform and a large number of horses or cattle were driven around and around. By using this technique 500 bushels of wheat could be threshed per day. The grain was separated from the chaff using a coarse sieve with two long handles. This contraption hung from cords and a pulley attached to the end of a flexible pole. So-called Dutch fans were used to finish cleaning the grain. Dutch fans were commonly used in England but not America because Americans threshed right after harvest to prevent damage by the weevil. Jefferson explained that "were our grain then laid up in bulk without the chaff in it, it would heat & rot."[23] Winnowing or removing chaff had traditionally been accomplished by throwing the grain against the wind.

A Colonel Dangerfield of Virginia substituted a series of rollers attached to a central axle in place of animals. By this method 100 bushels could be threshed per day.

By the end of the eighteenth century hand-powered threshing machines had been brought in from Europe. These had their flaws. They required too much care in their operation and repairs could not be made by the operators. Jefferson went to see a threshing machine with Washington in 1791 on a farm near Philadelphia. There was an admission charge of $1. The device was primitive and harvested only six bushels per hour. Its owner, Samuel Powel, thought a larger model might harvest 100 to 130 bushels a day. If Jefferson was impressed, he did not record it.

He turned instead to a Scottish thresher, a drum and beater patented in 1786 by Andrew Meikle. Jefferson's was the first in Virginia. He had read about it in Arthur Young's annals of 1791 and secured a model from Thomas Pinckney, U.S. Minister to England, near the end of 1793. His expectations were high. As he wrote James Madison in September of 1793:

> My threshing machine has arrived at New York. Mr. Pinckney writes me word that the original from which this model is copied, threshes 150 bushels of wheat in 8 hours, with 6 horses and 5 men. It may be moved either by water or horses. Fortunately the workman who made it (a millwright) is come in the same vessel to settle in America. I have written to persuade him to go on immediately to Richmond, offering him the use of my model to exhibit, and to give him letters to get him into immediate employ in making them. . . . I understand that the model is made mostly in brass, and in the simple form in which it was first ordered, to be worked by horses. It was to have cost 5. guineas, but Mr. Pinckney having afterwards directed it to be accommodated to water movement also, it has been it more complicated, and costs 13 guineas. It will thresh any grain from the Windsor bean down to the smallest.[24]

Jefferson wrote to George Washington in June of 1796 that he had "put the whole works (except the horse wheel) into a single frame, moveable from one field to another on the two axles of a wagon. It will be ready in time for the harvest which is coming on, which will give it a full trial."[25] Washington's comment on July 6 was, "If you can bring a moveable threshing machine, constructed upon simple principles to perfection, it will be among the most valuable institutions in this Country; for nothing is more wanting, & to be wished for on our farms."[26] The thresher's combination of gears and revolving beaters weighed almost 2000 pounds. To construct his version, based on the original, apparently took Jefferson three years.

With his new portable threshing machine his crews no longer had to erect a threshing floor outdoors at harvest. He made an undated explanation of his new method:

> Preliminary observation. My farms are divided into 7. field of 40. acres and in the center of each field is a granary of 2. rooms of 12. f. sq. each (1000 [illegible] contents) and an open passage between them of 12. f. When there is wheat in the field, it is brought as fast as it is cut to this granary & stacked round it. The threshing machine is fixed in the passage, and as the wheat is got out, it is put with it's chaff into one room and there kept till the winter. The threshing machine being removed, the fan takes it's place, the wheat passed thro' it, and the clean grain thrown over into the other room. The winter of that year our cattle have a moveable shed fixed up at the same granary, are fed with the straw and the manure is used in the same field the ensuing spring as will be explained. Many other conveniences result from having the little granary in the center of every field. In a large & hilly farm a great central barn is useless or injurious.[27]

Jefferson was satisfied his wheat was now cleaner than before, but he admitted to a correspondent in 1812 that it was still not clean enough. However, the straw was not bruised. As usual he did time studies on the machine's performance and concluded it doubled his output. With its use he could speed up the task of threshing, thereby eliminating infestation of the grain by the weevil, while at the same time allowing his workmen who would otherwise be treading, to begin plowing instead.

The number of horses he needed on his farms also was a concern. He explained to Randolph, "I found considerable hopes on the threshing machine expected, as 4. horses suffice to work that, & I had proposed to work my ploughs with oxen. Should that machine fail, more horses must be kept for treading wheat in the proper season, & to be employed in waggoning at other times. Or the raising horses for sale must be gone into so as to derive assistance in treading a year or two before they are sold."[28]

The number of horses needed, as mentioned in the Jefferson correspondence on threshing, depended in part on their size and strength, in part on the owner's incorporation of new ideas to the basic thresher plan, and perhaps in part on the owner's expectations. An 1812 letter of Jefferson's may summarize his success with threshing machines: "I have three of them myself, one going by water, & two by horses. Many have them in our neighborhood. Those moved by horses get out from 80. to 150. bushels a day with from 2. to 5. horses, & cost from 100 to 150 D. Those by water get out 300 bushels a day and more if they could be attended, & cost in proportion to their geer, canals, dams &c."[29] Jefferson used his sawmill as his souce of water power. Wood was still reasonably plentiful, so the thresher could be made cheaply. Jefferson hoped the machine would be commonly adopted in Virginia. But, as with the plow, threshing technology suddenly leaped ahead; his Scottish model was soon outdated.

The thresher which next dominated the scene was based on the type designed in the 1830s by Hiram and John Pitts of Maine. Horses walking a treadmill provided power for a revolving cylinder which knocked the kernels off the stalks. A fan blew away the husks. It was a stationary machine whose cost was high. Farmers banded together to buy and use it. Not until the early 1900s was a workable combine used on American farms.

One major farm task, reaping, apparently never challenged Jefferson's imagination. The sickle was the time honored tool for this job and was used throughout the Colonial period even though with it one man could reap only one acre or so per day. The long-handled scythe was substituted by some farmers from the sickle. Farmers favored the cradle in some parts of the South in the Colonial period and in the middle colonies in the latter 1700s, but not in New England until after 1800.

A cradle cut the grain and gathered it so the reaper could then throw it in a swath. Its virtues, once seen, slowly convinced farmers to rethink the task of reaping. By the Civil War the cradle had widely replaced the sickle and scythe. As Ruffin noted, though, even by the 1850s some of the largest and best farmers could cite solid reasons for staying with the sickle. Grain cradles continued through the early 1900s in hilly parts of America as well as in regions where little grain was grown.

Harvesting wheat was a major undertaking, requiring all available hands; Jefferson's estimate that one laborer was required to work ten acres did not apply to this work. His diary of 1795 gives the following glimpse. At Shadwell the crew began cutting the grain on June 27. There were 65 people involved, all duly categorized: seventeen cradlers, five reapers, seven stackers and thirty-six gatherers. July 3 to 6 the Monticello wheat was cut. Treading was begun July 8 at Monticello and finished at Shadwell on September 22. Meanwhile at Shadwell and Monticello, between August 20 and November 21, 305 acres were being sown for the new wheat crop. Barley and rye had been harvested, plowing was done, as were the multitude of other tasks incumbent on a farmer. Not surprisingly, Jefferson saw ways to improve the performance of his crew and drew up a new plan. But in agriculture the best laid plans frequently go awry and so did Jefferson's.

Cradles, sickles, and scythes were incapable of picking up the grain or binding it into sheaves. Raking, for those who did not have one of the horse-rakes which came into use by 1812, was done by hand, as was binding. The grain binder was not introduced until the 1850s. As with so much else agricultural, the first attempts to cut grain by machine were made in England and Scotland in the eighteenth century. How much American inventors were influenced by these earliest models is not known. Soon it would not matter, for changes in farming equipment became centered in the U.S. One inventor lived adjacent to Jefferson's Poplar Forest: Cyrus McCormick of Rockbridge County. McCormick began work on a grain reaper in 1809. William Manning patented a model of a thresher in 1831. Obed Hussey followed with a patent in 1833 and McCormick in 1834. McCormick's invention was modified over the years until it became, in essence, the modern reaper. It drastically reduced the number of workers needed for this labor intensive job. It has been considered the single most significant agricultural invention until after the Civil War.

Nevertheless the adoption of improved agricultural implements continued to be slow, particularly in the South. The Revolutionary War had been the first major watershed in changing farming methods, and the Civil War became the second. Farmers were turned into soldiers and those who remained on the land were forced to rely more on machines. With each war the country was fortunate the pace of invention had increased as much as it had and included the development of animal-powered machines. But the real transformation of agriculture did not occur until after the introduction of the gasoline engine, which effectively eliminated animal power for all except the smallest and poorest farmers. World War I hurried the process, once again because farmers were converted into soldiers.

The *U.S. Yearbook of Agriculture* for 1940 shows that agriculture at that point was still more like it had been in Jefferson's day than like it is today. The text discusses "20 acres and a mule" families who still were making an acceptable living in the South. In fact even on larger farms the change from animals to tractors was just getting into full swing. In a chapter titled "Agriculture Today" the authors saw nothing illogical about illustrating it with a picture of a team of horses pulling a hay wagon.

As for Jefferson, almost no part of the agricultural process escaped his attention or his inclination to devise a better method of doing the job. One of these jobs was seeding a field.

Despite Jethro Tull's invention of a horse-drawn seed drill in about 1701, which improved on a model of 60 years before, Young asserted there was not a good row drilling machine in England. The trick was to create a design which worked well under less than ideal soil conditions. Eventually a practical seeder evolved by 1840 and became common thereafter. Meanwhile Jefferson strove for a solution to the age old wasteful method of broadcasting seeds by hand.

He was excited by a new device invented by T. C. Martin of Virginia. It was sent to him by his friend John Taylor of Caroline County, Virginia. Jefferson therefore called it the "Carolina drill." In a letter to Washington in 1796 he said enthusiastically, "It is absolutely perfect. Nothing can be more simple, nor perform its office more perfectly for a single row. I shall try to make one to sow four rows at a time of wheat or peas, at twelve inches distance."[30] The device was duly constructed and proven, but it probably had the same flaws as others of the period: Its performance depended on soil preparation and the lie of the land.

Yet in characteristic Jefferson fashion Martin's drill was promoted to the board of the Agricultural Societies of both London and Paris. The idea behind Martin's drill was based on a band of buckets which raised the seed from the seed box into a funnel which directed the seeds into the furrow. Different sets of buckets were adapted to the different sizes of seed. Despite Martin's invention Jefferson did not give up on the "Jersey drill" which had been described in the *New York Agricultural Transactions*. He appreciated its design, which allowed four rows to be drilled at a time, but thought this could be increased to eight.

He also experimented with more efficient seeding of crops which were not amenable to growing in rows. As a result of discovering the idea in the *New York Agricultural Transactions*, he devised a seedbox for sowing clover. The box was seven feet long, six inches wide and four inches deep and divided into seven partitions, with appropriate holes in the bottom of each. He told Taylor he saved thirteen gallons of seed with the device and $13. Distribution was far more even and the job could be done even on a windy day by one man carrying the contraption.

Special cultivators were seldom used, cultivating being done with a hoe or plow. The horse-hoe, one of Tull's inventions, apparently never captured the imagination of Americans, including Jefferson, who had Tull's book on the subject in his library. A horse-drawn implement for cultivating between rows of tobacco was used infrequently.

Jefferson was more interested in the invention of a hemp-break, a machine for breaking and beating hemp into fiber. He grew hemp both at Monticello and Bedford, and processing by hand was slow, laborious, and distasteful to his workers. To a friend he gave a complete description of his device and included a drawing of it. After trying his sawmill as a power source, which he found unsatisfactory, he introduced the power of a horse to get the job done.[31]

As hemp formed a small part of Virginia's exports, Jefferson's devise had broader implications beyond his own plantations. He himself listed hemp as a primary staple, along with wheat and tobacco, when enumerating subjects the Albemarle Agricultural Society should pursue. Raising hemp and flax had been made compulsory by the Virginia Assembly in 1619 for all colonists having sufficient seed, but it never could compete with tobacco. Hemp had been promoted in the northern colonies as a possible staple for both British and American shipyards. As the job was so labor intensive, both in the cultivation and the preparation of the fiber, and grain was such a tough competitor for the fertile lands available, hemp was never established in New England either. It was grown more successfully in points in between, although never in sufficient quantities for American requirements.

Jefferson used hemp for making coarse shirts for his laborers.[32] Interestingly, this crop where grown, is usually still seeded broadcast, hoed by hand, harvested with a sickle and broken by hand or in primitive machines. Jefferson would feel right at home.

Making clothing was such an important job on his plantations that it is not surprising Jefferson created a fulling machine for his homespun. He described it as "the simplest thing in the world" before giving details and a drawing to Peale in an 1815 letter. He also improved a carding machine he had bought. Other tasks also needed new methods. To beat his corn into hominy Jefferson devised a gadget attached to the saw-gate of his sawmill. This he described to Peale in another 1815 letter. He developed a press for sesamum oil which he described to Georgia Governor John Millege in 1811. None of these improvements would change the course of a nation, yet they were remarkable nonetheless for a man whose time was so occupied in the political arena.

As a result of various time studies, Jefferson could record the length of time it took a workman to fill a two-wheeled barrow and carry it thirty yards, the amount of dung produced by a specific number of cattle, horses, and hogs, not to mention that "a pint of cotton seed contains of good seed 900" and "consequently a bushel will contain 57600." Few things escaped his observant eye.[33]

Jefferson in his lifetime witnessed the beginning of the fast-paced era when agricultural inventions and new practices came more rapidly than farmers could properly absorb them. That era continues. Instead of millennia between major advances there are decades. Jefferson would be delighted with the labor saving character of many of them, yet he could remind us that even with all our marvelous technology we have yet to resolve the problem of sustainable agriculture. American top soil still washes out to the oceans at alarming rates, while we have added equally serious problems unknown in his day: air and water pollution which hinders plant growth and takes its toll on human health, and the depletion of acquifers beyond their capacity to replenish themselves.

6

Mills and Home Manufacturing

Jefferson owned and operated various mills during the course of his life. The first was the gristmill his father had built on the Shadwell tract by 1757, the year of his death, and for years the only one on the Rivanna. As the river was then impassable, the products of this mill were for Peter's own use, although perhaps he ground for neighbors. Mill complexes were expensive to build and debt was a common denominator during this period. Furthermore, capital was almost nonexistent, as were needed engineering skills and men who knew how to manage and operate a mill. No wonder there were so few such enterprises.

Jefferson's frustration with this state of affairs is evident in a letter of 1793: "I wish to heaven the spirit of mill-building & manufacturing . . . could spread itself into Albemarle. We are miserably circumstanced there as to the disposal of our wheat. We can neither manufacture nor sell it there. And tho we have fine mill seats at the head of navigation of the Rivanna, we cannot get mills built."[1] But by 1806 he reported to James Madison there were now three mills on the Rivanna, his own, one five miles downstream, and another ten miles down, each grinding 40 barrels a day, indicating an increase in population and therefore need. The importance Jefferson attached to his mills is seen in the considerable space he devotes to the subject in his correspondence.

Despite the great freshet of 1771 which destroyed his gristmill, dam, and canal and thereafter formed a benchmark in his mind, Jefferson remained sanguine for years about his site. He was insisting in 1806 that it was one of the best in the entire country. The record after the 1771 disaster would have discouraged any other man.

His *Garden Book* for 1804 provides the highlights of past floods: "A great fresh in the Rivanna this day. It was above the top of the hopper in my toll mill. By marks at Henderson's distillery in Milton it wanted 6. feet of being as high as that in 1795. which wanted but 3. f. of being as high as the great fresh on the 26th. of May 1771."[2] Not included in his record here is one found in his *Account Book* of 1774 in which he noted a flood in the Rivanna eighteen inches higher than the one which had carried a neighbor's bridge away earlier, which was the highest ever known except for 1771.

The 1804 flood was hardly an auspicious beginning for the gristmill which Jefferson had finally replaced just the year before. More water related problems were to come. In January 1807 Jefferson wrote James Walker, who was hard at work on the President's new manufacturing mill as well as a new addition to the gristmill: "I receive with real grief the account of the tumbling down of the new walls of the toll mill. I had hoped that I had seen the end of my expenses for that establishment."[3] While a leak through the bank of the canal and water flowing over the bank were the direct cause in this instance, the results caused additional expenditures and lost time for grinding. Later that same year Jefferson wrote James Madison that a recent flood had swept away all the mills in his neighborhood and that half of his own mill dam was gone.

After operating only one year the dam was destroyed again by a freshet in 1808. Replaced soon thereafter based on a new plan, this dam was almost completely destroyed in 1810 by a freshet which also flooded the lowest floor of Jefferson's new manufacturing mill, just one year old. The gristmill must have been similarly flooded. Jefferson noted in his *Farm Book* that in the course of forty-eight hours some four and three-fourths inches of rain came down. This raised the river to such an extent that it carried away the middle of the dam and tore up sections of the eastern third. Worse was to come.

In 1814 he wrote in his *Garden Book*, "July 29. In the course of 20. hours there fell 12⅛ I. of rain, the earth being at the time extremely dry, it raised the river to the eves or upper floor of my toll mill. Or, more exactly half way up the joists.

"At the saw mill it was 10. I. deep on the barn floor, this seems to have been a rise of about 15. f. perpendicular from the surface of the river at the issue of the tail-race, or entrance of the ford. Hardware [River] is said to have risen 30. f. perpendicular."[4]

In February of 1815 a Boston visitor to Monticello, George Ticknor, reported he overheard his host telling Thomas Mann Randolph very quietly that the dam had been carried away the night before and it would cost $30,000 to rebuild. Ticknor did not know that Edmond Bacon, Monticello overseer, had witnessed this same quiet response in the flood of 1807. Bacon reported in his reminiscences this exchange: "'Well sir,' said he [Jefferson], 'have you heard from the river?' I said, 'Yes sir; I have just come from there with very bad news. The milldam is all swept away.' 'Well, sir,' said he, just as calm and quiet as though nothing had happened, 'we can't make a new dam this summer.'"[5] Jefferson then enumerated what must be done in the interim.

The 1815 damage is not recorded in either the *Farm Book* or *Garden Book*, which indicates perhaps that Jefferson had become reconciled to almost yearly damage to mills, dam and canal. In 1819 he told Bacon, after listing projects to be accomplished, "I have engaged here the best millwright [I] have ever known to go and rebuild the sawmill and the gristmill as soon as the canal is done."[6] Whether this damage was due to flooding is not made clear.

The problem of converting wheat to cash was not always too much water. Jefferson wrote to James Madison in July of 1806, "the drought in this quarter is successive. . . . Even the Rivanna, after taking out the water for my little toll mill, has not as much left as would turn another."[7] In 1820 there was enough water to run the mill but not enough to float the flour down the river.

Jefferson's apparent resignation to the inconsistencies of the Rivanna reflect his dependence on it. The Rivanna, a small shallow stream which flows into the James River, linked Monticello to Richmond eighty miles away by water and ultimately to the ocean itself. The little town of Milton, three-fourths of a mile from Monticello and six miles below Charlottesville, was at the head of navigation. In an era of poor roads the river was the most practical means of marketing crops and getting supplies. One of Jefferson's earliest projects was to begin clearing the Rivanna. He lists this undertaking first in his memorandum subtitled "Services to my Country," written in about 1800: "The Rivanna had never been used for navigation; scarcely an empty canoe had ever passed down it. Soon after I came of age, I examined its obstructions, set on foot a subscription for removing them, got an Act of Assembly passed, and the thing effected, so as to be used completely and fully for carrying down all of our produce."[8] The Declaration of Independence is listed as the second of his contributions to his fellow citizens.

For him personally the stretch of the river between his mills and Milton were of special concern. As noted, his crops were loaded in canoes or bateaux and floated to Milton where the hogsheads of tobacco and barrels of flour were transferred to larger boats for the trip to Richmond. This was his only way to get his crops to market.

The floods can be put into perspective only by considering what went into constructing and running his mills. He learned this part of farming soon after he moved to Monticello. After his gristmill, dam, and canal were destroyed in 1771, he began the laborious process of rebuilding. The first entry of 1773 in the *Garden Book* records that "Gordon, the mill-wright" had worked out the costs of the major components of a new mill. Jefferson apparently thought a new canal could be built quickly. The mill was in fact not rebuilt until 1803 when the canal was completed. The canal, begun in 1776 but not worked on continuously, proved a truly major undertaking, requiring ten to fourteen hired laborers. Cut through solid rock most of the way, it was six feet deep with sloping sides covered with grass. Gunpowder was used in blasting. Jefferson bought the powder in Charlottesville and Richmond. Its quality was low, a major reason why it took so long to build the waterway.[9] The eventual cost of the canal was $20,000.

This was not the end of Jefferson's capital outlay. He had determined to avoid the expense of building another dam to replace the one built by his father and destroyed in 1771 by moving the intake of the canal upriver three quarters of a mile to a natural ledge of rock. But the new canal did not deliver enough water to his mill. He was thus forced to build a dam after all. It was begun in 1805 and completed the next year. Due to floods this dam site proved a constant source of concern to Jefferson. These difficulties were certainly not needed by a President of the U.S.

Meanwhile the gristmill, rebuilt by James Walker during 1803, had ground its first grain the day of Christmas eve. Monticello overseer Gabriel Lilly did the honors. The mill was then out of commission for two years while an addition was constructed. It resumed grinding in December of 1805.[10] Jefferson ran through several millers before he turned the job over to Youen Carden who remained in charge almost continuously until 1824. If Jefferson could have found a man of Carden's abilities and personal integrity to run his manufacturing mill his vexations would have been reduced immeasurably.

As usual Jefferson began that project with the greatest of optimism. Always looking for a supplement to his income, he also wanted to serve his neighbors by grinding their grain on a major scale. In 1793, when his life was filled at last with crop rotations and gardening plans and everything seemed possible, he put out a notice for a tenant for his proposed mill, touting the location and its financial possibilities. However, politics intruded once again on his private life and it was not until 1803 that the mill site was actually laid out. Within four years it began operation. Fortunately Jefferson tended to remain tranquil under circumstances which would have floored a lesser man. Only in his relations with his immediate family and best friends did his emotions pour out. With this mill he would need all the fortitude he could muster.

The manufacturing mill, completed in 1806 in a competent, expeditious manner by James Walker, was plagued from the start by the lack of an onsite leaseholder and an honest, hard working, knowledgeable miller. By September 1806 Jefferson began looking in earnest for a tenant. In the interim he first used a slave, Moses, one of nine hired from the Dangerfield family of Spotsylvania County. He lasted but a short time as his year of work for Jefferson was soon up. Moses was replaced by Martin, one of Jefferson's own slaves, but the man failed to make the most of this opportunity to better himself.

As the President wrote Bacon at the end of December of 1806, "I am chagrined at the malconduct of Martin in the toll-mill. I fear I shall be as much disappointed in his principles as in his health. But if in addition to negligence & dishonesty, he disobliges our customers, he must be instantly removed & set to work with the other laborers. Were we to have recourse to a white miller, we should not be more secure as to honesty, & be at much greater expence. A black miller does not cost more than 100.D. a year including cloathing & finding."[11] Jefferson then discusses who among his slaves might replace Martin.

Attending to such matters from Washington via letter was not the same as residing full time at home. Jefferson did his best. In January of 1807 he made a five-year lease with Jonathan Shoemaker to be his new tenant. Trouble started at once. Rather than do the work himself, Shoemaker's son and partner, Issac actually ran the mill while the father lived in the vicinity of Washington. Whether the results would have been different had the father run the mill is doubtful or Shoemaker would surely have better instructed his son in proper management and operating methods. By March of 1809 Martha Randolph felt compelled to write her father, "I am afraid you will be very disappointed in your expectations from Shoemaker. It is the opinion of the neighborhood that it would be better for you to get the mill back upon any terms than to let him keep it. In the first place he is not a man of business. His bargains are ruinous to himself and more over he has not one spark of honesty. His credit is so low that nothing but necessity induces any one to trust him with their grain; and the general complaint is that it cannot be got out of his hands."[12]

Jefferson returned home shortly thereafter to begin his retirement, but even his presence did not improve Shoemaker's performance. George Jefferson, Thomas's factor in Richmond, complained: "I enclose you an account of fines against Shoemaker for which he is liable to you. His flour the Inspector informs me is frequently light. His barrels are not lined, which obliges us to have it done. The law does not compel the miller to do this, but custom compels the seller: or if he does not do it, a greater deduction is frequently made in the price than it would cost."[13]

Payment of rent was another problem. Shoemaker Sr. had agreed to pay $1250 per year cash on a quarterly basis, which Jefferson desperately needed if only to cover the cost of building and maintaining the mill. After Martha's letter he wrote what was for him a stern letter to the delinquent. He pointed out: "I am assured by the neighbors that from 40. to 50,000 bushels of wheat would have been carried there this year, but that people were afraid to trust them with it; & that the ensuring year there will not be 1000. bushels carried there."[14] Jefferson then reminded his tenant that after two years time Shoemaker had yet to pay any rent. To justify his nonpayment Shoemaker complained about the water supply to run the mill.

Shoemaker made a partial payment, but Jefferson's struggles to receive money from him continued to plague the relationship. While Jefferson apparently made no effort to find a new tenant, this may have been because a substitute was not likely to be found. Certainly his flour could not conveniently be ground elsewhere. In any event Shoemaker's cavalier disregard toward his obligations caused his landlord not only inconvenience in paying his debts, but also severe personal mortification, as he described it to the Dangerfields in 1810. The ex–President had been hiring slaves from that family for a number of years to supplement his own work force. In 1810 he was forced to apologize for his inability to meet his payment to the slaves' owners because Shoemaker had failed to remit his rent payment. This was the final blow to Jefferson's pride, long bruised because neighbors who used his mill could not get satisfaction from this tenant.

Thomas Mann Randolph, who was embarrassed to have to take his wheat to Richmond, assumed the lease in 1811, first in partnership with James McKenney of Culpepper and then with his brother-in-law, Thomas Eston Randolph. This Randolph was a merchant in nearby Milton and father of the young woman Jefferson's grandson, Francis Eppes, would later marry. Jefferson noted at that time that even under the Shoemakers' bad management they ground between 7000 to 8000 barrels in 1811, confessing to making a dollar a barrel. With his usual optimism Jefferson projected that under the new management the mill could receive 60,000 bushels a year and profit accordingly. After several years of unsuccessful results, Jefferson's optimism notwithstanding, his son-in-law left the venture. He was replaced by a Mr. Colclaser, a miller whose management skills were not the best. In the early 1820s he too left, and Thomas Eston Randolph took over as sole leaser. The latter, as Shoemaker before him, was delinquent in his rent and quarreled about the amount and other contractual obligations.

It seems doubtful that this manufacturing mill which cost over $10,000 to build was ever anything more than a drag on Jefferson's time, emotions and finances. In 1821 he wrote: "I offer for sale a merchant mill which would pay every dollar I owe in the world, but I know not when I may meet with a purchaser."[15]

Maintenance of the mills, canal, and dam were always a high priority in Jefferson's schedule for his work force. These tasks were never ending. In 1806 he told his new overseer Edmund Bacon, "When you have done the dam & pier-head before you go to digging at the mill, you should take a canoe & go down the canal, sounding everywhere to see if there is no place choaked with mud. I suspect there is from the circumstance of the canoe's grounding in it. It should be from 3. to 4. f. deep (I forget which) every where, & any obstruction found in it should be cleared out before it is too cold."[16]

In 1807 he wrote Bacon, "The finishing every thing about the mill is what I wish always to have preference to every kind of work"[17] In 1808 he wrote his overseer, "Consider as your first object the keeping a full supply of water to the mill, observing that whenever the water does not run over the waste, you should take your hands, and having put in a sufficiency of stone, then carry in earth and heighten till the water runs steadily over the waste. . . . Take Mr. Randolph's advice on these occasions."[18] While he was secretary of state Jefferson had entrusted building of the canal to young Randolph.

In 1819 Jefferson still had the mills on his mind. He wrote Bacon, "I look to the offal of the mill as our only resource for bread. I think it very certain that bread will not be made in the upper country generally. If we can keep the mill going it will be a resource for the present. After these two objects are secured, the next in importance is the river canal to the sawmill."[19]

The hazards of owning a mill were compounded in unexpected ways. One revolved around patents held by Oliver Evans. The President had worked earlier with Evans in the matter of his mills, asking advice and ordering parts. Having left the construction of his manufacturing mill in the hands of its builder, James Walker, Jefferson must have been astounded to receive a letter two years after the mill's completion contending that he had infringed upon Evans' patents. After looking into the matter, the President took time out to patiently explain that the mill had been built after the expiration of the first patent and before the date of the second. Nonetheless he inquired as to the amount due, for as he explained, "I make this paiment willingly as a voluntary tribute to a person whose talents are constantly employed in endeavors to be useful to mankind, and not as a legal obligation."[20] This act of generosity cost him $89.60, an expense he could ill afford.

Much more time and effort was involved in defending his rights against the Rivanna Company. Formed by a legislative act in 1806, its purpose was to improve navigation on the Rivanna between Milton and Charlottesville. Jefferson was, of course, in favor of this idea. The stumbling block involved the section going through the Southwest Mountains, a two-and-one-half mile stretch influenced by his dam and canal. To get boats downstream the directors decided to use Jefferson's canal and build locks just above his gristmill.

Jefferson's cooperative spirit was remarkable for he had good cause to worry about the locks, which would be of no possible use to him. They could cause problems in addition to diverting part of his water supply. "I only request such provisions by the Directors as may secure my mills against interruptions to which the boatmen have already shewn themselves wantonly prone," he wrote.[21]

Bickering went on about this stretch of the river until 1819, when Jefferson, in fear that the rotten state of the locks, now long in place, would damage his canal, pressed a friendly lawsuit he had initiated in 1818 as he put it "to quiet my title." The suit was concluded in November 1819. Jefferson's concern was not mitigated. He still feared the basic legal questions were not totally resolved, but for him the matter does not seem to have come up again. His mills continued to grind wheat and corn, presumably until his death in 1826.

The importance he attached to mills is shown by the fact that by 1812 he also had plans to build a canal and grist mill on the Backwater Creek on his property in Bedford. He had begun staying at his octagonal home there since 1809, although it, like Monticello, was still unfinished. He admitted the stream flow of the creek was meager, but as he owned the land around the head springs, he felt there would be sufficient water to grind flour for most of the year for a family. Although Joel Yancy, his overseer, wrote in 1819 to ask if the canal was to be started, there is no evidence these plans were carried out.

Sawmills were also a component of a self-sufficient plantation. In September of 1802 Jefferson's agreement with James Walker included construction of a sawmill to be completed by the end of the year. Walker did not fulfill this obligation; he was busy working elsewhere. The man who did build it rented the mill from Jefferson. By the end of January 1804, just three months before the disastrous April freshet, it was virtually complete. Jefferson does not record its fate in that freshet or subsequent ones.

A sawmill does not enter his records again until 1811 when Jefferson wrote Walker, "I am opening a canal at the hither end of my dam, and carrying it about 300. yards through the low grounds to where I shall have

6. f. fall, with a view of there building a saw mill, and joining to it a threshing machine. I can afford it but little water."[22] The first sawmill had presumably been located near the original grist and manufacturing mills. Whether it still operated is not evident. In any event Jefferson wanted one at this location. Would Walker build the mill? Once again he disappointed his former employer. Walker instead found another builder, who completed the structure in the spring of 1813. Due to lack of adequate water in the new canal which served it, operations did not begin until the following June.

After a heavy rain in the fall of 1813 Jefferson noted the low ground around the sawmill was so dry it absorbed most of the downpour. Damage to the sawmill was not recorded in the freshets of 1814 or 1815. Apparently he was not so fortunate in 1819 when he speaks of rebuilding the sawmill. The Rivanna had proven an inconstant friend.

For Jefferson self-sufficiency was not only a desirable philosophical goal; in his era it was a practical necessity. His mills were not the only machinery upon which he relied to sustain his large family. As clothing was essential, raising sheep and growing flax, hemp, and or cotton was an important part of the work schedule. These fibers needed to be manufactured into cloth. Once again his ingenuity was challenged.

In his day the most formidable problem was the availability of machines to process the wool or fiber. At first he had only a spinning wheel, the common loom and the hand card. In 1811 he added a spinning Jenny and a loom with a flying shuttle to his home manufacturing equipment. His search for improved machines would be a continuous one.

Jefferson's views on the subject of home manufacturing were laid out in his *Notes*.

> We never had an interior trade of any importance. Our exterior commerce has suffered very much from the beginning of the present contest. During this time we have manufactured within our families the most necessary articles of cloathing. Those of cotton will bear some comparison with the same kinds of manufacture in Europe; but those of wool, flax and hemp are very coarse, unsightly, and unpleasant; and such is our attachment to agriculture, and such our preference for foreign manufactures, that be it wise or unwise, our people will certainly return as soon as they can, to the raising raw materials, and exchanging them for finer manufactures than they are able to execute themselves.[23]

In the following decades an embargo he himself imposed on English trade and a new war would cause the same dilemma. Only gradually would this reliance on foreign fine goods decline and manufacturing on this side of the Atlantic increase—and then only in the New England states. After his renewal of friendship with John Adams, interrupted for more than a decade because of political differences, Jefferson in 1812 wrote his predecessor in the Presidency: "I thank you beforehand (for they are not yet arrived) for the specimens of homespun you have been so kind as to forward me by post. I doubt not their excellence, knowing how far you are advanced in these things in your quarter. Here we do little in the fine way, but in coarse and middling goods a great deal. . . . For fine stuff we shall depend on your northern manufactories. Of these, that is to say, of company establishments, we have none. We use little machinery. The spinning jenny, and loom with the flying shuttle, can be managed in a family; but nothing more complicated."[24]

Southerners in particular were caught by the embargo and War of 1812. Most, if not all, the planters bought most of the coarse cloth needed on their plantations and all of the fine cloth, including blankets. Until independence it had been British policy to make her colonies the source of raw materials, while workers in the homeland turned them into manufactured goods. It took the War of 1812 to jolt Americans into recognizing that, not only did they have the capability to manufacture their own cloth, but also the responsibility. As usual Jefferson pushed his fellow citizens into self reliance and higher standards. He had a dream of American perfectability, and he was not about to let it go in such an essential as making clothing.

As was true of other plantation owners, his needs were truly extensive. Yet optimism would always prevail and of course he would never admit to foreigners that his dear country was not performing superbly. In 1812 he wrote Thaddeus Kosciusko, the Polish general who served America in the Revolutionary War and was now pursing agriculture in France:

Our manufactures are now very nearly on a footing with those of England. She has not a single improvement which we do not possess, and many of them better adapted by ourselves to our ordinary use. We have reduced the large & expensive machinery for most things to the compass of a private family: and every family of any size is now getting machines on a small scale for their household purposes. Quoting myself as an example, and I am much behind many others in this business, my household manufactures are just getting into operation on the scale of a Carding machine costing 60. Dollars only, which may be worked by a girl 12. years old, a Spinning machine, which may be made for 10. Dollars, carrying 6. spindles for wool, to be worked by a girl also, another which can be made for 25. Dollars, carrying 12. spindles for cotton, & a loom, with a flying shuttle, weaving it's 20. yards a day. I need 2000. yards of linen, cotton, & woolen yearly, to clothe my family, which this machinery, costing 150. Dollars only, and worked by two women and two girls, will more than furnish. For fine goods there are numerous establishments at work in the large cities, & many more daily growing up, and of Merinos [sheep] we have some thousands, and these multiplying fast.[25]

To his Philadelphia friend James Ronaldson he wrote later in 1812:

> We shall in all events derive permanent benefit from the war, by it's giving time for the permanent establishment of our manufactures, to which the high duties you mention, will contribute, while they also enrich our treasury. We always manufactured a great deal in this state in the household way. But this was on the old Spinning wheel. The introduction of machines into our families is becoming common. Those of 6. spindles suit the smaller families. I have 36. spindles going myself & shall soon add 18. more. My son in law has 40. We find the old Jenny far preferable to the newer & less simple contrivances. In a year or two more, household manufactures will be so universally established in this state, that the British commerce in coarse goods will be compleatly extirpated, & never more will be of much value to them.[26]

With Dr. William Thornton in the patent office in Washington he was more frank: There must be a better way of making cloth. Shortly before leaving the Presidency he had given permission to two Boston men to import a machine which spun cotton, wool, and flax "equally." Jefferson understood that the spinning Jenny, while an improvement on the old spinning wheel because it had multiple spindles, had its limitations too. The question was how to make the Jenny better for home manufacturing. He thought he might have found an inventor who had done so, the New Yorker Oliver Barrett, Jr. He therefore wrote Thornton early in 1812, "I have seen in the hand of a friend an advertisement of a machine much simpler than the jenny, & which will do about 6. times the work of a spinning wheel. It's price, 15. Dollars shews there cannot be much work about it. This promises to be exactly what we want. But does it answer what is announced of it? . . . If we could but have a simple carding machine we should be fixed."[27] Then follows a succession of questions proposing different methods to make one. The tinkerer is once again attempting to solve his own problems.

The spinning machine was sent by Thornton and arrived by July of 1812. Despite its supposed simplicity, no one at Monticello could figure out the mechanism, which functioned as the common roving jack. Indeed, asked Jefferson of Thornton: What was a common roving jack? Another machine, the creation of Ebenezer Herrick of Massachusetts, was delivered the following year. As Jefferson explained to Robert Livingston, "Yet I have thought it a duty to my neighbors to take on myself the risk of disappointment. If the machines answer, a service will be rendered them; if they do not I only lose a few dollars."[28] Three years later Jefferson was corresponding with still another inventor of a spinning machine, but nothing appears to have come of the query.[29] Jefferson had also looked at a spinning machine in Washington exhibited by Jacob Alrichs. This did not capture his imagination or his pocketbook.

To Thornton in 1814 Jefferson concluded "that after trying several spinning machines I have settled down with the ancient Jenny, because it's simplicity is such that we can make it and repair it ourselves."[30] This proved to be the bottom line.

But Alrichs had also mentioned working on an improved carding machine. Would Jefferson buy one? Hand carding was a time-consuming job, and the carders could not keep up with the spinners. Alrichs' device arrived (with a bill for $97). As luck would have it, it did not perform properly. Alrichs provided an explanation as to the reasons why. As nothing more is mentioned about the carding machine, the difficulty was apparently resolved. During this period Jefferson ordered another wool carding machine for someone else.

Jefferson looked at new looms as well. He had started out with the common loom, then in 1811 he added a loom with a flying shuttle. Not entirely satisfied, in 1814 he described the improved loom of Janes as the most beautiful machine he had ever seen. Jefferson was denied this invention, as were most Virginians, because the man who had bought the patent rights for Virginia sales was too greedy. The machine did not sell as well as it did in other states where the price was lower. Jefferson suggested to Thornton that, of the 40,000 looms in Virginia, a quarter would be exchanged for the Janes model if only the price was commensurate to that charged elsewhere. One man's avarice thus denied a large number of people a machine crucial to their economic improvement; this was not Jefferson's way.

He noted the existence of another new loom soon thereafter, but concluded that his home manufacturing venture was too small an operation to warrant buying one. Now in his 70s, although interested in developments, he no doubt judged it better to stay with what he had, looms with flying shuttles. Jefferson admitted that they did not perform the marvels ascribed to them, but he thought they doubled the output of the common loom. He must have been interested, however, when in 1815 Thornton wrote to say he had seen a model which prepared cotton for spinning without carding—a very simple machine, according to the doctor. To show its merits he enclosed a sample of cloth made on it.

The problems involving cloth-making machines, their high price and or their suitability to the talents of his workers, must have been ever on Jefferson's mind. He expressed the dilemma he faced to his Poplar Forest overseer, Jeremiah Goodman in 1812: "I hope the spinning and weaving has got well underway. I am informed from Richmond that there is not a single yard of cotton or oznabrigs to be had there, nor is there another yard ordered or expected. We have no chance therefore of clothing the negroes next winter but with what we shall make ourselves."[31]

The ability of girls and older women to work the devices for making cloth was critical, for men could not be spared. Jefferson leaves a record of one failure: "Of Sally we can make nothing at all. I never saw so hopeless a subject. She seems neither to have the inclination nor the understanding to learn. She is now weaving one yard a day, with the flying shuttle and of such stuff as will not be worth giving to children."[32]

In 1811 Jefferson had done his best, engaging the services of William Maclure, a North Carolina weaver who agreed to teaching others the art. Maclure also made several spinning Jennies and a loom with a flying shuttle for the training program. Suitable housing, subsistence, and work areas were provided for Maclure and his pupils. By 1814 the instructor's task satisfactorily completed, his employer wrote a letter of recommendation for him.

Fine cloth suitable for Jefferson and his immediate family would continue to be made off the plantation. He had great expectations that his Merino sheep would supply the raw material, but their wool output was insufficient. In 1812 he wrote his Delaware friend, E. I. Dupont, "I shall shear this year, 3. fleeces only of imported Merinos, their wool of 1st. quality, and 15. of half blood. I have understood you are concerned in a manufactory of cloth, and will receive one's wool, have it spun, wove & dyed for the equivalent in the wool. I should be very glad to get mine into so good hands. Will you be so kind as to inform me more particularly on this subject."[33]

This request apparently came to nothing, for the following year Jefferson sent his wool to another friend, Judge Hugh Holmes, in Winchester, Virginia. He wrote Holmes in July of 1813: "Availing myself of your kind offer, I forwarded to Staunton by the stage 39. lb unwashed Merino wool which I hope has reached you safely. The cloth when made I would wish to have dyed of the darkest blue colour they can give it, which I think you said was what they called Navy blue. I yesterday wrote to Gibson & Jefferson to forward to the bank of Winchester, subject to your call, 30. Dollars which as well as I could judge from your information would cover the expenses of manufacture."[34] Not until a year later did Jefferson get the cloth which cost him more than he expected. Such manufacturers preferred buying their wool and selling the cloth.

While Jefferson apparently gave up his hope for domestic manufacture of fine cloth, common cloth was another matter. He wrote Yancy at Bedford in 1818, encouraging him to establish such an undertaking there. Bacon at Monticello recalled selling wagon loads of cloth to merchants.

Jefferson made no balance sheet of actual costs and benefits of his spinning and weaving. Considering the economics of the era, he really had no choice. He therefore modified his original political premise of the necessity for the predominance of agriculture to produce a happy citizenry to include a recognition of the importance of manufacturing beyond the home, provided it did not upstage farming. To this end he supported the tariff of 1816, which gave protection to infant manufacturing industries.

7
Animals

The New World had no native animals capable of being domesticated except the dog, guinea pig, turkey, duck, and llama.[1] European settlers until the 1700s, therefore, had to bring animals from home. Given the ships of the era, this proved a difficult task. Once here the problem was how to feed the animals, and how to protect them from wild predators and Indians who took exception to the fact the colonists were freely slaughtering deer and other animals which served as Indian livestock. Whites, no doubt, also occasionally made off with stock not their own. The weather, however, proved a more consistent threat.

Cattle, swine, sheep, and fowl were all at first expected to forage where they could. As long as populations of people and their animals were low, the food supply was reasonably satisfactory, except in winter in the more northerly colonies. Along river bottoms natural meadows were either grazed or made into hay. Meadows could be found all along the coastal plateau and in areas of limestone west of the Blue Ridge Mountains. Along the coast salt marshes dominated by Spartina and other grasses provided forage. Some farmers even cut the marsh grasses for hay. Hogs took advantage of the edible roots of some of the water plants. Yet as late as the Revolutionary War Virginia farmers generally did not use their wet areas.

Cattle, pigs, and sheep were usually turned out into the woods, a practice still followed by some American farmers. Mast was often available in large quantities in forests dominated by beech and oaks. In pine woods hogs ate young pine shoots, although the nutritional content was not great. Cattle browsed on a variety of herbage, even Spanish moss. Fowl ran free to scratch out their food wherever they could.

In time the better areas in which to grow livestock were determined. With the rise of towns and cities, a market developed for products from these domesticated animals. The high cost of farm labor also encouraged many farmers to turn to raising livestock. The animals themselves or products from them were sold to other colonies and abroad as well. Hay was in demand by urban private stables and liveries. When farmers saw the possibilities of profiting from their labor, especially when they were rewarded in cash, grasslands were established for the sole purpose of providing hay and pasturage. These may have been permanent in nature but more likely were planted as part of a rotation following two or three years of grain crops. Such practices were more common in the North than in the South.

Rotation of meadow grasses and legumes with grain crops was, of course, much more beneficial to the land than allowing the fields to lie bare during a fallow period and covered by a growth of miscellaneous weeds and even pioneer trees. By the mid-1700s meadow lands in German settlements of Pennsylvania were even irrigated where streams could be channeled onto adjacent flat areas. In this period Delaware River farmers increased their mowing acreage by draining the salt marshes and seeding them first to a grain, then to a permanent cover of clover or grass. This practice ultimately succumbed to the problems associated with keeping the dikes maintained.

A more permanent solution to providing animal feed became common in the eighteenth century—plowing and then sowing imported grasses and clovers. The grasses included timothy, rye, red top, orchard grass, foxtail and bermuda. Legumes included various clovers, lucerne (alfalfa) and sainfoin. Jefferson was an eloquent promoter of clover for its ability to fix nitrogen. As there are only occasional references to growing legumes before the Revolution, once again he was a leader. Instead of using the seed left over in the hayloft, an early practice, farmers began using selected seed. This was Jefferson's method. He wrote George Washington in June of 1796: "My exhausted fields bring a clover not high enough for hay, but I hope to make seed from it."[2]

To put this in better perspective we need to know something of the history of legumes. Legumes had been domesticated soon after wheat and barley, but their role in agriculture is not well documented until Roman times. Better Roman farmers had developed crop rotation as a method of retaining the fertility of their soils, using the powers of legumes to fix nitrogen. Legumes might also be plowed under green without collecting the seed for use by man and livestock. (Naked or weed fallows were still used by the common farmer.)

When Roman power declined so did good agriculture. After towns once again grew in size and began to prosper, agricultural innovation soon stirred, this time in northwestern Europe and England, where farmers had used the naked fallow to replenish soil bereft of nutrients from years of continuous cropping and permanent pastures. Field-grass husbandry,[3] with alternate cropping and pasturing, began developing in England by the sixteenth century and somewhat later in France and Germany. The process of switching over was very slow due to vestiges of the feudal system of land ownership with its attendant mental attitudes of subservience. Whereas fallows had been imposed every few years, the new method was based on the premise that fallows were not necessary except on the poorest, heaviest soils—provided crops were rotated between field grasses (including legumes) and grains. Until this point, production of cattle and sheep and consumption of their products was restricted to the wealthy, with the poor confined to the pig. At the same time there was little incentive to breed better animals.

Meanwhile other forces were acting on the agricultural field on both sides of the Atlantic. Manufacturing slowly became established, and commerce expanded with a better system of roads. Populations and incomes began to grow. People increasingly saw opportunities for innovation. This was particularly important when it involved food for residents of urban areas. With the payment of cash they expected better quality in their fruits, vegetables, and meat products.

Unlike many, if not most, farmers of his time, when it came to his animals Jefferson always sought out the best, not only because he appreciated fine stock but to elevate the tastes of his countrymen. With cattle he had little to choose from. Cows had originally been imported from England, Ireland, France, the Spanish West Indies, and Spain. After their numbers had increased there was no reason to import more, although there was some movement between colonies and later, between the states. Not only were few people interested in quality; any progress to improvement was virtually impossible as long as the animals foraged. John Beale Bordley, whose volumes were in Jefferson's library, described in his *Essays and Notes on Husbandry* that just prior to the Revolutionary War he began crossing native cattle with an English breed. The cow was described as small-boned, and well formed, with a gentle disposition and larger than usual milk production. Despite his influence, cattle breeding seems not to have been of interest to many of Bordley's peers.

Southern cattle in general were reported as being stunted, and poor milkers as well. Washington observed to Sir John Sinclair that in northern Virginia where cattle were properly fed and cared for as his were, they were found to weigh 700 to 800 pounds and more, as opposed to the more usual 450 to 500 pounds. Jefferson's cattle were certainly reasonably provided for, especially because he was concerned with the milk and butter they could produce in addition to meat and hides. Furthermore, Edmund Bacon, his Monticello overseer, indicated they got many fine cattle from western Virginia, so Jefferson must have been determined to improve the animals of Albemarle and Bedford.

Jefferson used oxen (and horses) for plowing, threshing grain and hauling wood, manure, and earth in wagons or carts. At the end of their working lives they were slaughtered for beef. The animals from Bedford were either fattened and then driven to Monticello or they were butchered, usually in mid-winter, and the meat was sent to Albemarle by wagon. Butter was also made at Poplar Forest for Monticello.

The cattle roamed the woods and pastures, as was customary, but they were not allowed to graze in cultivated fields. In addition to what they foraged, Jefferson fed them a variety of food. Two apparent favorites of his were Jerusalem artichoke in winter and succory in summer, the artichokes because they could be kept in the ground during the cold season and dug as wanted. The artichoke produced considerably more food than the potato. Jefferson had the satisfaction of reporting to John Taylor in 1808 that the French were cultivating this native American plant, finding it most productive there too. Jefferson got succory seeds from Washington who had gotten them from the Englishman Arthur Young. The cattle's diet was augmented by corn, wheat, stubble hay, potatoes, and pumpkins.

As a rule hogs fared better under American conditions than other livestock. Originally brought from England (with a few from the West Indies), hogs were able to fend for themselves much better than cattle, horses, and sheep except under extreme winter conditions. Their prolific breeding was an added bonus. Even under the harshest conditions and living almost entirely on mast, hogs in Virginia and northward were of high quality. Virginia pork in particular was much favored in England. Smithfield, Virginia, was a recognized center for excellent pork before the Revolution, and Jefferson was one of those who bought pork there for his own consumption. In 1801 his agent and kinsman in Richmond, George Jefferson, wrote him, "We have at length heard from the person in Smithfield (Mr. George Purdie) of whom enquiry was made sometime ago respecting hams. Mr. P. is a person remarkable for curing good bacon."[4] Jefferson also bought hams from Hanover, Virginia.

Part of the superiority of more northerly pork was attributed to the salt used in curing it. North Carolina, which enjoyed ideal conditions for raising livestock and from which many hogs and cattle were driven into Virginia for processing, was forced by British rule to use salt from England. Depending on its source, this was either too mild or too strong. North Carolinians could get salt of consistently better quality indirectly from

Spain and Portugal via New York and Pennsylvania, but this was more costly. Jefferson in his *Notes* of 1781 devotes a paragraph to the area west of the Alleghanies which abounded with salt springs. When a great scarcity of salt developed during the Revolutionary War, especially in the earliest years, these may have been considered a source. Virginians experimented with manufacturing salt by evaporation in coastal ponds. Virginia also traded with Bermuda and made the importation of salt a state monopoly to assure better distribution during the war.

In 1814 and 1815 Jefferson's overseer at Poplar Forest was responsible for obtaining salt for Monticello as well as Bedford, indicating that western sources were now proving their worth. Salt was generously supplied by Jefferson to his workers. In 1813 he wrote his Poplar Forest overseer Jeremiah Goodman, "Let the people have hereafter a fixed allowance of salt; to wit, give to their breadmaker a pint a month for each grown negro to put into their bread; and give besides to each grown negro a pint a month for their snaps, cymlins & other uses. This will be a quart a month for every grown negro."[5]

The following year he wrote Goodman, "I now send James with a small cart and 2. mules for the salt, which I am in hopes you have had packed in *strong* barrels, or such as can be well strengthened. I do not think he can bring more than 10. bushels, which with their barrels will weigh 700. lb. The rest of the salt (5. bushels) and the butter must come by the waggon at Christmas. . . . It will be well for you to accompany James to Lynchburg & see the salt put on board. He may rest a day at Poplar Forest."[6]

In his list of expenditures for 1769, Jefferson recorded paying to see a hog which weighed more than 1050 pounds. No doubt he would forever after mentally compare his own hogs against this standard. He was, however, ambivalent in his attitude towards this animal. He told Thomas Mann Randolph in 1793 that both he and his new overseer condemned hogs and Indian corn. However he felt, Jefferson could not do without them. They were in fact the most numerous animal he owned. Hogs were grown at Monticello, Shadwell, and Poplar Forest.

In 1812 he wrote his Bedford overseer: "Supposing there are 40. bacon hogs at this place [Poplar Forest] & 32. at Bear creek reserve 23. for the negroes, which allows a hog apiece for Hal & Jame Hubbard, and half a one for every grown & working negro, keep 6. for my use & Chisolm's then take out the Overseer's parts and send the rest to Monticello with the muttons."[7]

In spite of these numbers he was forced to buy pork from others. In 1819 he wrote a friend, "The last year was the only one of my life that I ever had pork to spare. This year as usual we have hardly enough for our enormously large family,[8] being equally deficient in the carcasses as well as the means of fattening."[9] The same year his Poplar Forest overseer, Joel Yancy, wrote him, "I shall fatten 70 good Hogs certainly, which I have now in the pens, and there are 5 others, which are a little shy & which I have no doubt we shall get in a day or two, so you may safely calculate on 75 hogs. . . . We have 25 or 30 more that would make good pork, but we can't spare the grain to fatten them, there is some mast sufficient I think (with a little corn to keep them gentle) to support them this winter & spring, and they will be large by next killing."[10]

Corn was more important than this letter would indicate and it limited the number of hogs Jefferson could grow. In his *Farm Book* under "hogs" Jefferson noted that every hog raised and fattened (including those stolen and lost) had eaten three barrels of corn. With the corn consumed by his workers, Jefferson's corn requirement was quite formidable.

Jefferson complained to Goodman in 1815 about the weight of the hogs driven from Poplar Forest to Monticello, which had ranged from a high of 101 pounds to a low of 47, too small to make bacon and fit only for salt pork for the negroes. Jefferson was no doubt unable to understand why Goodman had not achieved better results with the hint he sent from Monticello the preceding year: Grind the corn destined for hog consumption and boil the meal into mush. Jefferson pointed out at that time that the hogs at Monticello had fattened much sooner with half the corn on this regimen. Goodman was sent a pair of hogs of "the Guinea breed," some of which he had been given before with no apparent results. The master was quick to point out that at Monticello 18-month hogs of this breed weighed as much as 200 pounds, with most at 150 pounds. He compared these figures with Goodman's whose hogs averaged but seventy-three and three-fourths pounds.

By 1816 Jefferson was showing his exasperation. He told his new Poplar Forest overseer, Joel Yancy: "I send by the cart a boar & sow pig, Guinea, for the plantation, being the breed I wish to get into there as soon as possible. They take little more than half the corn to fatten them & breed much faster than the common hog."[11] The Guinea breed did better under Yancy. The figures supplied his employer in 1819 indicate hog weight was averaging 143 pounds.

The difference in weight between Goodman's and Yancy's hogs was due in part to the fact that Goodman's animals were weighed after being driven the almost 100 miles to Monticello. In 1814 Jefferson told Goodman: "Caution them [the four workers he had sent from Monticello] against whipping the hogs. The last year there was one so bruised all over that not a single piece of it could be used, & several were so injured that many pieces of them were lost."[12] In spite of the admonition Jefferson reported to his overseer that one hog was left at Lynchburg and one tired and was killed on the road. Two hogs represented a lot of meat. Raising them long distance was not a simple matter, but apparently the advantages outweighed the disadvantages. Perhaps the hogs were sometimes slaughtered in Bedford with their meat sent to Monticello by cart. Since swine foraged the woods and open fields, having this natural harvest supplemented at times with corn, potatoes and small grains, a mark on their ears was needed to keep track of the animals.

Hog breeding did not consume as much attention as did sheep. In his correspondence only two breeds of hogs—Guinea and Chinese (or Parkinson)—are noted. Maybe this lack of interest was because, although hogs were the primary meat for the Jefferson table, he himself preferred mutton, lamb, beef, and guinea fowl.

Raising sheep proved more difficult than raising hogs or cattle. Because of their vulnerability to attack by predators and dogs, they were not commonly grown until an entire area was well beyond frontier conditions. In general sheep were kept more for their wool than for meat; pork provided far more flesh per animal with a lot less work. Furthermore, many Southerners, it seems, never developed a taste for either lamb or mutton, and still haven't.

Accounts of the quality of the wool vary. This no doubt reflects not only the problems associated with breeding better animals on an open range, but also the possibility of damage to the fleece from briars, etc. To make matters worse, it was the usual practice to allow butchers to choose the best animals for slaughtering, leaving the rest to breed with no regard to the quality of their wool.

In addition to differences in quality related to breed, better fleeces also came with better care of the animals. Many farmers were frankly not fussy about the excellence of the wool during the Colonial period. On the other hand, Washington told Sir John Sinclair he paid particular care to his sheep. He was one of the few who culled out old and unthrifty animals from his flock and took care to save male lambs with the best wool and conformation. Washington's fleeces averaged five and one-fourth pounds of wool during the Colonial period while the average fleece was only three or four pounds.

Washington was responsible for Jefferson's interest in breeding sheep; it was the animal Jefferson preferred above all others except horses. Washington shared letters from the Englishman Arthur Young, who extolled the virtues of raising the animals. For one thing, Young said, sheep foraged more efficiently than other ruminants and foraged where other animals can't. After reading Young's letters Jefferson told the President he now intended to increase the size of his flock, saying, "I have never before considered with due attention the profit from that animal."[13] By the end of 1793 Jefferson had made arrangements to buy sheep from his good friend Archibald Stuart of Staunton, Virginia for the amount of $40.[14] The flock was small. By 1796 the Duke de la Rouchefoucauld-Liancourt noted that Jefferson had only enough sheep for his table.

About this time Jefferson was the recipient of a ram as a gift from Robert Morris, the Revolutionary War financier, smuggled from Spain (a smuggled ewe died). The ram was closely related to the famous Merino breed and Jefferson immediately set forth on a breeding program. Given a pair of Barbary broad-tailed rams in 1806, he anticipated a breeding program with them too. By the following year he owned four kinds of sheep. In addition to the first two, he wrote his granddaughter Ellen that he now possessed a specimen from Iceland and another from Senegal.[15] These too he planned to breed. The thinking of the era held that a pure breed of sheep could be obtained after four crossings.

Each of his sheep had its virtues. The Merino was prized for its fine wool. The Icelandic was noted for the softness of the resulting cloth. In 1808 Jefferson went so far as to send his Philadelphia friend James Ronaldson a fleece of this sheep to determine its possible profitability for manufacturing there. The report was negative. The Barbary broad-tailed sheep was extolled by Jefferson as the highest flavored lamb he had ever tasted, while the Senegal's flavor was said to equal that of venison.

In 1809 Jefferson got another Barbary ram from his friend, Dr. William Thornton, whose interest in gardening and farming was considerable. The two men had become close friends as a result of Thornton's job as the first architect of the new Capitol in Washington. Jefferson distinguished between the broad-tailed sheep from the Cape of Good Hope, those from Algiers and those from Tunis. He had the Tunis variety and continued breeding them for the table and the quality of their wool until at least 1817. Jefferson's devotion to these animals may be seen from the fact that during his presidency he grew sheep at the White House. One Icelandic ram, his "sheep of many horns," made a bit of history. In February of 1809, just before he left Washington on March 11, he received a curt note from one William Keough who "begs leave to state to your excellency that in February 1808 in Passing through the President's Square [now Lafayette Park] he was attacked and severely wounded and bruised by your excellency's ram, of which he lay ill for five or six weeks under the hands of Doctor Elsey."[16]

Cows, goats, and fowl were also sheltered and grazed on the grounds around the White House. In Andrew Jackson's day presidential sheep were still being used to crop the lawn. By Polk's term, while there was a presidential cow on the grounds, a neighboring farmer supplied the sheep, paying for the pasture privilege. This was not the last time the nation depended on four-footed friends to keep things tidy. During World War I sheep were called upon to mow the south grounds to save worker time.

At the end of his second term Jefferson's flock consisted of some 40 animals. They were driven to Monticello in November 1808.

The true Merino was to make the biggest dent into the previously nondescript flocks on American farms. The Merino is believed to have descended from a strain which was developed during the reign of the Roman Emperor Claudius (A.D. 41–54). Merinos produce the finest diameter wool fiber, with strands the width of a human hair. Originating in Spain, the breed deteriorated over time. It was revived by the Arabs who conquered that country in the eighth century. Under their care, trade in Merino wool was established throughout the civilized world. Late in the fifteenth century, when the Arabs including thousands of weavers, were expelled from the country, the Spaniards lost their wool trade. Merinos were still grown and provided considerable income, which, in part, financed Columbus's journeys to America.

To protect this source of wealth in the following centuries Spain refused all exports of ewes under penalty of death, except for a few permitted out of the country by special consideration of the royal court. Two of these exceptions were a large group given in 1765 and 1774 to Saxony, while in 1786 Louis XVI was allowed to import 386 ewes which he crossed with sheep at his estate at Rambouillet. The Rambouillet breed today is considered one of the best in the world. True Merinos are now grown mainly outside the U.S. Their heyday here was during Jefferson's lifetime.

After 1800 Spain's restrictions against exporting Merinos became largely inoperative, and foreigners abroad began to look at the breed in earnest. Jefferson described them as "a diminutive tender sheep, yielding very little wool, but that of extraordinary fineness, fit only for the finest broadcloths, but not at all for country use."[17] The quality of the wool had enticed Americans as early as 1785 when the South Carolina Agricultural Society tried to obtain some animals. Groups in Massachusetts and New York also made attempts, to no avail. Then opportunity beckoned. E. I. Dupont and the American ambassadors to Spain and France, Colonel David Humphreys and Robert Livingston, were prominent amongst Americans abroad who after 1800 took advantage of the lapse in Spanish restraints. One of Livingston's motives in accepting Jefferson's offer of the post in France was to see what agricultural knowledge he could gain which would be useful to America.

Jefferson's curiosity was aroused. In 1809 he called upon James Ronaldson again for help in evaluating fleece quality. This time he sent a sample of wool from the progeny of the ram given him by Robert Morris. Was it as good as that of the true Merinos owned by Colonel Humphreys, Robert Livingston, and E. I. Dupont? Would it be worthwhile for Jefferson to preserve these sheep descended from Morris's ram and encourage his neighbors to introduce them into their flocks? Jefferson asked the same questions of Caleb Kirk of Brandywine, Delaware. Kirk responded,

> I Received thy favor of 13th. with the Inclosed Specimen of Spanish Merinos wool. I have compared it with those in my neighbourhood. I have likewise had the Opinion of our principal Hatters, without having any knowledge of breed, before giving their Judgement, the result has generally been unfavorable. They uniformly make use of our *best* lambs wool of the *first* years growth being short and more suitable for their purpose than longer wool.
>
> I am Induced to believe that thy Original Stock have not been from the genuine Merinos.[18]

This analysis must have whetted Jefferson's appetite for full-blooded Merinos.

As late as 1809 Merinos were still difficult to get. One of Jefferson's sheep fancying friends begged him as the just-retired President to put his efforts into influencing certain individuals to expedite shipment. Merinos had become the "in" variety very quickly, due in part to their scarcity, in part to the genuine fine quality of their fleeces. Full blooded lambs which had sold in 1807 for $100, two years later were selling at $1000 for ewes and up to $1500 for rams. The bubble of high prices burst in 1810 when the current American consul to Portugal, William Jarvis, began shipping a total of 4000 Merino sheep home, dividing them between every state he thought could benefit from them. Jarvis gratified the ex–President, as well as sitting President James Madison, by allowing both a choice of a pair from a small group he sent to Alexandria, Virginia, in February of 1810.

Although the sheep arrived in May, Jefferson did not get them for several weeks. In the interim they were quartered at Montpelier where Edmund Bacon went for them in August. For some reason Jefferson did not acknowledge the gift until the beginning of December when he thanked Jarvis for four Merinos.

Characteristically Jefferson reacted differently than other Merino owners to his new acquisitions when he got them. He wrote to Madison:

> I have been so disgusted with the scandalous extortions lately practiced in the sale of these animals, and with the description of patriotism and praise to the sellers, as if the thousands of dollars apiece they have not been ashamed to receive were not reward enough, that I am disposed to consider as right, whatever is the reverse of what they have done. Since fortune has put the

occasion upon us, is it not incumbent upon us so to dispense this benefit to the farmers of our country, as to put to shame those who, forgetting their own wealth and the honest simplicity of the farmers, have thought them fit objects of the shaving art, and to excite by a better example the condemnation due to theirs? No sentiment is more acknowledged in the family of Agriculturists than that the few who can afford it should incur the risk and expense of all new improvements, and give the benefit freely to the many of more restricted circumstances.[19]

Jefferson then went on to outline his plan. With his usual mathematical precision he demonstrated the short period of time it would take to spread the culture of Merino sheep to every county in Virginia with a reasonable profit to the owner of the prized stock. This plan has since been identified as the forerunner of modern cooperative breeding associations. Madison acceded to this proposal.

Jefferson also outlined his plan to Joseph Dougherty, the caretaker of his sheep in Washington as well as presidential coachman and stableman. He said he had made up his mind that, instead of selling the valuable offspring of these animals for thousands of dollars, which his debts certainly warranted, he would instead give a full-blooded ram to every county as soon as he could raise them. Dougherty was quick to respond, asking permission of his former employer to make that part of his letter public. It seems Colonel Humphreys had recently been in Washington and "put us all to silence with the constant sound of patriotism and his great exertions to promote domestic manufacture."[20] Dougherty wanted to show his fellow citizens what true patriotism was, but Jefferson objected strenuously, pointing out he would seem as greedy of praise as some people were of money.

Jefferson embarked upon his program as soon as Bacon got the animals to Monticello. As Bacon described it:

When I got home, I put a notice in the paper at Charlottesville that persons who wished to improve their stock could send us two ewes, and we would keep them until the lambs were old enough to wean, and then give the owners the choice of the lambs, and they leave the other lamb and both of the ewes. We got the greatest lot of sheep—more than we wanted; two or three hundred, I think; and in a few years we had an immense flock. People came long distances to buy our full-blooded sheep. At first we sold them for fifty dollars, but they soon fell to thirty, and twenty; and before I left Mr. Jefferson [in 1822] Merino sheep were so numerous, that they sold about as cheap as common ones.[21]

Allowances must be made for an old man's reminiscences of his younger days. Jefferson's own writings on the subject would indicate his Merino flock was never numerous. In 1812 he stated he had lost one of his original full-blooded ewes to scab, a skin disease, and the other two had produced only ram lambs. James Madison was more successful with his pair and sold rams but not ewes. In 1813 Jefferson still had only two ewes.

The problem of supplying Merinos from Monticello and Montpelier quickly became academic. After William Jarvis' shipment other large importations followed. Prices of course fell accordingly, especially after the conclusion of the War of 1812 when demand for domestic fine woolens fell. Jefferson commented in 1813: "The wool sells high to the Northward to the hatters, but our hatters do not know how to use it."[22] By 1824, encouraged by a new tariff in 1816 to protect home manufacturers and the subsequent interest of some businesses in making fine wool, a second fad developed, this time with Saxony sheep.

Few Merino sheep are grown in America today. However, their wool is still prized for its softness and clothing made from it is imported into this country. Indeed the Merino supplies at least one third of the world's wool.

Meanwhile Jefferson himself was having second thoughts about the value of this breed. It had the misfortune, he found, of being very susceptible to scab. Less than a year after beginning their culture, Jefferson wrote George Jefferson in Richmond that two ewes had even introduced scab into his flock. His cousin replied he understood Merinos had similarly introduced the disease into the flocks of every person who had them. This was serious; ewes, and sometimes rams, could die as a result of the infection, and the ewes could lose their lambs. George Jefferson recommended one of several cures presented in the ex–President's correspondence, so the disease must have caused considerable concern.

As a practical matter the Merino project also did not work out for other reasons. Jefferson wrote Doughtery at the end of 1812 that "the Merino fever has so entirely subsided in this part of the country that the farmers now will not accept of them, because they produce less wool & less suitable for the coarse manufactures they want, than the sheep they possess, and there is no market for the wool in this state."[23]

The process of reducing flock size was slower than the letter to Dougherty suggests for four years later Jefferson repeated the same complaint to George Logan. Yet, with other discriminating farmers, Jefferson recognized quality wool when he saw it. He continued raising Merinos and in 1818 sent a full-blooded ram to Judge Archibald Stuart of Staunton, Virginia, from whom he had bought sheep in the past.

In 1812 Jefferson praised Livingston for his excellent book *Essay on sheep; their varieties—an account of the Marinoes of Spain, France, etc.*[24] Jefferson waxed enthusiastic regarding raising sheep and spoke of his own Merinos, but told Livingston his principal flock was broad-tailed Tunisian. While most farmers seemed to favor just one breed for both table and wool,

Jefferson had long been accustomed to raising more than one kind at a time, for it allowed him to experiment. He found, for example, that by cross-breeding his broad-tails, they were more easily propagated. (Tails of the pure-bred were so large they prevented unassisted mating.)

Jefferson wrote to John Adams in 1812 he reckoned that one sheep per person was sufficient to clothe that individual, in addition to the cotton, hemp and flax "we raise ourselves." In addition to wool the meat was important. He told Bacon in 1807 to "pay great attention to the hogs and sheep. We must get into such a stock as to have 30 killable hogs every year, and fifty ewes."[25]

Jefferson's sheep were a constant concern to him. His overseers were admonished repeatedly to carefully tend to them "as if they were children." The sheep were expected to forage by day, but were herded in for the night. Jefferson considered turnips a major food for both his sheep and cattle, supplemented by hay and dry fodder.

If an 1813 letter is any indication, Jefferson still preferred the descendants of the ram Morris had given him in 1794. These he now kept at Bedford. Neighboring farmers were using them to improve their flocks as farmers in Albemarle had earlier. Rams were given freely to those wanting them.

Dogs were an adjunct to sheep. Jefferson bought his first sheep dog, Bergere, in LeHavre in 1789. As early as 1791 he owned sufficient shepherd dogs of quality to send a pair of puppies to Washington; later he gave dogs to others as well. Comments on these animals are limited until his renewed interest in sheep upon his retirement. The Marquis de Lafayette sent dogs to him from France after he left office. Jefferson also requested his friend Pierre Samuel Dupont de Nemours to buy him a pair before his next visit to the U.S. As the visit did not occur for six years, Jefferson's habit of enlisting help from more than one source again paid off.

Jefferson never had many dogs. He told Judge Harry Innes in 1813 he kept four pairs at different places and allowed no other dog near. While an admirer of the abilities of these animals, he could not be called a dog lover and certainly did not think of them as pets. For the sheep man dogs presented a double-edged sword. Those not trained to protect sheep posed a threat as potential killers when allowed to fend for themselves. For anyone dependent on flocks for wool and meat this hard-nosed attitude was necessary. Jefferson went so far at one point as to order Bacon to have all the negroes' dogs killed, although he permitted Bacon to keep a couple for himself. The master's dogs were also useful for fetching cows, herding fowl to their quarters and as watchdogs.

Mules apparently started gaining acceptance as work animals during the Revolutionary War era. While they were widely used in France and southern Europe in the eighteenth century, they were slow to catch on in the Colonies, probably because the English were not familiar with their strong points. Like pigs, they required little care and could subsist on whatever food and shelter was available. They accepted hard heavy work and poor handling. Washington was one of the earliest promoters of mules in the U.S., importing breeding mares in 1785. Jefferson no doubt was once again inspired by his President and came to favor mules for hauling wagons between Monticello and Poplar Forest or Washington. Heavily loaded carts were pulled by three animals.

Jefferson bought mules in Virginia and Kentucky, also getting the best stock available. He mentions only one breed, the Don Carlos. Interestingly, considering the record of his saddle horses, he apparently never tried to cross mares and asses.

Through the end of the Revolutionary War draft horses were small and light, a reflection in part on their genetic heritage, in part on poor care. Riding horses were better treated, as they were the only practical method of getting around. Improving their stock was a top priority among the gentry.

Importing breeding stock began in earnest by the fourth decade of the seventeenth century. Pedigrees were recorded; one of the first activities of the Albemarle Agriculture Society was to obtain an outstanding Spanish horse to stud. Jefferson's love of fine horses is well known and riding them were one of his delights. When at home he could indulge himself. He wrote in 1795 that he lived on his horse from an early breakfast to a late dinner and very often until dark.[24] The horse helped him keep track of plantation activities. For some unknown reason a *Farm Book* notation on articles for contracts with overseers, noted that they were "not allowed to keep a horse."[25]

Jefferson's work horses were important to his farming. An undated calendar of work calls for four horses, four oxen and eight laborers for a farm of 280 acres in seven fields of forty acres each. Jefferson must have written this in about 1796, as the Duke de la Rochefoucald-Liancourt repeats these figures in his account of visiting Monticello. The numbers of horses fluctuated. Between 1809 and 1817 there were between one and three at Monticello, seven to ten at Tufton, three or four at Lego, five to seven at Poplar Forest and four to eight at Bear Creek. At times farm operations slowed for want of horses. Jefferson's horses were fed ten barrels of corn each per year, a cost which limited their numbers. Corn was supplemented by hay, fodder, chopped rye, and cut straw.

What part goats played on his farms is unclear. Only one sentence is devoted to them in his *Farm Book*, a note that "kids are fit for the table from 3. weeks to 3. months old."[26] Ten goats are listed at Shadwell in a 1795 inventory, but the animals are not mentioned on other inventories.

Fowl were common on American farms. They cost little, for they found their own food; feeding a little supplemental grain kept them domesticated. They found their own shelter if necessary, and they were easily propagated. Only those devoted to cock fighting appear to have considered improving birds until the mid-1800s when birds more exotic than the leghorn, Plymouth rock and Rhode Island red were introduced and grown in some number.

Jefferson had chickens, ducks, Guinea fowl, geese, and turkeys. He bought geese and ducks and made an effort to obtain a pair of wild geese and the crested turkey. He encouraged his youngest daughter Maria as a child to grow chickens. His oldest daughter, Martha, spent crucial years of her childhood abroad, but she was always the faithful supporter of her father's interests and was undoubtedly involved with the fowl. Two of Martha's children, Anne and Ellen, certainly were.

8
Farm Personnel

Jefferson was particularly dependent on his stewards and overseers because he was so frequently away from home. This situation was not helped by the fact that he had deficiencies as a manager of his estates, although he did not admit this to others until late in life. Perhaps he did not recognize his weakness until he turned over operations to his grandson, Jeff Randolph. Soon after Randolph came of age in 1815 he managed Monticello and in 1821 Poplar Forest was added to his charge. Jefferson then admitted that he had never had the supervisory skills his farms needed. The year of his death he deplored his lack of ability in this area to two friends.

It was not his fault that he had problems finding well-qualified overseers, but certainly a part of the difficulty was due to his temperment. He did not make employees and slaves toe the line; he was much too disposed to give his personnel the benefit of the doubt when things went wrong. Perhaps the most flagrant abuse of his good nature came from Jonathan Shoemaker, the first tenant of the manufacturing mill, who routinely ignored his responsibilities to Jefferson's pocketbook and reputation. In Shoemaker's case Jefferson's excuse was that he did not then need the money the miller owed, which was not true at all considering Jefferson's extensive debts. Only a handful of cases of punishment are recorded, resulting in jail for the miscreant slave (and lashes only once), while white workers were replaced without apparent ill feeling on Jefferson's part.

He apparently lacked interest in the details of farm management until 1794 when he returned to Monticello from his position as secretary of state in George Washington's cabinet. The unnamed overseer Peter Jefferson hired—or whom his wife Jane secured as a replacement after his death— must have been doing a reasonable job.[1] Thomas as a young man was absorbed in the study of law and then in the legal profession, and later, politics. The amount of time he spent on plantation matters, beyond going over the books and sanctioning whatever his overseers planned, must have been minimal.

This was entirely in keeping with the practices of the day. One of Jefferson's grandsons asked him how his father and friends had spent their time. The answer was: "My father had a devoted friend, to whose house he would go, dine, spend the night, dine with him again on the second day, and return to Shadwell in the evening. His friend, in the course of a day or two, returned the visit, and spent the same length of time at his house. This occurred once every week; and thus, you see, they were together four days out of the seven."[2]

Sarah N. Randolph, a great-granddaughter who had access to many family records, comments after quoting the above: "This is, perhaps, a fair picture of the ease and leisure of the life of an old Virginian, and to the causes which produced this style of life was due, also, the great hospitality for which Virginians have ever been so renowned. The process of farming was then so simple that the labor and cultivation of an estate were easily and most profitably carried on by an overseer and the slaves, the master only riding occasionally over his plantation to see that his general orders were executed."[3] This would explain some of Thomas's inattention under a one-crop system where the tasks were routine and straightforward, if tedious.

Although Jefferson was absent from Monticello for long periods prior to 1794, he was also absent much of the time after that year. When one reviews his pre-1793 correspondence, it is evident he was concerned with his personal family gardens and orchards and promoting the agricultural fortunes of others, but not so much in the farming operations taking place on his own land. What caused him to look closer at his affairs is difficult to say, except that he was determined to retire from public life. In the latter half of 1793 his interest in his farms becomes evident in his plans for crop rotation. In January of 1794 he was finally home; then he complained to President Washington, "I find on a more minute examination of my lands than the short visits theretofore made to them permitted, that a ten years' abandonment of them to the ravages of overseers, has brought on them a degree of degradation far beyond what I had expected."[4] The fact is, Jefferson appears to have been well content not to ask probing questions of his overseers and stewards an astute manager would have asked. Uncharacteristically he blamed others for what certainly was his own failing. His early interest in botany had never been transferred to agricultural matters except in an abstract fashion. From early manhood on he was noted for his agricultural expertise, but it was theoretical knowledge. In 1794, for the first time in his life, he took a hard look at his fields. From that time on he was a hands-on farmer.

Jefferson had gotten into the fix he described to Washington in spite of using experienced stewards. He began—or at least his chart in his *Farm Book* begins—with Thomas Garth, followed by John Key, Nicholas Lewis, and a Mr. Ballow. Each of these men were landowners in their own right, and Garth and Lewis were recognized leaders in the community as well. Each received payment from Jefferson for looking after the latter's interest. For his effort Key received eighty pounds per year, over twice what later overseers would receive. Key's tenure was for three consecutive years, Ballow's for two, and Garth and Lewis extended before or after. At times there seems to have been an overlap of stewards or their responsibilities. Garth and Lewis were certainly more important than the other two men, and Lewis was most valued by Jefferson.

Lewis was an early mentor and friend who owned land east of Charlottesville. He exchanged twenty-seven and one-half acres with Jefferson so the latter could consolidate his Monticello holdings. Jefferson was also gratified that Lewis became a trustee for the Virginia General Assembly Project for Making the Rivanna River Navigable. As Lewis had a mill on the river, the two had much in common. It is obvious from their correspondence that Lewis could be classified as a knowledgeable farmer, if not an ardent one. The two men exchanged agricultural information as well as plants. Jefferson described his neighbor as the best seedsman around. Lewis raised red clover seed for sale, which made him a true benefactor to Albemarle County. He also served as a captain in the Revolutionary War, a surveyor, a magistrate and a sheriff of Albemarle County.

Not surprisingly, Jefferson felt close to this man and regarded him highly. In 1792 he wrote to Lewis, "Unremitting business must be my apology, as it is really the true one, for my having been longer without writing to you than my affections dictated."[5]

In 1784 when he left for Paris Jefferson made an agreement with Lewis to manage Monticello and associated plantations in conjunction with Francis Eppes of Chesterfield County. That their business relationship was close can be determined from a letter Jefferson wrote Lewis in February of 1786: "mr Mazzei tells me that mr Key has left my service, but he does not know who succeeded him. I hope mr Key left with you the general instructions I gave him; so that his successor may have knowledge of them. If he did not, & you cannot recover them, be so good as to inform me of it, and I will send a new copy of them . . ."[6] This is an interesting letter, not only because Jefferson seems so unconcerned about his affairs, but because Jefferson is unaware that Ballow, who appears on his *Farm Book* chart, served as his steward (presumably at Lewis's instigation) in 1785–86. Bowling Clark was then appointed overseer. The incident shows how poorly Jefferson utilized the men who he had enlisted to help him.[7]

His curious lack of inquisitiveness about the farms upon which he depended for his income came home to roost with a vengence. Instead of asking Lewis hard questions regarding the agricultural activities at Monticello, he says only in the same 1786 letter: "The care of my trees, replanting them, & extending my grass grounds are objects of great concern to me. They are the more so as they are things which cannot be created in a moment. While I am absent they can be growing as fast as if I was present, so that all that time is saved to me."[8]

In their correspondence farm matters were seldom mentioned and such matters as were discussed involved finances. Lewis's health, however, soon interfered with this arrangement. Jefferson's inadequacies as a manager are also indicated in a letter to Lewis in June of 1791: "It is with infinite regret, my dear Sir, that I learn your purpose of withdrawing from the direction of my affairs. My confidence in you has been so entire, that since they have been in your hands I have never had an anxiety about them. I saw indeed that you took a great deal more trouble about them than I could expect or wish, & I feared it would lead you to an entire relinquishment of them. Instead of having a right to urge a continuance of such a drudgery on you, it is my duty to be thankful that you have submitted to it so long, and I am so, sincerely and thoroughly."[9] Lewis had been struck with an unnamed disease and by 1795 was dangerously ill. He lingered until 1808.

Garth also had business connections with Jefferson long before he became steward. Like Lewis he was appointed a magistrate and sheriff. Garth bought for Jefferson in 1775 the 819.25 acres which became known as Lego. While Garth served as Jefferson's steward from 1778 to 1782, he looked after his interests at other times too. While in France, Jefferson considered him a backup to Lewis. Garth probably functioned as Jefferson's attorney from 1791 until the secretary of state returned to Monticello in 1794. Garth also leased land from Jefferson during that period.

In 1790 Jefferson wrote Garth, "The letters I receive from the President are so pressing to go on to New York that I cannot wait the event of mr Lewis's illness nor even make any arrangement in case of his loss. I must therefore in that case beg that you will supply his place for me till I can have leave to come home or take some other final measure. I would not wish you to give yourself any trouble which may be avoided. The principal will be to sell & pay off the crop of tobo. & wheat now on hand, and to call in some balances of which he had made out a list."[10]

These instructions clearly show Jefferson's concept of a steward to be primarily confined to his finances. Yet without strong, knowledgeable and resourceful overseers on site at Monticello and Bedford, Jefferson was lost as a farmer.

Edmund Bacon, later overseer at Monticello, claimed in his autobiography that his older brother William "had charge" of Jefferson's estate while he was in Paris. The Bacon family, neighbors of Jefferson, probably served as interested friends. Thomas Mann Randolph, whose property, Edgehill, was adjacent to Monticello, could accurately be called a steward after he married Jefferson's daughter in 1790. Jefferson seems to have relied on the young man's judgement without hesitation.

By 1773 Jefferson had settled on the requirements he thought necessary in his overseers, if not his stewards, whose services he did not yet require. Lists, slightly different from one another, appear in the 1773 entry of his *Garden Book* and the *Account Book* and were repeated in the *Farm Book* after that volume was begun in 1774. They indicate the importance he attached to the subject. The duties and obligations on the lists were probably typical of the period. Jefferson drew up rules for contracts with tenants too.[11]

While these are interesting, they must be put into context. By 1805, upon looking for a replacement for his current Monticello overseer, he provided details to a friend he hoped could recommend a replacement: "My manager there has to provide for the maintenance of a family of about 40 negroes at all times, and for my own family about 3 months in the year; to hire annually, and overlook about 10. laboring men,[12] employed in a little farming but mainly in other works about my mills, & grounds generally; to superintend the gristmill, and a nailery of 10. to 15. hands, provide their coal, sell nails etc. I love industry & abhor severity."[13]

Jefferson's overseers were a varied lot and undoubtedly representative of what was available to plantation owners. Competition for their services, no matter what their capabilities, must have been keen. Even someone of Jefferson's prestige and extensive contacts had to scramble for men who were willing to face the challenge. The memoranda Jefferson made out for Edmund Bacon are daunting, and the responsibilities they imply indicate a good manager needed skills and experience few Americans who were not already landowners of some consequence possessed. Furthermore, wages were low, although they reflected the financial situation of the era; in 1792 they ranged from £25 to £30. Any intelligent, energetic man could go forth and be his own master and this is just what Bacon, Jefferson's last overseer at Monticello, did. It is probably remarkable the overseers and their employers managed as well as they did.

Who was in charge on Jefferson's plantations on a day-to-day basis prior to 1781 is not known. On the other hand, his chart in the *Farm Book* begun in

1783 does not include all the names which appear in the *Account Book* as paid overseers at Monticello and there are no names at all for Bedford. At Bedford the name Bennet emerges in 1781 and was still mentioned in 1788. There is nothing in the Poplar Forest records during the early years to indicate things were not running smoothly there. The tobacco crop remained steady in size. Tobacco growing was relatively easy to understand. Not until 1792 did Jefferson introduce wheat at Poplar Forest. Clark was overseer by then, and he had already served at Monticello and was accustomed to growing wheat there, so adding this crop should have gone smoothly.[14] To Washington he does not mention any concern for his Bedford land, so there at least his overseers appear to have served him well.[15]

In Albemarle Jefferson's chart lists Key as steward and a Chisolm (no first name) as overseer at Shadwell for 1783.[16] There is no information on Chisolm, but as Jefferson had not yet left for Paris he knew the man personally. No overseer is listed at Monticello for 1783, 1784, or 1785. Does this mean Jefferson could find no one to fill the slot? But why assign Chisolm to Shadwell with no mention of Monticello? The answer probably lies with George.

Of all the names on Jefferson's chart, that of George, or "Great George" as he came to be called, is by far the most interesting, for he was one of Jefferson's slaves.[17] In the slave roll entry in the *Farm Book* entry for 1774, Jefferson's first two slaves named George appear, father and son. The father, born in 1730, was on what Jefferson called his "proper slaves" list — those he inherited from his father or bought himself. George, who in 1774 was forty-four, and his wife, Ursula, were both designated as "a titheable person following some other occupation." In other words neither were field hands. In the 1773 *Account Book* Jefferson records buying Ursula, age thirty-five, and her sons George, fourteen years old, and Bagwell, five years old, from the Fleming estate. He paid £210 for the three negroes, which in an 1810 letter he called "an exorbitant price" since the woman was old and the boys infants. From whom Jefferson bought George, Sr., is not recorded, but he paid only £130 for him. However, his bride, Martha, needed a woman of Ursula's skills. William Fleming of Goochland County, who served with Jefferson in the Virginia House of Burgesses in 1773, no doubt mentioned Ursula's availability to his old friend from the College of William and Mary. Jefferson was willing to buy Ursula and her boys on twelve-months credit, not only to please his wife but because his finances at that point seemed to warrant it. George was the beneficiary of Jefferson's policy of keeping families together whenever possible.

Ursula was a pastry cook at Monticello and washed and ironed, according to the recollections of her son, Isaac. She later became nurse to the Randolph children. George, Sr., was known as the most efficient blacksmith at Monticello before a white man, William Stewart, arrived in 1801. While the first smith shop was built in 1774, George seems to have worked in some other non-field job in 1774, for Francis Bishop was the first smith, and a slave Barnaby was his helper.

A letter by Lewis's wife in 1770 to Jefferson, who was then busy pursuing his legal career, mentions: "George has been frequently hear and reports that all is well."[18] Such freedom of movement by a slave indicates that he was trusted and functioned in some capacity of importance.

Whatever his earlier jobs, George was singled out by Jefferson to be in charge of the house keys when the British intentions in the Charlottesville area in 1781 included capturing then–Governor Jefferson, a scheme which forced him to take his family out of harm's way, ultimately to Bedford. Isaac recalled his father's responses at the moment of truth.

> When the British come in, an officer rode up and asked, "Whar is the Governor?" Isaac's father [George] told him, "He's gone to the mountains." The officer said, "Whar is the keys of the house?" Isaac's father gave him the keys; Mr. Jefferson had left them with him. The officer said, "Whar is the silver?" Isaac's father told him, "It was all sent up to the mountains." The old man had put all the silver about the house in a bed tick and hid it under a bed in the kitchen and saved it too and got his freedom by it. But he continued to sarve Mr. Jefferson and had forty pounds from Old Master and his wife. Isaac's mother had seven dollars a month for lifetime for washing, ironing, and making pastry.[19]

While this is the only direct evidence that Jefferson manumitted George, there is an *Account Book* entry of April 15, 1782, that, among Jefferson's taxable property in Albemarle that year, were 129 slaves and two free negroes. As this record comes so soon after the British raid, Isaac's account is no doubt correct.[20] Jefferson had every reason to be impressed with George's fortitude in facing British soldiers and using his imagination in hiding the family silver. Giving George his freedom for this act is very much in line with the other known cases where Jefferson freed individual slaves.

In about 1782 George may have become *de facto* overseer, which would account for the lack of an overseer's name from 1783 on in the *Farm Book* chart. Jefferson was mostly at home from the latter part of the summer of 1781 through the growing season of 1783 and therefore could personally supervise what was going on at Monticello, while Chisolm worked as overseer at nearby Shadwell. Thus, when he left the country, we may assume Jefferson was not totally deprived of someone he could trust to look after his interests.

That Jefferson was depending on George is seen from several references to him in letters home from Paris. Anthony Giannini, who had been brought to the U.S. by the Italian Philip Mazzei in 1773 or 1774 and who worked for Jefferson thereafter, was told in a 1786 letter, after his employer gave detailed instructions regarding horticultural activities at Monticello: "I trust much to you for the replacing my trees which die, and extending them, and that George takes care of them thro' the year so that nothing may hurt them. . . . I hope on my return, which will not be very distant I shall find that you & George have kept up my plans well in my absence. Tell him & my other servants that I have their welfare much at heart."[21]

Lewis is told in a 1787 letter, in which Jefferson discusses leasing his lands in his absence from home, that George was to be assigned to take care of the orchards, grasses "&c." The following July he wrote Lewis that George, Ursula, Betty Hemings, Martin, and Bob were not to be hired out. By December, when he thought he would be returning home the following May, he told Lewis he would need only a skeletal staff for a projected two-month stay and named the same persons to serve. There are other references to George, both from Paris and later while Jefferson was secretary of state, which single out the man for his knowledge of what the master wanted done with his plantings and other outdoor work.

It is obvious George must have had some experience taking charge during this time, because when his name next comes up in January 1792 in a letter the secretary of state wrote his daughter Martha, he is given a vote of confidence. Martha was informed that her father would have to rely on her husband to supervise the overall management of his estates: "Having taken from other pursuits a number of hands to execute several purposes which I had in view this year, I can not abandon those purposes and lose their labor altogether. I must, therefore, select the most important and least troublesome of them, the execution of my canal, and (without embarrassing him with any details which Clarkson [the overseer] and George are equal to) get him to tell them always what is to be done and how."[22]

This letter was followed by a letter to Randolph himself regarding digging the canal for his mill: "George, aided by Clarkson will be sufficient to see that the work is done, and to take all details off of your hands. But they will need to be instructed in what manner to conduct it." After listing the men who should form the crew, Jefferson adds, "I consider George rather as their foreman, and should not require him to lay his hand to the hardest work."[23] The fact that Jefferson's carpenters were to be part of this crew indicates George must have been a reasonably strong leader.

By 1794 George became the first manager of the Monticello nailery, a project dear to Jefferson's heart. Jefferson wrote, obviously savoring the words:

I am myself a nail-maker. On returning home after an absence of ten years, I found my farms so much deranged that I saw evidently they would be a burden to me instead of a support till I could regenerate them; & consequently that it was necessary for me to find some other recourse in the meantime. I thought for a while of taking up the manufacture of pot-ash, which requires but small advances of money. I concluded at length however to begin a manufacture of nails, which needs little or no capital, & I now employ a dozen little boys from 10. to 16. years of age, over-looking all the details of their business myself & drawing from it a profit on which I can get along till I can put my farms into a course of yielding profit. My new trade of nail-making is to me in this country what an additional title of nobility or the ensigns of a new order are in Europe.[24]

Monticello boys, like farm boys in every age, would make a useful if unusual contribution to farm finances.

Jefferson told another correspondent in 1795, "my groceries come to between 4. & 500. Dollars a year, taken & paid quarterly. The best resource of quarterly paiment in my power is nails, of which I make enough every fortnight to pay a quarter's bill."[25] George's efforts at the nailery were therefore crucial to Jefferson's solvency. While the owner took care of ordering nail rod and selling the finished nails and no doubt looked in at the nailery from time to time, it was George who kept the operation going. It is true Jefferson wrote John Adams in 1795: "What with my farming and my nail manufactory I have my hands full. I am on horseback half the day, and counting and measuring nails the other half."[26] This was no reflection on George's capabilities, for Jefferson was in his element in such surroundings and loved to make things, including keys, locks, and chains.

Yet there were problems with the nailery. Jefferson found nail rod more costly than he apparently anticipated and it had to be bought with cash. He found the competition from British nails a problem and, when he tried consigning nails to single dealers, he found them slow to pay. None of this of course reflected on George. Indeed Jefferson's *Account Book 1795* notes a large sale of nails. Such a fast start-up indicates George's skill as a supervisor. The nailery continued to flourish in 1796 and 1797 when George, Jr. (called Smith George) took over at the nailery while his father assumed the duties of overseer.[27] When Great George's health began to fail, so did the nailery. Jefferson wrote in May of 1799, the year of the older George's death, "A long illness of my foreman, occasions our work to go on so poorly that I am able to do little more than supply [nails to] this part of the country."[28] George's replacement at the nailery, William Stewart, while expert at his trade, proved so eccentric that the man was ultimately fired in 1807. The nailery kept up production until the War of 1812 and after its conclusion on a much reduced scale.

At harvest time all hands were put into the fields. Jefferson notes in his diary of 1795: "Great George, with tools & a grindstone mounted in the single mule cart, should be constantly employed in mending cradles & grinding scythes. The same cart would carry about the liquor, moving from tree to tree as the work advanced."[29] Although George was merely plying his trade as a blacksmith, the fact that he was trusted to ride with the liquor indicates his character and ability to make sound judgments.

By 1797 George is listed in the Monticello column of overseers in the *Farm Book* and again for the years 1798 and 1799, at which time he was sixty-nine. He died on November 29, 1799. George had been a blacksmith and had been in charge of the nailery and the crew on the new canal. As an overseer he was in charge of the fields. The letters which follow show the man had considerable experience growing crops and caring for farm animals. In 1796 Jefferson wrote in his *Farm Book* that he and George had concluded that they would keep a dozen breeding sows. In 1798 Randolph wrote the vice-president that George was "under great apprehension his corn wd. be lost before you came home from the weakness of his ploughs, he *must* make a crop of it this year for every body seems to be neglecting it for Tobo. I have bought 40 Barrels for him @ 11/. & had it hauled to him by James: he was quite out."[30]

George was also growing tobacco that year, but he encountered some problems, as Randolph explained to his father-in-law: "Your affairs at Shadwell go on well, the whole crop of Tobacco (46000) is planted & stands. George is not so forward, he cannot command his force: there were in my absence some instances of disobedience so gross that I am obliged to interfere & have them punished myself. Several of the people had actually planted considerable crops of tobacco before I knew they designed it. I have refused permission to cultivate it, & insist on their planting something which you have always suffered when at home, in its place."[31]

There was no doubt some resentment on the part of other blacks for George's authority over them, no matter how well deserved. White overseers, of course, had the same problem with discipline. Growing tobacco, which the slaves had tried before on the sly, was particularly lucrative that year, so field hands wanted to grow their own small crop. Jefferson had written Randolph in January of 1798 that "George should be hurried to get his tobacco down. . . . good tobacco sells here at 13. D."[32]

In 1798 another letter to Randolph relates that Jefferson had ordered clover seed, so important to rejuvenating his fields, and "mr Page [overseer at Shadwell] & George have written directions where to sow it. . . . I wish them to keep a look out for the arrival of the seed at Milton or Charlottesville that no time may be lost for sowing it."[33] Evidently George may have known how to read. Randolph wrote later that year, "Agricultural affairs proceed both at Montio: and Shadwell: George is steady & industrious—Page I think is as anxious about his duties as an overseer I ever knew."[34]

The history of Great George, illustrates Jefferson's willingness to train his slaves and give them the responsibilities. Indeed these were the criteria he insisted upon before granting freedom to any slave. When referring to his experiences at the nailery where he made nails, Isaac recalled that Jefferson encouraged the children "mightily." Isaac, at age seventy-two when he was interviewed, was still a practicing blacksmith, with his own shop near Petersburg, Virginia.

Two other blacks held notable leadership capacity in farm work. Nace lived at Poplar Forest, and as Jefferson had little to say in his records and correspondence about his slaves there, only the bare facts are available. Nace was born in 1773. On Jefferson's listing of Bedford slaves in 1810 a " + " appears next to Nace's name, indicating he was not a field hand but a titheable person following some other occupation. This presumably was a headman, a dependable slave put in charge of a slave gang. In an 1811 memorandum to his new Bedford overseer, Jeremiah Goodman, he details the jobs of each slave. "Nace, the former headman, and the best we have ever known is to be entirely kept from labour until he recovers, which will probably be very long. He may do anything which he can do sitting in a warm room, such as shoemaking and making baskets. He can shell corn in the corn house when it is quite warm, or in his own house at any time."[35]

As late as March 1821, Nace was responsible for delivering cattle and sheep to Monticello, over 90 miles away. Unfortunately this man ultimately let down his advocate. John Hemings, another talented slave and a carpenter, wrote to Jefferson in November of 1821 from Poplar Forest where he was still hard at work on the house:

> Sir, I am sorry to complain to you so near the close of my work, above all things on earth I hate complaints. . . . the moment your back is turned from the place Nace takes everything out of the garden and carries them to his cabin and buries them in the ground and says that they are for the use of the house. I don't set up myself for the things that are made for your table but as common a thing as [illegible] which we are suffering for the want of now. . . . [T]he pipel tels me that he is making market of them at the first opportunity. . . . In my situation I am at work in the morning by the time I can see and the very same at night."[36]

The other black headman or overseer worked at Monticello. The only reference to him is by Bacon, who gave his name as Jim. He was noted for making the best pork among the overseers.[37]

A white overseer of interest is Bowling Clark, the first named for Monticello for 1786 through 1787. His background is unusual for such a position. His grandfather, Christopher, had been a wealthy tobacco planter in adjoining Hanover (now Louisa) County and an early settler in that part of Virginia. His father, Bowling, one of seven children, inherited only 400 acres of his father's holdings and ten young slaves. His own personal fortunes apparently never rivaled his father's.

As the senior Bowling Clark married in 1742, Bowling, Jr., was Jefferson's age or younger—in his late thirties or early forties—when he began working for America's envoy to France. Due to Clark's background, Jefferson no doubt felt secure about his affairs at Monticello, especially because George and Giannini were there. There is no hint of concern in Jefferson's correspondence home that his mind was not at ease on the management of his farms. His agricultural concerns in this period centered, except for plows, on the financial interests of others.

When Clark left Albemarle is not known. He may have moved to Bedford County in 1788 where his father had been buying land as early as 1771. In any event Jefferson called upon him again in 1789 to serve as overseer at Bedford, a post he held until 1801. The younger Clark had begun buying land in Bedford County from 1794 on, obviously planning for his own future. Perhaps he began farming it at once, spreading his time and attention. In any event Clark's efforts seem to have been satisfactory until February of 1801 when Jefferson's buyer in Philadelphia complained about the poorly packed tobacco originating at Poplar Forest. The President was much upset; he needed every bit of cash his crop would bring, for his new office was costing him sizeable amounts of money. Whatever passed between employer and overseer as a consequence of this information, the relationship by October was again on solid ground. Jefferson assigned Clark to the task of laying out a tract of Poplar Forest land for each of his sons-in-law. In his letter to Randolph he refers to Clark as "an honest & judicious man." Nevertheless, Jefferson had already made up his mind to replace Clark and by August was deep into negotiations.

At the other extreme were at least two overseers who were illiterate (Clarkson and Lilly). Clarkson served only one year, but Randolph reported favorably on him. Lilly remained for five years, and Jefferson, then President, was well pleased with the man and wished him to stay. Unfortunately he could not afford the increased wages Lilly was demanding and he later discovered the overseer had left a large debt with a merchant at Milton.

Age, like literacy, was not a factor in Jefferson's selection process. Bacon, who served him longest, was barely 21 when he assumed the post. Bacon lived within two to three miles of Monticello and had worked for Jefferson at various jobs prior to this appointment as overseer. His father, according to Bacon, had been raised with Jefferson and went to school with him. When Bacon gave his autobiography at age seventy-six he made several claims of familiarity with his employer which were contested later as inaccurate. It does seem clear that Jefferson knew the Bacon family well and was satisfied the young man had been well trained by his father. While it is apparent from correspondence that in the earliest years Bacon did not always make sound judgements, he served his employer well for almost twenty years. He then moved west and became a prosperous farmer.

One- or two-year tenures plagued the overseer vocation. For his choices of men Jefferson had to rely on the recommendations of friends and acquaintances, even those out of state, which were not always reliable. There is no doubt, however, that when the relationship failed, the fault was not his. He was an eminently fair employer, slow to anger. Carpenters and other skilled tradesmen who worked for him also received considerate treatment, as did the tenants of his mills and his plantations. Yet he was a realist; his analysis of the situation in 1799 was, "I find I am not fit to be a farmer with the kind of labor we have, & also subject to such long avocation."[38]

Jefferson has been chided for the discrepancy between his concerns regarding slavery and the fact he himself was a slave holder. In the Virginia of his day, though, the plantation system could not have functioned without them. It was hard to find free laborers,[39] and tobacco was the only saleable agricultural product abroad until the Revolutionary War—a labor intensive crop. Although the earlier growth stages did not, the grain harvest required all able-bodied workers. Thus, unless a man was content to be a hard scrabble farmer, the slave system was essential. Although after the Revolution Virginians became increasingly less dependent on slaves and they could even have been called a liability in some respects, by then the institution was firmly entrenched and became increasingly established in states to the south.

Jefferson was philosophically against selling slaves whenever possible. After explaining to his brother-in-law, Francis Eppes, that he would not sell more land, he wrote in 1787, "I am also unwilling to sell negroes, if the debts can be paid without. This unwillingness is for their sake, not my own; because my debts once cleared off, I shall try some plan of making their situation happier, determined to content myself with a small portion of their labour. I think it better for them therefore to be submitted to harder conditions for a while in order that they may afterwards be put into a better situation."[40]

Unable to manumit them because of his enormous debts, Jefferson did what he could to modify what could have been a harsh relationship. In 1814 he wrote Edward Coles on the subject of slave emancipation, "It shall have all my prayers, and these are the only weapons of an old man. . . . My opinion has ever been that, until more can be done for them, we should

endeavor, with those whom fortune has thrown on our hands, to feed &
clothe them well, protect them from all ill usage, require such reasonable
labor only as is performed voluntarily by freemen, and be led by no
repugnancies to abdicate them, and our duties to them."[41] If this sounds
feudal in spirit, hardly any spot on earth at this time had better conditions
for any race.

Jefferson was also well aware that free blacks were free in name only.
Few whites extended a helping hand to integrate these generally unskilled,
unlettered people into the greater white community. He foresaw the
conditions which would prevail after the Civil War decades later. Until the
attitudes of non-slave holding as well as slave holding whites changed, his
people were better off under his protection.[42] He wrote in 1788:

> as far as I can judge from the experiments which have been made to give liberty
> to, or rather, to abandon persons whose habits have been formed in slavery is
> like abandoning children. Many quakers in Virginia seated their slaves on their
> lands as tenants. They were distant from me, and therefore I cannot be
> particular in the details because I never had very particular information. I
> cannot say whether they were to pay a rent in money, or a share of the produce:
> but I remember that the landlord was obliged to plan their crops for them, to
> direct all their operations during every season and according to the weather,
> but, what is more afflicting, he was obliged to watch them daily and almost
> constantly to make them work, and even to whip them. A man's moral sense
> must be unusually strong, if slavery does not make him a thief. He who is
> permitted by law to have no property of his own, can with difficulty conceive
> that property is founded in any thing but force. These slaves chose to steal from
> their neighbors rather than work. They became public nuisances, and in most
> instances were reduced to slavery again.

Jefferson continued,

> Notwithstanding the discouraging result of these experiments, I am decided
> . . . to import as many Germans as I have grown slaves. I will settle them and
> my slaves on farms of 50. acres each, intermingled, and place all on the footing
> of the Metayers [Medietarri] of Europe. Their children shall be brought up, as
> others are, in habits of property and foresight, and I have no doubt but that they
> will be good citizens. Some of their fathers will be so: others I suppose will need
> government. With these, all that can be done is to oblige them to labour as the
> labouring poor of Europe do, and to apply to their comfortable subsistence the
> produce of their labour, retaining such a moderate portion of it as may be a just
> equivalent for the use of the lands they labour and the stocks and other
> necessary advances.[43]

These ideas were never put into practice.

Jefferson inherited slaves from his father. He also received some from
his mother and from John Wayles through Martha Wayles Jefferson's
inheritance. There was, in addition, a natural increase in numbers. In his

1774 listing he claimed ownership of 187 slaves. The numbers fluctuated over the years from births and deaths, a few purchases (primarily to reunite families) and more sales as he struggled with his debts, principally the one his wife had inherited upon the death of her father. Sometimes Jefferson sold slaves at their own request to be united with family members, and in a few cases he sold one for delinquency.

The health and well-being of his slaves was always a prime considera-tion. When doctors were needed they were sent for. Jefferson even saw to it his people were inoculated against smallpox with Jenner's new vaccine soon after it became available. Lists of food, clothing, and bedding were faithfully maintained for each person to assure proper treatment. Ellen Randolph, Jefferson's granddaughter, recalled: "Bad year or good year, crop or no crop, these dependents were to be clothed and fed—well clothed and well fed."[44]

Slaves who showed ability were routinely pressed into assuming more responsible positions. Some learned to read and write. Letters written by carpenter Hemings and by a house servant named Hanah at Poplar Forest survive. While it was to Jefferson's best interests to teach skills to his slaves so he would not need to spend cash to hire men from outside the plantation, there can be no doubt that he was personally interested in the development of each of those people who depended on him.

He was also solicitous about his slaves' personal wishes. He wrote to his Poplar Forest overseer, Jeremiah Goodman, in 1812, "I have given Moses [who was sent to Bedford to bring back a yoke of steers] leave to stay a day with his friends."[45] Later that year to Goodman he wrote: "I will send up some of the young people from Monticello who want to visit their relations . . . and they will return with the waggon & drove & assist in driving [the hogs]."[46] Messages between Albemarle and Bedford slaves were frequent, courtesy of Jefferson family members.

The Duke de la Rochefoucauld-Liancourt summed it up this way:

> His negroes are nourished, clothes, and treated as well as white servants could be. As he cannot expect any assistance from the two small neighboring towns, every article is made on his farm; his negroes are cabinetmakers, carpenters, masons, bricklayers, smiths, etc. The children he employs in a nail factory, which yields already a considerable profit. The young and old negresses spin for the clothing of the rest. He animates them by rewards and distinctions; in fine, his superior mind directs the management of his domestic concerns with the same abilities, activity, and regularity which he evinced in the conduct of public affairs, and which he is calculated to display in every situation of life.[47]

These observations are corroborated by Isaac, son of George, who said in his memoirs: "Old Master very kind to servants" and "Isaac calls him a mighty good master."[48] Bacon recalled, "No servants ever had a kinder master" and "Mr. Jefferson was always very kind and indulgent to his servants. He would not allow them to be at all overworked, and he would hardly ever allow one of them to be whipped. His orders to me were constant: that if there was any servant that could not be got along with out the chastising that was customary, to dispose of him. He could not bear to have a servant whipped, no odds how much he deserved it."[49] "He did not like slavery. I have heard him talk a great deal about it. He thought it a bad system. I have heard him prophesy that we should have just such trouble with it as we are having now [1861]."[50]

While it concerned an overseer well before Bacon's time, Jefferson himself put it this way to Randolph: "Your account of Clarkson's [the overseer] conduct gives me great pleasure. My first wish is that the labourers may be well treated, the second that they may enable me to have that treatment continued by making as much as will admit it. The man who can effect both objects is rarely to be found. I wish you would take occasion to express to him the satisfaction I recieve from this communication."[51]

Bacon remembers servants being rewarded what would now be called bonuses for good conduct and good work. In the *Account Book* for 1811 he recorded giving Hemings the carpenter $15 dollars (the wages of one month) as an "encouragement." To Randolph he wrote: "I forgot to ask the favor of you to speak to Lilly [the overseer] as to the treatment of the nailers. It would destroy their value in my estimation to degrade them in their own eyes by the whip. This therefore must not be resorted to but in extremities. As they will be again under my government, I would chuse they should retain the stimulus of character."[52]

There was one instance when even this patient man could no longer tolerate abuse. Several hundred pounds of nails had been stolen by one Jame Hubbard, who worked at the nailery. This Jefferson overlooked. Later Hubbard ran away. Jefferson wrote to Reuben Perry of Bedford

Having received information in March that Jame Hubbard had been living in Lexington upwards of a twelvemonth, I engaged a man (Isham Chisolm) to go after him. He got there five days after Hubbard had run off from there, having committed a theft. He returned of course without him. I engaged him to start a second time, offering a premium of 25. D . . . he took him and brought him here in irons. I had him severely flogged in the presence of his old companions, and committed to jail where he now awaits your arrival. The course he has been in, and all the circumstances convince me he will never again serve any man as a slave. The moment he is out of jail and his irons off he will be off himself. It will therefore unquestionably be best for you to sell him. I have paid for his recovery 70. D. All I ask for it is that he may be sent out of the state.[53]

There were a few other cases of runaways as well as insubordination which Jefferson solved by selling the individuals. Interestingly, one of two Hemings women who ran away in 1822 were later freed. The slaves who ran off with the British were from Jefferson's plantations in Goochland and Cumberland counties. According to his official records at the time, fourteen were involved, two of them preteens. As the incident occurred under the conditions of a raiding party of enemy soldiers, there is no way of telling whether the flight was voluntary. Two of the women and one child returned on their own and later died of camp fever. Jefferson indicated ten of the others died while with the British.

Jefferson hired slaves from others while his canal was being built and during the presidential years. This was done reluctantly for it required cash. In 1806 the bill totalled $590 for nine slaves. After the canal was completed in 1803 the slaves involved worked on the mills, leveled garden grounds and made roads. Where possible Jefferson asked for the same individuals each year.[54] Since he rented out some of his own fields while he was President he also had to lease out forty-five of his own slaves to his tenant to farm the fields. Although he leased some of his slaves earlier, they too had remained on his own land at Monticello.[55]

His thoughts regarding leasing his servants to someone who lived elsewhere can be seen in an 1820 letter. "You have been quite misinformed as to my having any intention to lease my possessions in Bedford. Nothing could induce me to put my negroes out of my protection."[56] Considering he was nearing the end of his long life and was desperate for cash, Jefferson's sense of noblesse oblige to his slaves is nowhere more apparent. The exception to this reluctance to lease slaves would have been to his grandson Jeff, to whom he gave a five-year lease of Tufton and Lego in 1818 with the slaves living thereon.

9

Monticello Gardens

Agriculture was not the only facet of botany which consumed Jefferson's interest; indeed his curiosity was at first confined to flowers and landscaping. On his twenty-first birthday in 1764 he planted sycamore and locust trees at the Jefferson home, Shadwell. At age twenty-three he began his *Garden Book*, a record covering fifty-eight years. Flowers, not trees, dominate the entries for the first year. To what extent he was involved with planning and or planting these beds at his birthplace we do not know.[1] During these formative years he spent many happy hours with his favorite sister, Jane, until her death in 1765, botanizing as they wandered the Jefferson property. What he saw and learned of the native species during these excursions became the basis for his extensive knowledge on the subject. As he did not marry until he was twenty-eight, Jefferson had an opportunity to solidify these early interests before assuming the responsibilities of matrimony.

By age seventy-one, with more experience behind him, he wrote to a friend, "Botany I rank with the most valuable sciences, whether we consider its subjects as furnishing the principal subsistence of life to man and beast, delicious varieties for our tables, refreshments from our orchards, the adornments of our flower-borders, shade and perfume of our groves, materials for our buildings, or medicaments for our bodies. . . . To a country family it constitutes a great portion of their social entertainment. No country gentleman should be without what amuses every step he takes into his fields."[2]

As an up-and-coming young lawyer Jefferson thought of building a house of his own. Great Virginia plantation homes of the period were normally situated on rivers which provided the means for transporting people and goods through virgin forests. Although he had property traversed by a river, albeit small, he chose a mountain top as the site of the mansion itself. As a disciple of the great sixteenth-century architect, Palladio, he may have followed this mentor, who recommended an elevated location. Perhaps he was merely enraptured by the view of his land. By choosing this high point, far from his thriving legal practice and what concentrations of inhabitants Virginia possessed, Jefferson made a statement. Like others who were his peers he could easily have chosen to build his residence far to the east, allowing an overseer to run his Albemarle plantations, as he was compelled to do later for his other estates. This he seems never to have considered. He was to be a man of the country, not the town.

For his house Jefferson departed from the usual Georgian architecture of Virginia in favor of a Palladian design. For the setting he would ignore the formality of the French garden for the more naturalistic curves and plantings of the English. In 1768 he put his plan in motion by having a 250-foot square leveled on the northeast end of the top of his mountain in exchange for 180 bushels of wheat and twenty-four bushels of corn. The project of clearing land continued for several more years. In 1768 he also bought quantities of grass and clover seed for both Shadwell and Monticello from a variety of individuals. Even then he understood the need to cover Virginia soil at all times to protect it from the heavy downpours of rain typical of the region.

In 1769 the mansion was begun. From the very beginning of his plans for the house and grounds at Monticello, Jefferson was well aware he would have problems with a supplemental water supply for his plants, as well as for making bricks and normal household use. Mountain tops, even his small one which was not very high, are not the best places to find adequate water, especially for a man devoted to gardening. He could not rely on rainfall to supply it and thus had to turn to natural springs on the mountain, a well, cisterns, and artificial ponds. He was lucky to have at least fifteen springs upon which to draw for the mansion and outlying workers' houses, in addition to the nailery.[3]

The well, dug in 1769, was sixty-five feet deep. Lacking modern drilling equipment, this was probably as deep as could be achieved without blasting. Some years adequate water was produced, while in dry years when the water table was low the well did not produce at all.

In 1808, toward the end of his Presidency, Jefferson made plans to solve his water problems by constructing a series of cisterns. These would double for fire protection. Four were built by 1810. Typically he went to great lengths mathematically to determine how much water his proposed system would collect. Unfortunately, the cisterns were not water tight. In 1819 he was trying to secure Roman cement, the latest in a series of ploys to solve the leakage which plagued the holding facilities. By 1822 he still had not redone all of them.

Of course he thought of a pond for catching rain water which could incidently serve to retain fish for the table until needed. Although appearing in his plans of 1804, none was actually built until 1808. It was located near the south pavilion. Because the brick of the bottom and parts of the sides were found during restoration of the grounds, we can see today an exact replica of this pool.

Along with work on his house and well, Jefferson started planting fruit and nut trees in 1769. He understood how long it would take for them to begin producing. Thus was begun what would become a state-of-the-art botanical garden.

From the beginning Jefferson kept meticulous records. Even without these notations it would be obvious that this gardener had done his homework before anything was actually planted. The orchard location on a southeastern slope and his spacing of the trees there show that he was aware of their requirements for optimum growth.[4] In his *Garden Book* he designated the first row at the bottom of the ridge for pears (to be planted sometime in the future). He planned nine rows of fruit trees in all, each row approximately 300 feet long. To the west of this grouping "in the hollow" were five rows starting from the bottom of the hill.

In 1769 he again bought clover seed but was also able to reap from his own clover and goose grass seed. To cap this year's efforts he had a park-like area 1850 yards in circumference cleared on the north side of the mountain. Some 8000 chestnut rails were split to fence it in.

The timing of all these activities proved fortuitous; Shadwell burned in February of 1770. Thus Jefferson continued his horticultural work that year with a new urgency, acquiring nectarine and apricot grafts and grape vines from George Wythe, his teacher in law. In his accompanying note Wythe said prophetically, "You bear your misfortune [the burning of Shadwell] so becomingly, that, as I am convinced you will surmount the difficulties it has plunged you into, so I foresee you will hereafter reap advantages from it several ways."[5] Wythe also sent seeds of garden peas from his wife. To round out his garden for the year Jefferson planted raspberries, gooseberries, currants, strawberries, asparagus, and artichokes. He worked on his sod and pruned his cherry trees for good measure. By November he was settled at Monticello.[6]

In 1772 he harvested his first fruit, two plumb peaches, probably off trees planted in 1769. He had good reason to concentrate on his food supply, by 1775 his family, as he called it, was composed of 34 free individuals, including his young wife and daughter, Martha, and eighty-three slaves.

After adding a small group of fruit trees in 1773, in 1774 Jefferson began expanding his orchard in a significant fashion. Besides twenty-four apple trees and nineteen cherry trees from a plantation in Albemarle County, he acquired stones of apricot plus 198 cherries of different kinds from Philip Mazzei. Jefferson also planted some 1500 olive stones.

By 1778 he drew a plan of the orchard as it then stood. While he had a very respectable number of trees, he craved more. In 1811 things got sufficiently out of hand to necessitate recording another tally, along with the location of his prizes. He had done the same for his new nursery the preceding year. He had a total of 384 trees: sixty-nine apples, fifteen Taliafers (which he named after Colonel Richard Taliaferro, George Wythe's father-in-law, who had discovered this excellent cider apple near Williamsburg), seven apricots, forty-eight cherries, five nectarines, 160 peaches, two pears, two plums, five quinces, and seventy-one vacancies. These he intended to fill with seven cherries, fifteen pippin apples, seven Spitzenburg apples, eleven calvite apples, sixteen pecans, six pears, and 8 Taliafers. There was an additional enigmatic entry: "1. Qu? 16."

The overlap between garden plans caused landscaping reconstructionists some problems. While Jefferson's notes are far more complete than most gardeners make, they were not meant as a guide to anyone who wished to duplicate his efforts 200 years later. Still soil stains left by decayed tree roots in the orchard subsoil were of great help. Thus far 57 such stains have been found on the southwest slope in Jefferson's grid patterns of 1778 and 1811. There were similar marks 600 feet to the northeast. Spacing in both locations was generally twenty-five feet apart north to south and forty feet apart east to west. Although an attempt was made to identify plants through seeds, pits and pollen which survived, the effort provided little practical information.

There was a second large orchard on the north side of the mountain, which was in the process of being planted in cider apples in 1786, a priority item for Jefferson. In 1794 peach trees, 263 in all, were planted between these apples. Both orchards were underplanted, the north orchard to Irish potatoes (at least in 1806), the south orchard in 1808 in part to Irish potatoes, in part to cow peas and Ravenscroft peas. Jefferson said the underplanting was "because in cultivating them we shall get rid of the briars, bushes, weeds &c."[7] Both orchards were bordered with a thorn hedge Jefferson had bought for the areas he wanted most to protect from depredations by animals.

There were other smaller orchards at Monticello, but no location was given for them. An orchard was begun at Poplar Forest in 1782.

As with other facets of farming, Jefferson was the beneficiary of a revived interest in agriculture abroad. Fruit trees had been given attention, as shown in the publication in England in 1640 of *The Countrymans Recreation, or the Art of Planting, Graffing, [sic] and Gardening.* Grafted trees were sent to America very early. In 1620 one George Thorpe was provided with books on English "husbandry and huswifery" by a friend in addition to young stock and apple trees grafted with pippins and other of the best apples, as well as apricot and plum stones.

By 1705 Robert Beverly wrote in his *History and Present State of Virginia* that apples were improved greatly by grafting and good management. Yet there were very few planters who grafted and fewer still who took any care to get choice fruits. Beverly reported that the stone fruits grew so well they did not need budding or grafting, and he had heard of no one doing so. As long as peaches were grown as animal feed, cider, or vinegar, top quality was not needed. It would take connoisseurs like Jefferson, who wanted excellent peaches for dessert, to go to the trouble to raise grafted trees. He explained to a friend in 1786 while in Paris, "The fruits of the peach-class do not degenerate from the stone so much as is imagined here. We have so much experience of this in America that tho' we graft all other kinds of fruits, we rarely graft the peach, the nectarine, the apricot or the almond. The tree proceeding from the stone yields a faithful copy of its fruit, & the tree is always healthier."[8]

Americans continued to be slow to improve their fruit trees until after the Revolutionary War. In 1735 Peter Collinson, the English Quaker botanist, was urging his American Quaker botanist friend, John Bartram, to try the grafted pears, plums, nectarines, and apricots he sent. By 1772 a Boston widow of a gardener advertised a large collection of grafted and inoculated English fruit trees, as well as other nursery stock. These examples, though, were still the exception. Most apples and pears in the colonies north of Virginia were propagated as seedlings. The situation changed quite quickly with independence. The William Prince nursery catalog for 1771, for example, offered twenty-nine peaches, most of which appear to be seedlings, but by 1791 Prince offered thirty-five varieties of peaches that were all inoculated (grafted).

While Jefferson planted stones and seeds in his orchards, named varieties were more prominent. In 1767 he inoculated cherry buds onto stocks he already had. Two years later he used peach stocks for inoculating apricots and almonds and also planted grafted pears and apples. He probably performed the inoculation himself. If so, he does not mention where he acquired the art. As a passionate lover of fruit, however, learning the technique would have been high on his list of priorities.

In 1773, according to his records, one of his workmen grafted a group of fruits. The same man did more grafting for him in 1780. Jefferson wrote from Vermont to ask his son-in-law, Thomas Mann Randolph, in 1791 to have "Anthony" inoculate all the spontaneous cherry trees in the fields with good varieties. In 1794 Jefferson grafted and planted in the nursery a variety of fruit trees. After that he seems to have relied on nurseries for named varieties.

It is fortunate for us that most people were not as fussy as Jefferson, for many of the tree fruits commonly grown in America have been derived from local chance seedlings. While Europeans had made significant improvements over the wild stock by selecting from this natural variation, horticultural history indicates perfection had not been reached at the time colonists started coming to America. Fortunately these immigrants continued the process of selection from chance seedlings that showed promise, using budding and grafting to incorporate good characteristics into future generations. The task still goes on.

Twenty varieties of apples which originated by accident here and were thereafter propagated in the colonies were still standard commercial varieties in 1950, with the remaining ten considered choice. Even today Rhode Island Greening and Baldwin, which go back to colonial days, and Jonathan and York Imperial, which date to the early 1800s, can be found on the market and in mail-order nursery catalogs. Other oldies, like Jefferson's Spitzenburg and Albemarle (Newtown) pippin, are being promoted again as well.

Pears were not so popular, despite French plantings in the New World. Only four were under cultivation by 1800: Bartlett, White Doyenne, Tyson and Seckel. Only the last two are of possible American origin.[9] Although pears were a favored fruit in New England, if not in other colonies, seedling pears are the poorest of all seedling fruit trees. Therefore, grafting or using suckers is imperative. Unlike apples and peaches, new varieties were few and the farmer needed to know how to graft or had to buy his pear trees.

Almost none of the peach varieties grown in the Colonies came from Europe. This trend continued, yet, despite the innumerable seedling trees and stones set out in America from the earliest days, virtually all U.S. peaches grown today originated in America after the Civil War. Nectarines, cherries, plums, and apricots have always been minor fruits in the East. Quinces, popular in colonial days, are seldom grown today.

The number of trees involved in Jefferson's operations are estimates. Deaths of seeds, stones, and trees are impossible to untangle. Neither were varieties identified in today's terminology. There is no way to tell how many kinds of fruit Jefferson experimented with or how many he had at any one time or in total except when he actually counted. In his correspondence concerning peaches there are references to plum peaches, peach apricots, apple peaches, melon peaches, and lemon peaches. Jefferson and his contemporaries also gave names which described certain qualities, color, time of ripening, where the tree originated, the name of the individual who discovered it, or from whom it was obtained. To further complicate matters, Jefferson's spelling was variable, as was usual in his time.

Peaches, it can safely be said, were his favorite fruit. His determination to enjoy them outweighed the probability of their survival on his little mountain. In 1775 he lost all he had planted previously to frost. In the spring of 1790 cold weather claimed the replacements. He bought eight more trees in 1791, and planted 60 stones in 1802, with an unrecorded number in 1804. All were killed in 1804. He replaced them that year with 119 trees. In 1807 he planted over 500, only four of which were trees; the remainder were stones. In 1809 he added sixty-eight peach stones and the following year, in addition to new peaches from friends, he transplanted forty-six trees from his nursery. Yet in 1811 when he recorded that he had only 160 peaches, and he gave up his professed intention of making a collection of the choicest peaches available.[10]

This eclectic mix caused some problems for modern reconstruction of the main orchard; trees were sought from all over the world. American selections were not necessarily easy to locate either. State experimental stations were the source of many. Word of varieties needed was also circulated to members of the North American Fruit Explorers. Only a dozen or so are available to the public from retail sources.

As mentioned, in 1769, the year he planted his first fruit trees, Jefferson began his nut tree collection. He budded English walnuts and American black walnuts. In 1773, after he was settled at Monticello, he planted almonds and at least one French chestnut and grafted five French chestnuts to the common American chestnut. The following year he added numerous almonds and a filbert, gifts from Philip Mazzei.

As the years passed the number and types of nut trees Jefferson tried increased, and as he reorganized his gardening areas, the planting locations changed. By 1790 he wrote Randolph to instruct George to make a nursery in a suitable spot and plant the enclosed "Paccan" nuts at once. Pecans were not new to Jefferson, even though they are not native to Virginia. He knew of two young trees planted in 1780 in his area. However, as he explained to a New Orleans man from whom he had just received a parcel of nuts, although the trees had flourished, they had not borne nuts. His correspondent thought perhaps Monticello was too high or dry a location for Jefferson's experiment, but an inhospitable site did not deter this Albemarle gardener, who continued to try for years thereafter with pecans.

In 1809 Jefferson proposed "to make me one large orchard of Paccan and Roanoke and Missouri scaly barks [hickory] which I possess [undoubt-edly from the Lewis and Clark expedition], and of Gloucester [Virginia] and common scaly barks of which I shall plant the nuts."[11] This idea, like others, was not pursued, although Jefferson's nursery chart of 1810 did designate one terrace to "nuts" and one to almonds, while his orchard plan of 1811 included pecans among other trees to fill vacancies in his rows.

As with other plants, Jefferson promoted nut growing to others. As early as 1789 he sent pistachios from Paris to a South Carolina friend just for experimentation, as he explained.

Not until 1791 did Jefferson begin patronizing nurseries in earnest for his planting needs; before that year he relied on stock from friends and probably his woods. That year he ordered a large number of plants from William Prince in Flushing, Long Island, New York. He had visited the Prince nursery earlier.

The extent of Prince's offerings is remarkable, ranging from the various fruits and nuts to deciduous trees such as sugar maple to evergreens such as spruce and fir to roses. Later Bernard McMahon of Philadelphia and Thomas Main of Washington became Jefferson's favorite sources for buying plants. He must have been a favored customer, not because of his name and position but because of his insatiable desire for more plants. Jefferson never met a plant he didn't like.[12]

His income could support his addiction at least initially. He was following the example set by earlier Americans and even British adminis-trators of the Colonies. Sir William Berkeley, governor of Virginia, had 1500 apple trees in 1642. He was, in fact, instructed in 1641 by the Virginia Company to require every man with 100 acres or more to establish a garden and orchard and to protect it with a fence, hedge, or ditch.[13] Several years later every man granted 500 acres or more was ordered to enclose a quarter acre near his house for an orchard and garden. To what extent this order was carried out is open to question, yet large landholders through the Revolutionary War period seem to have counted it an honor and even a duty to be patrons of horticulture, taking pride in their own ventures. In this they were emulating the examples of the upper class on the other side of the Atlantic.

Our knowledge of early farming endeavors in America is based in large part on orchards, for trees are easily counted. Thus we know that in 1686 William Fitzhugh's orchard in Westmoreland County, Virginia, had 2500 apple trees—proudly described as "most grafted [and] well fenced with a locust fence" according to its owner. Other known orchards of great size include a Maryland plantation which featured 600 bearing apple trees when the property was put up for sale in 1783. An Accomac County,

Virginia, orchard of 1814 had 63,000 peaches. Jefferson's own plantings were in keeping with what the gentry did.

These quantities of trees in the Colonial period, as well as later, might confound today's gardener. The European upper class drank wine; the working class, beer. In the New World American grapes generally made unacceptable wines and attempts to grow the European vinifera were usually futile. Apple cider, peach brandy, and perry (pear juice, often fermented) were thus made in large quantities. The Maryland plantation's 600 trees, mentioned above, were touted as producing 8,000 or 10,000 gallons of "very fine cider" and the 63,000 peach trees yielded 10,000 gallons of brandy. Both apples and peaches were also used as food for livestock, while choice specimens were served as dessert at the owner's table.

Such large orchards would seem to have required enormous numbers of laborers. Yet as late as 1800 the trees were basically untended. Disease and insect control were not the problems they are today. Another reason is that, despite having been practiced in Europe for centuries, American fruit growers were often of the opinion that pruning, another time-consuming chore, was somehow unrewarding except for heading trees high to keep the fruit out of the reach of the cattle and pigs. Livestock often pastured in the orchard despite their droppings, which were thought to cause trees to overbear. Not until experiment stations were set up after the Civil War were orchard management practices changed.

Knowledgeable hired help was always in short supply and better care may not have been feasible anyway. Gardeners—usually immigrants with experience gained in England or on the Continent, advertised their availability in such newspapers as the New York *Gazette* and the South Carolina *Gazette*, but not until the late twentieth century have American growers had a large enough trained work force to adequately cope with commercial farming and horticultural ventures. Even this has been due as much to labor saving machinery as to increased numbers of college trained people.

The labor situation, as well as the problems associated with the reproduction of quality trees eventually spawned nursery businesses. William Prince's nursery began in 1737. By 1768 another Long Island nursery won a prize for having 27,123 apple trees in nursery rows, the most on the island. By the turn of the century these would be joined by such influential nurseries as Thomas Main's and Bernard McMahon's.

But Jefferson did not dine on fruits and nuts alone. In 1771 he mentions his first harvest at Monticello: peas, his favorite vegetable, perhaps from the seed he had received from Mrs. Wythe.[14] He planted numerous varieties of peas in the years to come. In 1771 he also planted two beds of asparagus seed, another apparently welcome vegetable. The variety of vegetables he grew increased dramatically; and in this he was again a pioneer.[15] The typical English diet until the beginning of the seventeenth century was grain and dairy products, perhaps with fish or poultry. Meat was eaten only by the rich. Vegetables did not catch on until after 1600 and then only because of London's increasing population. The colonists who landed at Jamestown and Plymouth Rock brought a very slender arsenal of vegetables across the Atlantic. Furthermore, they did not have a tradition of growing them.

The mainstays of vegetable gardens today are of New World origin: maize, beans, squash, peppers, tomatoes, and white and sweet potatoes. The colonists learned to grow these vegetables from the Indians. Of Old World vegetables grown today, the globular beet dates only to the mid-1500s, as does the carrot. The modern heading broccoli was developed within the last three centuries. Brussel sprouts and celery are relatively recent, as are kohlrabi and rutabagas, which were introduced at the end of the 1700s. Even the pea was not a common vegetable at the close of the seventeenth century. Thus Jefferson's ventures in his vegetable garden were with plants whose requirements and potential had hardly been tested. His contemporaries, by and large, were not much help; few doted on fruits and vegetables for the table as he did.

On March 31, 1774, he laid out a new vegetable garden on the southeastern slope where his main orchard was located; the site is not known. In order to create a level surface for his plants he had his workmen cut into the hillside below Mulberry Row. His plans called for a garden 668 feet long and eighty feet wide with triangles at each end.[16] He now mentions his new garden wall, which was to be built below the terrace. This wall was an integral part of his garden scheme for excavated soil was deposited behind it to make a level shelf which grew to eighty feet by 1000 feet.

The wall was a monumental undertaking. Stones weighing up to a half ton each were set without mortar. Needless to say it was built over a period of years. Yet, despite its massiveness, it did not survive intact. Much of the stone was removed in the late 1800s to line the exit road of the estate. The rest seemed unstable and were taken down after the construction was recorded with the help of photogrammetry. Workers found the wall averaged seven feet high, and some sections reached twelve feet. Some 650 feet of its length was uncovered. The stone work has been restored. In the process of reconstruction the archeologists, relying on information Jefferson left in his notes, were delighted to find numerous shards of broken plates and glassware from the master's house.

In addition to holding back the dirt for the vegetable terrace the wall was exposed to the southeastern sun, a dream-come-true of every advocate of solar heating. Jefferson made full use of its warmth for tender new plantings or for figs, pumpkins, squash and gourds which thrived in the extra warmth.

Jefferson had considerable difficulties with his garden and orchard layout, in part because of changes in his overseers. Being President didn't help. In 1804, when leveling of the vegetable garden Jefferson had used since 1774 began in earnest, Gabriel Lilly was still the overseer. He was followed by John Freeman who lasted only one year. Even Edmund Bacon, who was hired before the end of 1806 and proved an efficient overseer until 1822, was not able to cope with Jefferson's plans. By the beginning of 1808, while 250 feet of the platform had been completed at the southwest end, Bacon found the amount of dirt which needed to be removed beyond the capacities of his labor force. Jefferson apparently had not foreseen the extent of the difficulties involved. He therefore called upon Thomas Mann Randolph to help Bacon lay out the terraces on an alternate plan. To overcome the problems the overseer was facing Jefferson planned four different levels of 250 feet each. Only three were completed. Bacon in his memoirs noted laconically: "It took a great deal of labor. We had to blow out the rock for the walls for the different terraces and then make the soil. . . . It was a fine garden."[17]

From his earliest entries onward, Jefferson provides us with fascinating insights into his life and times. For example, in 1767 he notes that 2500 "midling peas" fill a pint and in 1768 that 2000 Charlton Hotspur peas do so "accurately." He notes that with strawberries the average plant bore twenty, but that 100 were required to fill a half pint. While we may cringe at the physical labor involved with gathering and preparing such tiny berries, at least their flavor was good, which cannot always be said of strawberries on the market today.

He frequently mentions where he got his seeds or plants, and this information provides insight into distribution methods as well as the extent of Jefferson's own friendships. Only a few people developed small businesses to cater to the need, and Jefferson does not record buying his vegetable seed from any business establishment. Yet they are worth recording. A surgeon in Richmond and another man in Petersburg, Virginia, both advertised Spanish morotto peas in the Virginia Gazette in March of 1767 and again in 1768. In this same time frame similar ads appear in the New York Gazette and the South Carolina Gazette. Englishman David Landreth in Philadelphia, established the first proper seed business in America, in 1784. As a resident of that city from the late fall of 1790 through 1793, Jefferson was certainly aware of Landreth's undertaking and undoubtedly checked it out. Landreth first advertised his offerings in the November 22, 1793, Federal Gazette. The ad provides little information.[18]

Jefferson does not seem to have purchased seed from the Shakers. This is surprising because, from his assumption of the presidency until his death, Shaker seeds were acknowledged to be among the best in America. Perhaps it was because most of the seeds were grown in New York and were distributed to stores near Shaker Communities. However, Jefferson should have been intrigued with a Shaker innovation—putting their seeds into packets.

Like the orchard, the vegetable garden evolved over time. In 1774 the beds were simple plots in which Jefferson indicated his different plantings by means of numbered sticks. This system was soon abandoned when he expanded his vision and determined to regrade his garden. When that awesome project was finally completed in 1809 (without the assistance of a bulldozer) Jefferson, now free of the presidency, could plunge into his garden activities without unwanted distractions. This time he chose to arrange his vegetable garden into squares of varying sizes. A border strip next to the wall was also divided into sections. It must have pleased him to be able to arrange his crops with such precision.

Naturally he showed the results to visitors. Mrs. Samuel Harrison Smith, wife of the founder and editor of the *National Intelligence* newspaper, later described what she remembered seeing in 1809: "When we rose from the table, a walk was proposed and he accompanied us. He took us first to the garden he has commenced since his retirement. It is on the south side of the mountain and commands a most noble view. Little is as yet done. A terrace of 70 or 80 feet long and about 40 wide is already made and in cultivation. A broad grass walk leads along the outer edge; the inner part is laid off in beds for vegetables. This terrace is to be extended in length and another to be made below it. The view it commands, is at present its greatest beauty."[19]

This is how Jefferson saw his garden that year. There were 18 squares,[20] each numbered, stuffed full of vegetables. In the border were his earliest crops, the lettuces, spinich, endive, and radishes that could benefit from the heat trapped by the adjacent wall. Additional vegetables spilled over into the nursery, orchard, asparagus bed, and vineyard. Thomas Jefferson was very serious about his vegetables.

"Square II," for example, contained one row each of rhubarb, long pod soup pea, African early pea, lentils and three rows of Windsor beans. The rhubarb entry is puzzling. Jefferson identified it as "rheum undulatum" and comments its leaves were excellent as spinach. Bernard McMahon in 1806 reported that Rheum rhaponticum grew in American gardens and listed as its virtues roots which afforded a gentle purge, esteemed use for pies and tarts, "and very wholesom for children." This is the same rhubarb grown today. McMahon himself preferred Chinese rhubarb, R. palmatum, which he promoted. The leaves of both species must never be eaten; they contain amounts of oxalic acid and its salts which can cause death. Are the leaves of undulatum different, or did Jefferson mistakenly believe them safe, or did he err in recording the information? In any event, the plants were still in his garden in 1811, although they were then located beneath the wall.

His plan of 1812 shows how he grouped his vegetables. The platforms were arranged according to the part of the plant which was harvested. The upper platform was designated for "fruits," such as peas, beans, tomatoes and melons. His roots were in the middle platform, and his leafy vegetables, including the cole crops, were on the lowest level. His border continued to contain early and tender crops. He also had squares of gooseberries, raspberries, and currants.

He also locates various vegetables in areas designated "submural," "low grounds," and "islands." Where these latter locations were is impossible to determine. Nevertheless, it demonstrates that Jefferson was well aware of variations within his planting area and experimented with their potential.

Because planting dates are frequently noted we can tell he extended his season as long as possible, putting in his peas in early February and sowing various crops throughout summer and into fall for winter use. Where possible he planted successive crops in the same plots to extend their season. These might be of the same variety or early, middle, or late bearers. Archeologists found the evidence for the warming beds adjacent to the wall, which would permit the earliest and latest harvesting.

To help himself in following years, the charts he began in 1809 have columns labeled to record where the crop was sown, the date it was planted, when transplanted if that were the case, when it came to table, and when it was finished. A column reserved for "observations," was soon changed to "miscellaneous."[21] He records his failures dispassionately. Under "miscellaneous" he at times exhibits his attention to detail. With frame peas he notes that two quarts sowed 440 feet at a one-half-inch distance.

These charts were essential for he tried some 250 vegetable and 150 fruit varieties. His garden was not just a backyard home garden. It was truly an experimental one. As Jefferson wrote to McMahon in 1810, "I am curious to select only one or two of the *best* species or variety of every garden vegetable and to reject all others from the garden to avoid the dangers of mixture & degeneracy."[22] He also tried planting pumpkin and squash together to see the variations which might result from cross-fertilization.[23]

The qualities Jefferson was looking for are not necessarily those we desire today. Cucumbers were for pickling, other crops were chosen for their ability to withstand long storage over the winter months in the cool dry rooms beneath the house. Such essential characteristics aside, it is evident from his records that Jefferson, over the course of his life, tried virtually every vegetable available in his day. Many he ordered; others he discovered; still others were sent by friends and acquaintances. With beans he was not content with just one kind; he had forty. There are almost as many varieties of cabbages, and even more kinds of peas. We cannot ascertain now whether each of those he named was indeed a different variety from the rest of its tribe, but the numbers indicate a willingness to experiment, not only for his personal tastes, but for what might be suitable for his countrymen at large. It is doubtful that any other contemporary American grower had in his home garden more types than did Jefferson.

In view of his reputation as a master gardener, three vegetables common today must be singled out: tomatoes, sweet corn, and white potatoes.

The tomato, native to tropical America, came to what is now the U.S. via Europe. It was considered poisonous in colonial New England, as were the white potato and eggplant. In England tomatoes had been grown more as a curiosity than the staple they became in Italy. That undoubtedly explains the attitude of the colonists, who were predominantly English transplants. Jefferson's earliest written reference to this vegetable seems to be in his *Notes* (he called them tomatas), but he does not give the Latin name or where they were grown in Virginia.[24] He himself does not seem to have tried them until 1809 when he got seed from his friend George Divers of Farmington in Albemarle County. The two often visited, discussing agriculture and exchanging plants and seeds. Jefferson also got Spanish tomato seeds that year from General John Mason, who described the fruit as "very much larger than the common kinds."

Jefferson apparently became acquainted with the tomato during his eight years as President. He made a chart showing the earliest and latest appearance of numerous vegetables and fruits on the Washington market. He found tomatoes were to be had as early as July 16 and as late as November 17. Presumably he became accustomed to them and determined to grow them himself. Except for 1810, when he neglected to make a chart of his vegetables, he lists tomatoes in each year's chart thereafter through 1824. In 1813 he shared seeds with his brother. If tomatoes were once a curiosity, they were beginning to be accepted in Jefferson's region. McMahon mentioned that there tomatoes were grown in Philadelphia but gave no varieties, indicating this vegetable was not much sought after. Not until about 1850 did tomato breeding begin in earnest; the improved fruits then quickly gained their current popularity.

Sweet corn is native to the New World, but Indian tribes were slow to accept sweet corn, if they purposely cultivated it at all. White colonists became aware of it when in 1779 an officer in General John Sullivan's army is said to have found it growing in Indian corn fields on the banks of the Susquehanna and brought seed back to Plymouth. It did not spread to Virginia quickly enough to be mentioned in Jefferson's *Notes* in 1781 or by McMahon in 1806. The only reference to sweet corn in Jefferson's writings comes in 1810, with the notation that sweet or "shriveled" corn was growing in his garden. There is no explanation of where he got the seed or what he thought of it. Sweet corn continued in obscurity until the Golden Bantam variety was developed in 1902. Hybridization later made a lot of improvements to sweet corn.

Until fairly recently field corn served the purpose of roasting ears, at least for country people. Jefferson even grew Indian corn while in Paris. Naturally he wanted to try more than one kind. He wrote his steward and neighbor Nicholas Lewis in 1787, asking him to send an ear or two of "drying" corn from Cherokee territory. He was gratified with the results. "The homony corn is a precious present. The corn of this county and of Italy, as far as I have seen it, cannot be eaten, either in the form of crop or of bread, by any person who has eaten that of America."[25] Farm hired help, slaves, and livestock were not as fussy.

White potatoes were a novelty in Jefferson's time. Except in Ireland, Europeans shunned them. Colonists to America seldom grew them until the mid-1800s. This is hardly remarkable as Irish potatoes were not the size of those today and were of poor quality, variable in shape and color. They were even thought to shorten one's life because of their supposed un-wholesomeness. Jefferson tried them as early as 1772 and grew them in later years. However, while in Paris he requested seeds of the sweet potato (which is in a different family), charging his manager at home not to attempt sending roots as they would rot en route.

The Indians, from whom the settlers learned so much, were inclined to the less demanding American perennial, the Jerusalem artichoke. Jefferson grew the artichoke in his garden for most of his life, no doubt as a substitute for the Irish potato. McMahon included that vegetable in his list of American esculents, saying they were a healthful, tasty food. They could be used in salads, soups, and stews.

Just as gardeners who today introduce into their vegetable plots plants grown for their flowers, Jefferson used castor bean shrubs to border the nursery in 1811, perhaps as a mole repellent, if not for their ornamental value. The following year Jefferson planted white, scarlet, crimson and purple arbor beans (probably the scarlet runner) in several areas. He tried sprouting broccoli in white, green, and purple grown in adjacent rows. He grew the white and green from 1794 and the purple from 1809. Other oddities included many-headed cabbages and a serpentine cucumber sent to him by an Ohio man. But for all this, as visitors to the restored gardens are aware, the varieties available in his day do not, by and large, measure up to those to which we are accustomed. His cucumber, really a West Indian gherkin, is small, seedy, and dry if productive. His tomato helps one understand its lack of popularity before hybridization. The same holds true for the flowers.

Much as Jefferson treasured the gardens which provided his food supply, he did not spare young, able-bodied field hands for their maintenance. Less energetic older men would suffice. In 1801 Jefferson in a letter to Randolph refers to "Goliah & his senile crops" who prepared his garden. Several months later it is interesting that Jefferson in a letter to daughter Maria puts it this way: "Goliah is our gardener, and with his veteran aids. . . ." The switch in adjectives is surprising as the father did not ordinarily spare words when writing to his family.

The entire garden area, some eight acres, needed protection. Archeologists found post stains which indicated as many as three separate fence lines had been built as the garden evolved. The fence of 1808 was the responsibility of a Mr. Watkins, who was employed for the purpose. He was hired for the fall to get the components for the paling fence assembled so Jefferson upon his release from the presidency the following spring could lay out the precise course the 4000-foot fence was to take. The chestnut pickets or pales were ten feet high, the locust posts twelve feet, the rails of heart poplar or pine. Mr. Watkins was admonished to make the fence strong with the pales so close together "not to let even a young hare in." Jefferson gave detailed instructions as to how to proceed and estimated the number of parts needed: 300 posts, 900 rails, and 7500 pales. Mr. Watkins had his work cut out for him. This fence would seem to have been Jefferson's crowning achievement against animal predation. If it could not protect his precious plants, what could?

He tried other types of fences too. One of these involved peach trees. The orchard does not reflect Jefferson's most massive fruit tree planting project. This occurred in December of 1794 when he planted 1157 peach trees. While 263 were planted between his apple trees in the north orchard, the remainder were used to replace the rail fences, which were in a state of disrepair and overgrown with weeds, that had delineated the fields of his farm land.[26] The peaches were to serve for beautification purposes as well as food for farm animals, if they needed further justification. Always careful to preserve his forest trees, Jefferson reused serviceable rails for outer fences to keep out animals.

There seems to be no record of the losses in his peach fences. However, as he is soon referring to work on rail fences, the peach trees apparently were not the answer he had hoped for. They no doubt succumbed to frost, as had those in his orchard.

Despite his experience with peaches, Jefferson remained partial to living fences, as wood suitable for fencing was a commodity he desired for other projects. In 1805 he settled on what is now known as the Washington thorn, ordering 4000 of them from Main's nursery in Washington. It grew wild around the city in abundance. Hardy, large, and strong when full grown it was ideal for repelling animals; 10,000 additional thorns were bought in 1806, with 200 more for his nursery to replace those that did not survive. Jefferson ended up buying an additional 4000 in the spring of 1807 and 2000 more that fall. The numbers are mind boggling, but at six inches apart and with slaves to plant them, both the quantities and the work involved become understandable. This was not a one-person job, even for an ardent gardener. The south orchard and vegetable garden, except for the Mulberry Row line, were bounded by thorn, as were the north orchard and the roads. The instructions sent with the plants by Main are of interest for their specificity. Jefferson's subsequent instructions to his overseer tell much about his technical expertise as a gardener. He was soon promoting thorn to William Hamilton of Philadelphia, yet they proved not to be the total answer. In response to another friend's inquiry in 1816 as to which type of hedge to plant, Jefferson was somewhat equivocal but could suggest nothing better.

Jefferson put in a rail-covered ditch as a fence too, one he had seen on at least one English estate in 1786. This "ha-ha," fence was common in eighteenth-century gardens. He would certainly have seen George Washington's, which was constructed in 1765. As McMahon explains in his *American Gardener's Calendar*, while there was no set design to a ha-ha, the structures had a common purpose: "It being absolutely necessary to have the whole pleasure ground surrounded with a good fence of some kind, as a defense against cattle, &c. a foss [ha-ha] being a kind of concealed fence will answer that purpose where it can conveniently be made, without interrupting the view of such neighboring parts as are beautified by art or nature, and at the same time affect an appearance that these are only a continuation of the pleasure-ground. Over the foss in various parts may be made Chinese and other curious and fanciful bridges, which will have a romantic and pleasing effect."[27]

Although the ha-ha appears in Jefferson's 1804 plans to improve Monticello, the ditch apparently was not built until 1814. It was constructed along Mulberry Row. Now that the unsightly wooden buildings had been removed, Mulberry Row no longer needed to be screened off by an upright fence. The ha-ha would not interfere with the view, yet it would prevent damage to the west lawn by animals. A visitor who saw it reported it looked as if a post-and-rail fence had fallen across the void. The rails were spaced far enough apart so the legs of any animal attempting to cross would fall through. Jefferson's records indicate that his ha-ha was 500 yards long and enclosed the entire west lawn of the house. Archeologists have found three sections of it, which averaged four feet wide and two feet, eight inches deep.

McMahon perhaps inspired him to begin a new project in 1807, a garden pavilion or, as Jefferson terms it, a "structure in the garden terras." It became a favorite retreat to read and sit in at the center of the garden wall. A twelve-and-one-half-foot square, it had Tuscan arches on each side, a pyramidal roof, plus a Chinese railing. Next to it were stairs.[28] McMahon in his book advocated "light ornamental buildings," and perhaps this served as a prod to the President. The structure was destroyed by a storm after Jefferson's death.

It is interesting that this pavilion was built at this site, for Jefferson in his 1804 plans had discussed various similar structures, concluding, "But after all, the kitchen garden is not the place for ornaments of this kind. . . . these temples will be better disposed in the pleasure grounds."[29]

How much time did Jefferson spend in his garden? Did he himself count the 2500 midling peas into a pint jar and pace out the length of the row? With the scope of his other activities and obligations, it is probable he seldom did much more than supervise Goliah and Wormley, who figure in his correspondence to family members, and Bailey, a gardener who came to him in 1794, served for many years and is still remembered because of the walk bearing his name near his former house below the orchard. But when he did manage some hands-on gardening all dedicated fellow gardeners will empathize with Mr. Jefferson's deep feeling of satisfaction at the task.

10

Landscaping

With his new house underway since 1769 and his park on the north side of the mountain cleared, Jefferson could begin to flesh out his landscaping plans. This he did in 1771 near the eve of his wedding, which proved the commencement of the most fulfilling period of his life. Yet two-thirds of the plan looked forward to his death. He sketched a layout for a burying place in a secluded valley in the park, half for family, the other half for "strangers, servants, etc." with a proposed Gothic temple in the center.[1] This description is followed by the name "Jane Jefferson" with a brief verse, indicating that his late sister still stood atop her pedestal in his thoughts. He also recorded other decorative ideas, equally imaginative. During this period he made several drawings of proposed temples and other garden structures from which to view the landscape. Such buildings, so clearly influenced by the English romantic school, were new to America, especially on such a scale.

The remaining third of his resolution included notes common to owners of uncleared property: "Thin the trees, Cut out stumps and undergrowth. Remove old trees and other rubbish, except where they may look well."[2] A list of desirable plants and animals to lodge there follows. The animals range from the common (rabbits) to the exotic (peacocks) to those whose habits Mr. Jefferson failed to take into account (a buck elk and a buffalo). This clearly went beyond George Washington's deer park and similar preserves on the estates of country gentlemen. A visitor to Monticello in 1782 reported a score of deer as the noteworthy inhabitants at that point. Jefferson's dreams had a habit of dying hard; in 1785 he wrote to the Reverend James Madison, President of the College of William and Mary, that he proposed to colonize the European "hare, rabbit, red and gray partridge, pheasants of different kinds, and some other birds."[3] However, this plan apparently remained a proposal.

166

The plants, broken down into their various categories of trees, shrubs, climbing shrubby plants, evergreens, and hardy perennial flowers, show a more realistic evaluation of their potential. The names appear under a heading of "The Open Ground on the West—a shrubbery." With the exception of fig which had already been planted elsewhere two years earlier, all of these are duly listed in the same order in the *Garden Book*, dated September 30. Most likely he had written the plan in his small pocket-size *Account Book* while he traveled and transferred the information about the shrubbery in to the *Garden Book* upon his return home. Despite this attention to the subject, there is no definite statement by Jefferson that any of these plants were put into the ground either in 1771 or later.

We can wonder where he thought to get this mixture of species in sufficient quantities to create a landscaped unit. Perhaps he meant at first only to make a nursery. More probably he was merely daydreaming.[4] In 1771 he could hardly foretell how often government service would keep him from home for extended periods. Given the difficulties of communication at that time, Samuel Adams and his constant provocations against the British in Massachusetts and even the Boston Massacre, must have seemed remote to Virginians. As for Jefferson, 1771 did mark one notable planting—the famous Mulberry Row. Part of the first round-about, it lay just above the terraced garden and in front of the outbuildings necessary to the plantation.

During the first years of Jefferson's married life basic work continued on the house and grounds. The newlyweds had moved into the South Pavilion, the first building completed at Monticello and the one to which Jefferson had moved after Shadwell burned. Obviously its cramped quarters would not do for two, let alone the family which was soon begun.

As for the grounds, a first order of business was to make the round-about roads to service the mountain. There were eventually four, each fifteen to twenty feet wide and cut into the mountain 100 feet to 200 feet apart, with oblique links connecting them. This was a time-consuming job. Jefferson notes: "In making the Round-about walk, 3 hands would make 80. yds a day in the old field, but in the woods where they had stumps to clear, not more than 40. & sometimes 25. yds."[5] Jefferson of course did the surveying. The first round-about was completed in 1772; the second is mentioned in 1782, although it is not known when it was begun or completed. The lowest or fourth round-about is mentioned in 1792. Road building was obviously on ongoing project. An 1807 memorandum notes that a priority was to "finish that Roundabout or rather finish the 4th Roundab[t] in order—in winter to move the fence to the 4th. Roundabout."[6]

The round-abouts were no ordinary roads. The following year Jefferson instructed Edmund Bacon, the overseer. "In all the open grounds on both sides of the 3ᵈ. & 4ᵗʰ. Roundabouts, lay off lots of the minor articles of husbandry, and for experimental culture, disposing them into a ferme ornee by interspersing occasionally the attributes of a garden."[7] One wonders what Bacon thought of all this, despite the accompanying drawing.

The round-abouts, four miles in all, were supplemented by sixteen miles of roads. One segment led straight up the mountain to a main gate. The rest served various points on the plantation.

Jefferson was proud of his system of roads. Considering the methods of road building available, they were, no doubt, admirable. Nevertheless, his guests were not necessarily impressed. One woman visitor, the wife of Dr. William Thornton, designer of the national capitol and a good friend of the President, left an account of the direct road up the little mountain. In 1802 she, her husband, and her mother paid a visit to Monticello with James and Dolley Madison and Mrs. Madison's sister. Arriving at the foot of the incline at dusk, with a backdrop of lightening, the party ascended on foot through the woods to beat the approaching storm rather than take a chance with their host's road. Mrs. Thornton's elderly mother alone faced the terrors of going up the drive in the carriage. The thoughts of the servants as they maneuvered the two vehicles up the mud-rutted path were not recorded.[8]

Margaret Bayard Smith's enthusiasm for Monticello was tempered when Jefferson took his visitor from Washington, along with his granddaughter, Ellen, on a tour of the round-abouts during the summer of 1809. She had already navigated the first circuit on foot. She wrote, "The first circuit is not quite a mile round, as it is very near the top. It is in general shady, with openings through the trees for distant views. We passed the outhouses for the slaves and workmen. They are all much better than I have seen on any other plantation, but to an eye unaccustomed to such sights, they appear poor and their cabins form a most unpleasant contrast with the palace that rises so near them."[9]

Then she was invited on the grand tour. She found the experience of descending the little mountain alarming. She reported in her reminiscences that Jefferson told her, "you are not to be afraid, or if you are you are not to show it; trust yourself implicitly to me, I will answer for your safety; I came every foot of this road yesterday, on purpose to see if a carriage could come safely; I know every step I take, so banish all fear."[10] In Mrs. Smith's estimation the road Jefferson saw was not the road she saw. At the worst places she therefore got out of his small carriage and walked.

In 1772 Jefferson followed up on his conviction that man does not live by bread alone. He had palings made to enclose the park he had laid out in 1769. He noted that the pales should alternate high and low, the first to have five nails, the second, four. The following year he made unexpected use of his graveyard near the end of Mulberry Row. His dearest friend from his youth, Dabney Carr, died. Carr had married Jefferson's sister, Martha. The two men had made a pact that whoever outlived the other would bury the deceased at the foot of a favored oak on the Jefferson mountain. While in his plan of 1771 Jefferson must have been thinking of his late sister Jane, the foresight proved timely. Carr died on May 16 and was buried at Shadwell. Jefferson, who had been at Williamsburg, had clearing begun at his proposed location after he returned home; at its completion Carr was reinterred, the first person to occupy the graveyard. Jefferson then took Martha[11] and her six children into his own home.

Jefferson's shrub plantings in 1778, his first at Monticello, were 19 calycanthus.[12] These apparently were dug from the Green Mountain, a range in southwestern Albemarle County. He does not record where he put them. Interestingly he does not mention this shrub on his plan for 1771. In fall he planted 32 umbrella trees[13] and 59 aspens which formed what he later referred to as his "aspen thicket," the location of which is unknown. In addition, he planted 14 pride of China trees[14] he had started from seed that spring in the nursery. It is possible he had started the umbrella trees and aspens at the same time.

The following years were not kind to Jefferson's personal life, between the war and his wife's precarious health. Of note here are his flowers planted in 1782, for which he made a chart of their blooming period. He was at Monticello for the first ten months this year to be with his dear spouse before her death on September 6. Perhaps this garden was put in for her benefit. In the future he would plant flowers for his ladies.

Jefferson's vision of landscaping his estate went much further than mere flowers. Unfortunately for his plans, after Martha's death service to his country again intervened. While he no doubt lamented having to leave his beloved Monticello, the prospect of a European trip in 1784 as Minister Plenipotentiary to France could not have been entirely disagreeable to him. He could see for himself the places, plants, and people he had long known through books. Now a widower for over a year, he would take his oldest daughter, Martha, with him. His youngest daughter, Maria, would follow later.

In his European travels he was first a representative of his country. His free time, though, could be spent on subjects more to his liking. Predominant among these were architecture and gardening. How his time abroad influenced his architectural plans for redesigning Monticello and creating Poplar Forest and other American buildings is not relevant here. Gardens and landscaping are another matter.

Jefferson and Martha arrived in Paris August 6, 1784. Having settled his daughter in school by the 26th and presumably having attended to other matters, by September 15 Jefferson was already at the gardens at Versailles which he went to frequently throughout his stay in that city. We can assume he visited other Paris gardens too. In 1786 Jefferson went to London at the request of John Adams to participate in various state-negotiations. He made good use of his time there touring English gardens, guided by Thomas Wateley's *Observations on Modern Gardening*, published in London in 1770. Jefferson may have owned his copy even before going abroad. These gardens were to make a lasting impression on him, their naturalistic designs appealing to his sense of what was appropriate for America. The formal gardens he found in Paris did not fit the temper of the American spirit, which was derived as much from the predominantly English background of its settlers as from the vast land resources those settlers occupied.

After he returned to Paris Jefferson wrote to a Virginia friend, "The gardening in that country [England] is the article in which it surpasses all the earth. I mean their pleasure gardening. This, indeed, went far beyond my ideas."[15] Due to his habit of taking notes on everything that interested him we have his observations of the sixteen gardens he visited. As he explained it, "My inquiries were directed chiefly to such practical things as might enable me to estimate the expense of making and maintaining a garden in that style."[16] On a subsequent trip through southern France and northern Italy he did not record his observations regarding landscaping, concentrating instead on agriculture and wine-making. He may have seen nothing of interest, or perhaps he had already decided on future plans for Monticello.

It was during this period that Jefferson began a project he pursued for the rest of his life. His new European friends were interested in plants from America; he thought his friends at home could profit from plants of European origin. He would act as the intermediary.[17] To supply gardeners abroad he enlisted help where he could, including John Bartram, Philadelphia plantsman. A prime recipient of European plants was the South Carolina Society for Promoting Agriculture, of which Jefferson had been elected an honorary member in 1785. General Lafayette's aunt, the Comtesse Noailles de Tessé, received several American species.

Seeds and bulbs were commonly brought to the Colonies with each wave of settlers. At first they came via the women's apron pockets, a reminder of home which might brighten lives as well as provide food and medicine. Weed seeds also came in the ship's ballast and in the farm animals' feed and bedding, not to mention human clothing and possessions. Then came a period of trial and error. Did the hyacinths and pinks respond to American conditions in Boston? In Savannah? At least seeds and bulbs were designed by nature to keep over a period of time without much further attention.

Plants were a more immediate concern. It was not until 1829, after Jefferson's death, that the Englishman Nathaniel Ward, a doctor and avid botanist, developed the Wardian case, in effect a modified terrarium. Until then only a few plants could withstand being out of the ground for the weeks involved in crossing the ocean, not to mention the time it took to get them on board and launched or disembarked on arrival. Jefferson preferred exchanges of seeds.

In an era when American flora were just beginning to be catalogued Jefferson was in the vanguard of American botanical identification. In his *Notes* written in 1781 he included a long list of the more prominent Virginia plants, giving the Latin name for each. He indicates that he was relying on Dr. John Clayton, "our great botanist." "This accurate observer," said Jefferson, "was a native and resident of this state, passed a long life in exploring and describing its plants, and is supposed to have enlarged the botanical catalogue as much as almost any man who has lived."[18] Jefferson must have been delighted when in 1792 another prominent botanist, Benjamin Smith Barton, physician and professor of botany at the University of Pennsylvania from 1790 to 1813, named a native Virginia flower for him: Jeffersonia diphylla (twinleaf). It had previously been called Podophyllum diphyllum. As he explained in a paper read to the American Philosophical Society, the honor was bestowed not because of Jefferson's political status but because the knowledge of natural history Jefferson possessed was equalled by that of few people in America.

After returning to America late in 1789, Jefferson hardly had time to gather his thoughts and marry off his oldest daughter, Martha, to Thomas Mann Randolph before he agreed to President Washington's request that he become secretary of state. The stimulus of English gardening ideas had to be put on hold. It was not until 1791 that he could anticipate retiring from public life for good. Counting on his new son-in-law to plant them while he himself labored in Philadelphia, he placed a large order with William Prince's nursery. In addition to numerous fruit and nut trees these included sugar maples ("all you have"—60 were sent), six cranberry trees, three balsam poplars, six Venetian sumachs, two hemlock spruce, three large silver firs, three balm of Gilead firs, six monthly honeysuckles, three Carolina kidney bean trees, three balsam of Peru, six yellow willows, six rhododendrons and thirty roses of various kinds, not all of which he actually received. Where these new treasures were planted is not recorded.

At least some were near the house, for he wrote Martha in 1793 when he lived for some months across the Schuylkill River from John Bartram's ". . . I never before knew the full value of trees. My house is entirely embossomed in high plane-trees, with good grass below; and under them I breakfast, dine, write, read, and receive my company. What would I not give that the trees planted nearest round the house at Monticello were full-grown."[19] As he wrote Madame Noailles de Tessé in 1803, planting trees had always been his passion.

His love affair with trees would continue for years. As he explained to Andrew Ellicott in 1812: "All this will be for a future race. . . . Yet I do not wish it less. On the same principle on which I am still planting trees, to yield their shade and ornament half a century hence."[20]

The year 1793 was devoted to farming plans for his impending retirement. When he arrived home in January of 1794 agriculture consumed his time and interest, as well they might after such a lengthy absence. However, he must have been well aware that time was flying by, and his landscaping needed attention as well. In 1794 the *Garden Book* shows 2400 cuttings of weeping willow were planted, along with a notation as to their location. Although they would provide beauty too, the trees were to be used as a crop for their wood, a group to be lopped every three years. A small number of purely ornamental specimens were also planted.

These fits and starts on planting continued. In 1798, his next recorded planting spree, he added three rhododendron, three Scotch pines, two Norway firs, three balm of Gilead firs (which he had not received in his 1791 order), three dwarf "ewe," three juniper, four horse chestnut, three balsam poplar, two sugar maples, and three bush cranberries. Since he ordered such specific numbers he must have had sites in mind for each tree and shrub. Indeed he mentions where he wanted most of them planted in his letter to Randolph. By then, however, it seems to have occurred to him that, as de facto leader of the Republican faction, currently vice-president and with a distinct possibility of becoming president, he was doomed to remain away from his beloved Monticello for years to come.

If he could not conveniently continue landscaping at home, Jefferson made plans for the grounds at the new White House. John and Abigail Adams had lived in the mansion only briefly. Outdoors Adams left but one imprint—a vegetable garden on the northeast side of the building. For him this was a sine qua non for moving in. It was therefore left to his successor to make some order out of both the interior and exterior of the President's official residence. Having experienced life at Monticello Jefferson must certainly have felt right at home with the unfinished state of his new surroundings.

Yet this man was a committed planner. The disorganization at Monticello and the capitol was in the minds of others, not his. He had the uncommon facility of being able to visualize in considerable detail the end result he wished. Others saw only bare ground, perhaps with stakes; he saw mature trees and shrubs, walkways, and even garden buildings. For all the disorder he might live in without complaint, he was in truth a very orderly man. The raw grounds around the still uncompleted Washington mansion must have teased his imagination. With his usual take-charge attitude he must have mentally toyed with possible solutions to the bareness around him, but as only the third president of a fledgling nation, he seems not to have done anything about actually landscaping the White House until the very end of his second term.

Considering the fact construction was still going on within the mansion, not to mention on the four adjacent buildings that housed the Departments of the treasury and state on the east and war and navy on the west, plus the capitol itself, laborers on the public payroll had more than enough to keep them busy and the U.S. treasury empty for extraneous projects. He was burdened by the problems of reestablishing a bankrupt national government only a few years old to a new location that was devoid of amenities and overwhelmed by demanding officials and the curious public, all of whom claimed his attention and time. It is therefore remarkable that the chief executive of the United States should even think of creating a landscaping plan, let alone make a dent in its execution.

The man's enormous energy is nowhere more apparent than during this time frame. In addition to these Presidential duties, by 1804 he was beginning a new round of plans for landscaping at Monticello and completing the renovation of his house there, and in 1806 beginning a new house in Bedford County. It is curious, though, that while there is a considerable body of correspondence by Jefferson during the presidential years on horticultural matters, there is none regarding landscaping in Washington except to his employees.

Fortunately an undated drawing showing landscape plans for the White House still exists, as do drawings showing landscaping plans for Pennsylvania Avenue. The lower (south) half of the first drawing is vintage Jefferson with dramatic sweeping curves and large areas of massed plantings. The upper (north) half is an adaptation to Major Pierre Charles L'Enfant's plan for diagonal streets which would converge on the President's house like sun rays. Jefferson, whose landscaping plans elsewhere avoided straight lines, is not likely to have been the originator of this design for the north grounds. The technique of the unsigned drawing is not his nor is the writing on it.[21]

Benjamin Henry Latrobe was the likely executor. Latrobe was hired in 1803 as surveyor of public buildings to replace L'Enfant, who had proven impossible to work with. Advice by Latrobe, a professionally trained architect, was honored by the President, but Jefferson's judgement was final. For the post which concerned itself with two subjects so dear to his heart—landscaping and architecture—Thomas Jefferson would not have chosen a man who could not produce what Thomas Jefferson wanted. But as the President was never the prima donna, the undated, unsigned drawing can be seen as a combined effort.

Trees naturally dominated the plan, just as they did Jefferson's plans for Monticello. They screened the President's house to provide the privacy he treasured. They also provided a relaxing place to work for the inhabitants of the house and members of the public. Equally important, masses of trees would make the sumptuous mansion less overpowering to Americans unaccustomed to large European castes, and they softened its lines. Surrounded by such an extensive, barren yard, the house desperately needed planting materials on a large scale.

The grounds were divided into public and private sections. The public area was on the somewhat higher ground to the north of the mansion,[22] the private to the south. At Jefferson's request a stone wall eight feet high on the south side was built by Congressional order around the border of the grounds, excluding the executive offices. It replaced a rail fence and was sufficiently impressive to be one of the few things recalled by Edmund Bacon about his last visit to Washington as overseer at Monticello. Jefferson had some help in getting the new wall. Federalist William Plumer complained that the rough fence was "not fit for the yard of a barn."

The public part of the grounds was uniformly covered with trees except for open swaths which, without the stone wall, would have been the visual extensions for the four diagonal streets approaching from the north.[23] From these streets the focal point was house. Sixteenth Street ended at the north entrance to the grounds. This entrance was flanked by stone piers. The wide graveled driveway coming from the north entrance ended in a grand circle, directly in front of the mansion.

The private south grounds overlooked the Potomac River and were intruded upon only by the entrance to the mansion on the east from Pennsylvania Avenue, which proceeded southeast to the capitol building. L'Enfant's original plans for a "palace" had been exchanged for those of a smaller (although still large) "White House," so Pennsylvania Avenue was no longer centered on the President's house. To overcome this design problem, entrance gates for both pedestrians and coaches were planned to provided a suitable terminus for the street. The entrance was a triple-arched brick structure trimmed with stone and complemented by iron pickets.[24]

After an appropriate sweep of driveway, with the house at first screened from view, visitors were to pass through a dramatic archway-guard house which divided the wing that connected the mansion from the offices to the east. Unfortunately in their hurry to finish this arch Jefferson and Latrobe persuaded the stone masons to keep working well after temperatures dropped. Consequently the mortar did not set up properly, and when the supports were removed, the arch collapsed. It lay in ruins until the stones were finally removed in 1819 during James Monroe's administration.

The drive ended at the great circle in front of the house. A similar pavilion-like structure appears in the drawing of the west wing, but there is no indication this was ever built.

Garden beds bordered the lawn, running the width of the south facade, while a large area of the south grounds was designated as a garden. Jefferson no doubt expected it to be divided into parterres filled with both edible and ornamental plants, but there is no indication it was ever planted during his term of office. It served as the White House flower garden for half a century after being planted during James Madison's tenure.

Pictures of the President's house during this period show the starkness of the reality. One of Jefferson's very first improvements was to abolish the outhouse; he deemed it inappropriate for the public to observe presidential habits of the toilet, and two water closets were installed upstairs. However, some of the wooden sheds left over from construction of the mansion were economically converted to lodging for goats, sheep, and fowl. Cows were put up in makeshift shelters. Only a few were kept since meat, poultry, fish, and shellfish were available from vendors. Still, livestock grazed on the grounds throughout the terms of many presidents to come. Horses were similarly accommodated.

The President, his family, guests, and servants depended on the Washington market to provide adequate fruits and vegetables. The eight-year chart Jefferson made of their availability indicates Washingtonians had a remarkably varied diet in what was essentially still a frontier town. Lettuce, parsley, and spinach were sold year round. No less than twenty-eight other vegetables and six fruits are listed. Thus the Washington market was not representative of city markets either in the North or South. Vegetables commonly sent to market were cabbages, turnips, carrots, onions, parsnips, and, later on, beans, watermelons, dried apples, and peaches. Private gardens were more likely to have a wider selection. On the frontier itself the pioneer was lucky to eat field corn and apples.

Due to a lack of government funds, Jefferson took it upon himself to provide at least some greenery for future presidents. Bacon fortunately kept the memoranda Jefferson wrote him during the presidential years. One made out in 1807 instructed: "As soon as the Aspen trees lose their leaves, take up one or two hundred of the young trees, not more than 2 or 3 feet high; tie them in bundles, with the roots well covered with straw. Young Davy being to carry Fanny to Washington, he is take the little cart, (which must be put into the soundest order,) to take these trees on board."[25] Where these aspens were planted is not recorded. On December 19, 1808, shortly before the end of his term, Jefferson gave instructions to Bacon to send another 200 young aspen.

While Jefferson was replenishing, others were cutting trees, to his great distress. Margaret Bayard Smith commented:

> Not only the banks of the Tiber, but those of the Potomack and Anacosta, were at this period adorned with native trees and shrubs and were distinguished by as romantic scenery as any rivers in our country. Indeed the whole plan was diversified with groves and clumps of forest trees which gave it the appearance of a fine park. Such as grew on the public grounds ought to have been preserved, but in a government such as ours, where the people are sovereign, this could not be done. *The people*, the poorer inhabitants cut down these noble and beautiful trees for fuel. In one single night seventy tulip-Poplars were *girdled*, by which process life is destroyed and afterwards cut up at their leisure by the people. Nothing afflicted Mr. Jefferson like this wanton destruction of the fine trees scattered over the city-grounds. I remember on one occasion (it was after he was President) his exclaiming "How I wish that I possessed the power of a despot." The company at table stared at a declaration so opposed to his disposition and principles. "Yes," continued he, in reply to their inquiring looks, "I wish I was a despot that I might save the noble, the beautiful trees that are daily falling sacrifices to the cupidity of their owners, or the necessity of the poor.[26]

Beyond what trees had been brought from Albemarle, ornamentation of the White House grounds was dependent on scarce funds from the public treasury. Although Jefferson's expenditures for Monticello were lavish, public money was something else. In his instructions to Latrobe regarding construction of the wall, he had made it clear that planting the grounds, putting in gates and a porter's lodge must be held in abeyance until funds were on hand. Meanwhile grading continued, and would not be completed until after Jefferson left the presidency. By the time the wall and drives were completed, funds had run out. So had his second term of office.

Beyond the White House environs, Jefferson had also been actively involved with the plantings along Pennsylvania Avenue. He gave orders to plant trees on this main street. It was necessary to box them to prevent damage from horses and cattle. While boxes would obviate the need for stakes (reported to equal the cost of the trees), they would drive up the total cost to $1 per tree. Three planting plans were submitted to the President. A double row of Lombardy poplars on either side of the road was ultimately put in.[27] These poplars are fast growing and quickly give a finished look.

Thomas Munroe, who was in charge of such matters, informed the President he would get the trees from Mount Vernon and General Masons Island. They would be of good size and priced at twelve and one-half cents each. Jefferson had visions of more trees. He told Munroe later in March, after first sketching what he had in mind, "It will allow us also next autumn either to plant our oaks,[28] elms &c. in the same lines with the lombardy poplars, giving to these trees of large growth a distance suitable to their size, or we may plant them midway [between the double rows of poplars] . . . so as to make a shaded mall."[29] This was followed by precise planting instructions.

Jefferson's hopes for these additional trees were dashed by reality. He wrote Munroe in June of 1807 that "on a view of the expences incurred & engaged for the Pennsylvania Avenue, that the funds will admit only to gravel it *where* it is wanting and *as much* only as is necessary to make it firm. The planting with oaks et. & additional arch to the bridge must be abandoned."[30]

The result of the combined efforts of those involved was recalled by Latrobe's son, John H. B. Latrobe in 1811:

> The Pennsylvania Avenue, in those days, was little better than a common country road. On either side were two rows of Lombardy poplars, between which was a ditch often filled with stagnant water, with crossing places at intersecting streets. Outside of the poplars was a narrow footway, on which carriages often intruded to deposit their occupants at the brick pavements on which the few houses scattered along the avenue abutted. In dry weather, the avenue was all dust, in wet weather, all mud; and along it "The Royal George"—an old-fashioned, long bodied four horse stage—either rattled with members of Congress from Georgetown in a halo of dust, or pitched, like a ship in a seaway, among the holes and ruts of this national highway.
>
> The Capitol itself stood on the brink of a steep declivity, clothed with old oaks and seamed with numerous gullies. Between it and the Navy Yard, were a few buildings, scattered here and there over an arid common.[31]

In 1803 Jefferson was able to further his horticultural interests in a manner not given to many: He was in a position to initiate the Lewis and Clark expedition. This was not the first time he had attempted to learn more about the botany of western lands. In 1792 he had suggested such an expedition to the American Philosophical Society, to be paid for by private funds. He had become a member of that group in 1779, and by 1792 was among the first vice-presidents. This was the year a wildflower was named for him, and botany was much on his mind. As he attended Society meetings regularly while in Philadelphia, it was most logical and appropriate that he should think a western expedition to be a proper Society endeavor.[32] The venture was actually undertaken by the French botanist André Michaux under Jefferson's instructions but was curtailed when Michaux was recalled by the French minister. Now President, Jefferson saw his opportunity to complete his dream.[33]

This time his point man was his own private secretary, Meriwether Lewis. William Clark was selected to serve as his chief aide for the proposed group of about ten outdoorsmen.[34] It seems clear Jefferson intended this expedition, like the first, to be a journey to pursue botanical and other natural history information while fulfilling the ostensible purpose (as far as Congress was concerned) of determining the commercial possibilities of the Louisiana Territory newly acquired from France. The audacious object was to explore the Missouri River to its source and whatever river then flowed to the Pacific.

Lewis did not perform traditional secretarial duties, as Jefferson wrote his own letters. Under the President's guidance Lewis instead polished his knowledge of the outdoors, preparatory to the great undertaking Jefferson expected the Congress to underwrite. Lewis was well suited for the task. Jefferson described his qualifications: "It was impossible to find a character who, to a complete science in Botany, Natural History, Minerology and Astronomy, joined the firmness of constitution and character, prudence, habits adapted to the woods, and familiarity with the Indian manners and character, requisite for this undertaking. All the latter qualifications Captain Lewis has. Although no regular botanist, etc., he possesses a remarkable store of accurate observation on all the subjects of the three kingdoms."[35]

To overcome any deficiencies in botanical knowledge, Lewis was duly sent by Jefferson to Philadelphia by March of 1803 to the renowned American botanist Benjamin Smith Barton, who had named *Jeffersonia diphylla*. Barton was instructed to point out what was most important for Lewis to look for on the trip. Jefferson's old friend, Dr. Benjamin Rush, was asked to add his thoughts on the subject to Lewis while the latter was in the city. Philadelphia nurseryman Bernard McMahon was brought into the circle, and it is said the final planning of the expedition took place in his house.[36]

The great undertaking officially began at St. Louis in May of 1804. The men covered some 8500 miles before their return to that town in September of 1806. The results, botanically and otherwise, must have been most gratifying to Jefferson. Seeds which Lewis sent him before his return were given to the American Philosophical Society. The large collection of seeds that Lewis brought back with him were eventually put into the hands of McMahon[37] and Philadelphian William Hamilton, whose advice on landscaping was sought by Jefferson. McMahon also got Lewis's entire collection of dried specimens. It was McMahon who took the responsibility of making sure Lewis was given the opportunity to name his discoveries. Unfortunately the explorer died in 1809 after serving as Governor of the Missouri Territory.

One other individual also got a gift of seeds and plants: André Thoüin, the director of the French National Garden whom Jefferson had met in Paris. Jefferson's response was delayed until 1813. He was of course delighted to return Thoüin's many favors, since the director had sent seeds of choice specimens annually whenever shipping permitted. In this case there was a serious problem. As Jefferson explained, "At present we are blockaded by our enemies; as we were indeed for many years while they called themselves our friends. I know not therefore how the present letter is to get to you."[38] Jefferson enlisted McMahon's help in sending a collection of seeds and plants to the Frenchman.

Jefferson's long-time gardening friend, Madame de Tessé, to whom he had repeatedly sent American plants, was also promised a selection from the bounty should she wish it.

As for himself, he explained to McMahon: "I reserved very few of Govr. Lewis's articles, and have growing only his salsafia, Mandane corn, and pea remarkeable for it's beautiful blossom & leaf. His forward bean is growing in my neighborhood."[39] These articles included the snowberry, the sweet-scented currant, and Pani corn, which Jefferson called "the best."

Considering the habitats these plants represented, it is not surprising so few were actually introduced into eastern cultivation, especially given the knowledge of American gardening of the day. The climate and soils of Philadelphia or Albemarle County are not those of the Northwest. The most important finds of the expedition were the Oregon grape holly,[40] which immediately found popularity despite its selling price of $20 per shrub, and the osage orange. While the former was useful as a landscaping plant, the latter became an essential to farmers in the prairie states for fencing. Wood fences were prohibitively expensive, if even possible to obtain wood for, while wire fences were yet unknown. The thorny osage orange grew fast and was eventually set out in the millions.

Jefferson had a great fascination with American plants. According to Margaret Bayard Smith he had a long list arranged according to their shapes, colors, and the seasons in which they showed to best advantage. He wanted the White House grounds planted exclusively in them. For other sites Jefferson's horizons were broader. His long-time interest in foreign plants could be facilitated while he was President in a more formal manner than heretofore. Smith fells us:

> By his desire, our consuls at every foreign port, collected and transmitted to him seeds of the finest vegetables and fruits that were grown in the countries where they resided. These he would distribute among the market-gardeners in the City (for at that time there was abundant space, not only for gardens, but little farms, within the City bounds), not sending them but giving himself and accompanying his gifts with the information necessary for their proper culture and management, and afterwards occasionally calling to watch the progress of their growth. This excited the emulation of our horticulturilists, and was the means of greatly improving our markets. For their further encouragement, the President ordered his steward to give the highest prices for the earliest and best products of these gardens.[41]

During this time Jefferson's attention once again returned to Monticello. By 1804 he was at the pinnacle of political power as President of the United States and in November would be reelected by a tremendous majority. After this he could realistically expect to retire from public office for good in 1809. Both his increasing age and his devotion to plants spurred him on to complete his landscaping at home.

He was aided in his goal by the fact the enlargement of his house was well under way and its precise outlines were not established. Thus he could with confidence plan the ultimate setting for it. Naturally he wanted to take every advantage of the views made possible by the elevation of his mountain top. Individual trees and groves had to be carefully located to provide a frame that would not in time become a screen. As a start on actual planting he put in some 40 hemlock and Weymouth pines[42] near his aspen thicket. This represents the earliest known nursery of forest trees in this country. Jefferson also continued development of what he called the "Grove," an eighteen-acre area which contained a large assortment of native and exotic trees. It was located on the north slope, opposite the gardens and orchards on Mulberry Row, between the first and fourth round-abouts. Incorporating trees already growing on this side of the mountain, it must have been the earliest, or one of the earliest, arboretums in America.

More importantly, about 1804 Jefferson once more set down overall sketches for the grounds. The concept was quite elaborate, entailing massive amounts of work. Because of Presidential duties, these ideas were laid on hold and many did not come to fruition.

The year 1805 saw the beginning of what proved to be extensive plantings of thorn for his live fences. Jefferson appears to have been uncertain as to how to proceed with the general landscaping. This is shown in a lengthy letter in 1806 to William Hamilton, from whom he had gotten many species of plants. Located in the Philadelphia area, Hamilton's estate, The Woodlands, is considered the finest example of landscape gardening in this period in America. Jefferson himself believed this, telling Hamilton, "The Woodlands [is] the only rival which I have known in America to what may be seen in England."[43] Jefferson also told his grandson, Jeff, that The Woodlands was the finest model of pleasure gardening he would ever see.

The design of The Woodlands was based on the ideas of English landscape gardener G. F. Parkyns. Jefferson also found much merit in Parkyns *Six Designs for Improving and Embellishing Grounds with Sections and Explanations* which was published in 1793. For whatever fame the Englishman was to enjoy, Jefferson and Hamilton were certainly responsible. Jefferson told his Philadelphia friend he had tried to get Parkyns "to go and give me some outlines, but I was disappointed."

After thanking Hamilton for plants received and promised, Jefferson explained his problems regarding landscaping Monticello. The gift acknowledgment becomes a request for advice and an invitation to see his mountain top first hand. Jefferson had, after all, been corresponding with the Philadelphian since at least 1800 when the seat of government was moved to Washington. As he told his friend, "my views are turned so steadfastly homeward that the subject runs with me whenever I get on it."

Jefferson explained to Hamilton that he was waiting to improve his grounds until he returned home. This was to be his challenge: "The grounds which I destine to improve in the style of the English gardens are in a form very difficult to be managed. They compose the northern quadrant of a mountain for about 2/3 of its height & then spread for the upper third over its whole crown. They contain about three hundred acres, washed at the foot for about a mile, by a river of the size of the Schuylkill."[44] In 1809 he was still deviously enticing Hamilton to come to Monticello, but there is no evidence the owner of The Woodlands ever did, nor in fact is there evidence he ever gave the President any advice.

Jefferson, of course, was quite capable of making up his own mind. Furthermore, his talents were commensurate with the task of designing his grounds by himself. Sometime in 1806, presumably after he had written Hamilton in July, he busied himself drawing the locations of the various features of his land.

In 1807 he drew up two landscaping plans. The first must have been drawn prior to mid–April when he was actively planting around the mansion itself. He was at Monticello during this period and made the most of it. For some reason the information was put in his *Weather Memorandum Book*, as were most of his records that year for planting. Trees were sited, some in clumps, others individually, at strategic locations. At the four corners of the house he put circular beds of mockorange. He also added flower beds and laid out both the gravel walk and the ellipse in front of the house. During restoration of the grounds a few yellow willows and shrubs, notably lilac were still growing as indicated on his sketch of the ellipse.[45] The beds around the house are notable for the fact that they include flowers. In his house plan of 1772 rectangular flower beds behind the house were drawn but appear not to have been dug. Where he put his flowers in 1782 is not known. These beds of 1807 would be more permanent.[46]

In a letter to his granddaughter Anne in June of 1807 Jefferson provides an overview of a second plan for that year. He drew it on the back of an envelope. He told her, "I find that the limited number of our flower beds will too much restrain the variety of flowers in which we might wish to indulge, & therefore I have resumed an idea, which I had formerly entertained, but had laid by, of a winding walk surrounding the lawn before the house, with a narrow border of flowers on each side. This would give us abundant room for a great variety. I enclose you a sketch of my idea, where the dotted lines on each side of the black line shew the border on each side of the walk. The hollows of the walk would give room for oval beds of flowering shrubs."[47]

Nothing further was done about this until 1808 when the walks and flower borders were set out. The letter to Anne might have been addressed to one of his peers. Although this granddaughter was only sixteen in 1807, her correspondence with Jefferson shows that he was fully justified in enlisting her as his chief gardening assistant.

When Anne was fifteen he had put her in charge of tending some tussocks of Peruvian grass over the winter months. She duly reported: "I planted the former [the grass] in a box of rich earth and covered it for a few nights until I thought it had taken root and then by degrees for fear of rendering it too delicate exposed it again. It looks extremely well indeed. If you think it will not stand the winter out it is not too late to take it in."[48] By the next year she had demonstrated sufficient enthusiasm and responsibility to provide intelligent commentary on his plans.

Flowers had not been of great interest to Jefferson. He explained to his French gardening friend Madame de Tessé in 1803: "I rarely ever planted a flower in my life. But when I return to live at Monticello . . . I believe I shall become a florist. The labours of the year, in that line, are repaid within the year, and death, which will be at my door, shall find me unembarrased in long lived undertakings."[49]

Letters by Anne and her younger sister Ellen to their grandfather and his to them provide not only information on the newest flower beds and accompanying plantings, but insight into their relationship as well. While in 1807, as mentioned, Anne was sixteen during this exciting period on the mountain top, Ellen was only ten.

Even as a youngster Ellen's letters are those of someone far older, both in content and expression. She observed in December of 1806: "Fine weather has at length returned and the grass and wallflowers look remarkably well."[50] And her observations of April of 1808: "We have had blue & white lilac, blue and white flags and jonquils. I found in the woods a great many mountain cowslips and wild Ranunculus besides other wild flowers. I have got the seed of the Jerusalem Cherry which I am told is very beautiful."[51] No wonder her mother worried about the academic abilities of Ellen's older brother Jeff. Cornelia, five years Ellen's junior and next in line, would also be a scholar and was an artist as well.

Jefferson's confidence in Anne's abilities as a gardener is indicated in this letter of November of 1807: "I wish to learn from you how the tuberoses &c. do, and particularly to have a list from you of the roots and seeds you have saved that I may know what supplies to ask from Mc. Mahon for the next spring. When Davy comes I shall send some Alpine strawberry roots, and some tussocks of a grass. . . . These I must consign to your care till the Spring."[52]

Even Meriwether Lewis's pea from the great expedition west was in Anne's care. She wrote in February of 1808, "I shall plant Governor Lewis' Peas as soon as the danger of frost is over. The bed they were in last summer was so much shaded that all of them did not ripen and as there are a good many empty one's I think it will be better to change it. The shady one will suit violets or any other flower's that like shade."[53]

Jefferson must have treasured the information. For her part, although she was a devoted gardening disciple of her grandfather, Anne had other things on her mind in 1808. In September she married Charles Lewis Bankhead and left the Monticello area. Late in November she wrote the President, "On coming from Edgehill I left all the flowers in Ellen's care, however, I shall be with you early enough in March to assist about the border."[54]

Jefferson's timetable for flower beds then went askew, perhaps for lack of Anne's presence and Ellen's tender age. Not until 1810 was mention made of the flower borders on the west lawn where he planted larkspurs, poppies, and balsam apple.

He was encouraging Ellen's interest in plants throughout 1808 and 1809, trying to tempt her to take over from Anne as his gardening assistant. In March of 1808 Ellen (then age eleven) and Anne (age seventeen) had made a pact that they would write to their grandfather every post their parents did not. Consequently Ellen, an exceptionally literate and talented child, made—and received—numerous comments regarding plants, but she never caught the gardening spark, despite obvious abilities and her grandfather and mother's proddings.

In 1809 Jefferson wrote to Anne: "What is to become of our flowers? I left them so entirely to yourself, that I never knew anything about them, what they are, where they grow, what is to be done for them. You must really make out a book of instructions for Ellen, who has fewer cares in her head than I have. Every thing shall be furnished on my part at her call."[55] Later letters between Jefferson and Ellen, though, are not concerned with gardening.

Gardening confidences continued with Anne after her marriage. In October of 1808 Jefferson wrote Martha, "Tell Anne that my old friend Thoüin of the National garden at Paris has sent me 700. species of seeds. I suppose they will contain all the fine flowers of France, and fill all the space we have for them."[56] By December Jefferson finally came to grips with the sheer number of seeds and sent them on to McMahon, explaining that they were from every country except the U.S. The following February he got in return a collection of flower seeds, apparently gratis, from McMahon, although not treasures as were the Thoüin specimens.

Jefferson's attachment to Anne is shown in this letter to her mother in February of 1811 when he was at Poplar Forest: "I have wished for Anne but once since I came here, and that has been from the moment of my arrival to the present one. . . . I had begun to prepare an Asparagus bed, and to plant some raspberry bushes, gooseberry bushes &c. for Anne. But it has been impossible to go on with it, the earth is so deep frozen, and I expect to leave it so."[57]

Jefferson still had hopes that this oldest granddaughter and her husband might settle at Poplar Forest. Unfortunately Bankhead succumbed to all the problems of a drinker, causing Anne and her four children no end of anguish. Later Anne herself came to an untimely end, dying just months before her grandfather.

The special bond between these two is beautifully shown in this letter Jefferson wrote to Anne from Monticello in May of 1811: "Nothing new has happened in our neighborhood since you left us. The houses and trees stand where they did. The flowers come forth like the belles of the day, have their short reign of beauty and splendor, and retire like them to the more interesting office of reproducing their like. The hyacinths and tulips are off the stage, the Irises are giving place to the Belladonnas, as this will to the Tuberoses &c."[58]

Ellen's recollections of this period capture the pleasure grandfather and grandchildren shared in the Monticello gardens:

> He loved farming and gardening, the fields, the orchards, and his asparagus beds. Every day he rode through his plantation and walked in his garden. In the cultivation of the last he took great pleasure. Of flowers, too, he was very fond. One of my early recollections is of the attention which he paid to his flower-beds. . . . When spring returned, how eagerly we watched the first appearance of the shoots above ground. Each root was marked with its own name written on a bit of stick by its side, and what joy it was for one of us to discover the tender green breaking through the mould, and run to granpapa to announce, that we really believed Marcus Aurelius was coming up, or the Queen of the Amazons was above ground! With how much pleasure compounded of our pleasure and his own, on the new birth, he would immediately go out to verify the fact, and praise us for our diligent watchfulness. Then when the flowers were in bloom, and we were in ecstacies over the rich purple and crimson, or pure white, or delicate lilac, or pale yellow of the blossoms, how he would sympathize in our admiration, or discuss with my mother and elder sister new groupings and combinations and contrasts. Oh, these were happy moments for us and for him! It was in the morning, immediately after our early breakfast, that he used to visit his flower-beds and his garden."[59]

During this time Jefferson was painfully aware how slowly his dream would be realized. In 1810 he wrote his Washington friend, Samuel Harrison Smith, who along with his wife, Margaret Bayard, had visited Monticello the previous year: "I have made no progress this year in my works of ornament: having been obliged to attend first to the utile. My farms occupy me much, and require much to get them underway."[60]

The following year, however, the flower borders got some overdue attention. Unfortunately there is no surviving planting plan for them. Martha and her family were living permanently at Monticello, and had been since Jefferson returned home for good in the spring of 1809, so we may surmise that Ellen, now fourteen, was pressed into duty. Jefferson explained to McMahon in April, "I have an extensive flower border, in which I am fond of placing *handsome* plants or *fragrant*. Those of mere curiosity I do not aim at, having too many other cares to bestow more than a moderate attention to them."[61]

McMahon had offered more seeds and bulbs. This is typical of how Jefferson got them. He informed the nurseryman: "Small parcels of seed may come by post; but bulbs are too bulky. We have always medical students in Philadelphia coming home by the stage when their lectures cease in the fall who would take charge of small packages, or they may come at any time by vessels bound to Richmond, addressed to the care of Messrs Gibson & Jefferson [his factors there]."[62] Only an ardent gardener would go to such trouble.

In 1812 Jefferson refined the size of the beds in the borders. With his new arrangement groups of like flowers could be planted in each compartment, instead of the mixed species he had originally contemplated. Such a massing of the same species, as modern professionals are quick to note, provides a greater visual impact. More seeds and bulbs were received from McMahon in spring and again in fall.

As all serious gardeners know, it takes time to establish trees and shrubs, and Jefferson fretted about his inability to make better use of it. He wrote in August of 1813 to Samuel Harrison Smith: "mrs. Smith would find I have made no progress in the improvement of my grounds. All my spare labor having been in constant demand for the improvements of my farms, mills, canals, roads &c. having given me constant occupation. To these are added our establishment for spinning & weaving, which occupy time, labor & persons."[63]

However, overseer Edmund Bacon recalled that the grounds were "most beautifully ornamented with flowers and shrubbery. There were walks, and borders, and flowers, that I have never seen or heard of anywhere else. Some of them were in bloom from early in the spring until late in the winter. A good many of them were foreign. Back of the house was a beautiful lawn of two or three acres, where his grandchildren used to play a great deal."[64]

Jefferson was finally realizing that to be successful at it, especially on the scale of his holdings, required undivided attention by one person who could make decisions and carry them through. This long-standing dilemma had to be resolved. While an enthusiastic and dedicated farmer and gardener, he had always had other interests and occupations too. Besides, in 1813 he was seventy years old.

He was fortunate to have at hand what he needed most—grandson Jeff, Martha's oldest boy. In 1815 at age twenty-three Jeff took over the supervision of Monticello and managed Poplar Forest from 1821. While never a scholar as his younger sisters, Ellen and Cornelia, Jeff had all the personal characteristics needed for his new role, not the least of which was a total devotion to his grandfather's well-being. Married in 1815 to the daughter of family friend Wilson Cary Nicholas, who later would, unintentionally, burden Jefferson with a $20,000 debt, Jeff had considerable incentive to settle down and produce an income on Monticello's fields.[65] Needless to say he enjoyed his grandfather's complete confidence, and as a grandson he was able to avoid the difficulties inevitable with the usual hired overseer.

It was late in his life, and Jefferson wanted to complete the landscaping at Poplar Forest. He was spending more of his time there now that the house he had started building in 1806 was finally liveable. Early in February of 1782 he had sent the first plants to Poplar Forest: six apricot trees, two morellas, two Kentish cherries, two May dukes, two carnations, two black hearts, two white hearts, two Newtown pippings, two russetins, two golden wildings and some white strawberries. It is difficult to believe they were meant for anyone else to enjoy, but Jefferson could hardly have expected to use them soon. His wife's health was declining, and she died that September. While he made a brief trip to Bedford in July of 1782 and in the following years, it was not until 1811 that additional planting occurred. His Bedford house was well under way by then, and he had finished his public career.

As at Monticello, he added a variety of fruits later: gooseberries, raspberries, and grapes with a bed for tomatoes, lettuce, and asparagus. Oddly, he did not mention peas. Rose bushes, pinks[66] and bear grass[67] provided some purely aesthetic touches. He also began landscaping the mounds between the house and each necessary. For this he used weeping willows, golden willows, and aspens. Athenian poplars and more weeping willows were planted elsewhere. Additional specimens of all these trees were in his nursery, as were three Lombardy poplars.

In 1812 the nursery trees were put in their permanent locations. Trees and shrubs also were added around the house: locusts, European mulberry, balsam poplar, red buds, dogwoods, paper mulberries, calycanthses, altheas, lilacs, and lirodendrons. More aspens and mulberries were started in the nursery. Sixty-four paper mulberries were planted in the nursery in 1815 and nineteen in a clump at each outhouse or "necessary." Jefferson had come to favor the paper mulberry. He described them to a friend in 1816 as "the most beautiful & best shading tree to be near the house, extremely clean, bearing no fruit, scarcely yet known in America."

By 1816 the house at Poplar Forest was considered fit for Jefferson's women so he hurried to make it appeal to them on the outside by adding a flower garden, in addition to the roses, pinks, and bear grass he already had. These were supplemented by additional trees and shrubs, including 190 tulip poplars. This was Jefferson's first planting of the tree for which Poplar Forest had been named by a previous owner. It is not a true poplar, but rather a member of the magnolia family and is a common tree in Bedford County.

Martha's help was sought, and by 1816 he had introduced the wonders of gardening to granddaughter Cornelia. Next in line after Ellen and age seventeen that year, she frequently accompanied her grandfather to Bedford. Martha observed in a letter to her father Cornelia knew all of the tulips and hyacinths she was sending from Monticello at his request. As

Jefferson had been retired since 1809, there is no correspondence between him and Cornelia to indicate their gardening relationship. However, a letter by Cornelia to Ellen in 1826 shows her love of flowers and general knowledge of plants.

While the aspens at Poplar forest were identified as coming from Albemarle, as were the Pride of China trees planted in 1817 and a few trees from Bedford friends and neighbors, no mention is made of where all these many other plants were secured. They represented trees and shrubs growing at Monticello, so those easily propagated probably came from there or were cuttings or seeds from trees already growing at Poplar Forest. Others, such as the redbuds and dogwoods, undoubtedly were taken from the surrounding woods. When the final 20 balsam poplars, given by a neighbor in 1819, were installed, another Jefferson planting program ended. Most home owners would only term it a "landscaping extravaganza."

11
The Final Years

Despite his advanced age and deteriorating health, the usual charts and notes appear in the *Garden Book* through 1824 when this long-running account was finally laid aside at age 81. Jefferson supported the establishment of the United States Botanic Garden in the District of Columbia in 1820. The federal government assigned five acres for it to the Columbian Institute of Arts and Sciences, which had been established in 1816, and increased the property to 12.5 acres in 1824. Jefferson, John Adams, James Madison, and the Marquis de Lafayette were all members of the Institute and active in promoting the project. These superstars, however, were all at the end of their respective long careers and lesser lights did not assume the work necessary to get the garden going. Little came of the idea, and after twenty years the effort was discontinued. Jefferson must have recognized that from Monticello he could do little for it beyond lending his prestige.

An effort with more lasting consequences was the establishment of the Albemarle Agricultural Society. Considering Jefferson's knowledge of and honorary membership in such organizations elsewhere, the comparatively late establishment of an agricultural group in his own county must be attributed to the concerted efforts he was making to get his own house in order. At age 74 he was the Albemarle citizen who got things started. On May 15, 1817, a group of men gathered. Five were appointed to prepare rules and regulations which would govern the group, including Jefferson. After consulting with the others via letter, he drew up the rules and also a platform of the "Objects for the Attention and Enquiry of the Society." His age had not impeded his vision; except for a few crops such as hemp and flax which decreased in importance over time, his recommendations anticipated what agriculturists throughout the 1800s actually applied themselves to.

With Monticello and Poplar Forest under control, Jefferson, ever restless mentally, was free to concentrate on his last major project, the establishment of the University of Virginia. By 1804 the Virginia legislature was exploring the idea of a state university with a liberal bent. Jefferson was thrilled and immediately created a blueprint for the school.[1] While nothing further was done at this time, he had an opportunity to promote his vision in 1810 when he was approached by letter by trustees of East Tennessee College to sell tickets to a lottery to benefit the projected school. Jefferson bowed out of this task, but sent the trustees his proposed design for the University of Virginia.

The thought that his own state might fall behind must have gnawed on his mind until at last he could squeeze in the time. Always the champion of education, a school of higher learning was a logical final endeavor for a man whose thoughts were always on the future.

The choice of site, Charlottesville, was favorably near Monticello — and incidentally to the other two U.S. Presidents, James Madison and James Monroe, who were involved in the initial phases of the university. The cornerstone of the institution, Central College, was chartered and renamed the University of Virginia in 1819. The campus was laid in 1817 and from that point on the school was Jefferson's major concern. He described it to a friend as the last of his mortal cares and the last service he could render his country.

One wonders, though, what went through his mind upon the receipt of a letter from John Adams in 1817: "I congratulate you, and Madison and Monroe, on your noble employment in founding a university. From such a noble triumvirate the world will expect something very great and very new; but if it contains anything quite original, and very excellent, I fear the prejudices are too deeply rooted to suffer it to last long, though it may be accepted at first. It will not always have three such colossal reputations to support it."[2]

Jefferson's own optimism prevailed. The expansion of a privately funded Central College to a full-state-supported university merely provided new challenges. By 1820 Jefferson was able to report that "seven of the ten pavilions destined for the professors, and about thirty dormitories, will be completed this year; and three other, with six hotels for boarding, and seventy other dormitories, will be completed the next year, and the whole be in readiness then to receive those who are to occupy them."[3]

Money, always his bugaboo, proved one for his university too. Yet Jefferson was sanguine. He wrote in 1822: "Our University of Virginia, my present hobby, has been at a stand for a twelve-month past for want of funds. . . . The institution is so far advanced that it will force itself through. So little is now wanting that the first liberal Legislature will give it its last lift."[4]

Jefferson's own crowning horticultural and architectural achievement is seen in the design of his university buildings and the landscaping which flowed from it. There he showed his total command of both disciplines. Before construction buildings and grounds had been designed as an integral unit. Instead of a solitary large structure or perhaps two or three buildings grouped together, he created a U-shaped composition with a rotunda which housed the library at the center. He had earlier promoted the idea of a university as an academical village. Each side of the complex he designed had five pavilions for faculty residences above, with office and classroom space below. These were joined to fifty-four lodging rooms for students. Colonnaded arcades connecting each set of pavilions provided shelter from the elements and contributing to the overall design. The extreme length of the arms of the "U" resulted in a visual problem of perspective which Jefferson solved very neatly. As the rotunda was to be the central vantage point, the pavilions could not be equidistant because the more distant buildings would suffer from foreshortening. The spacing was increased accordingly. As no building was planned opposite the rotunda, faculty, students, and visitors had an uninterrupted view of the Piedmont hills in the distance.

"The Lawn," as the enclosure is still called, measured 200 feet by 600 feet and has remained the central focus of campus life. Peter Maverick, a New York engraver, in 1822 made an engraving of Jefferson's plan of this grassy area and its buildings. While the engraving shows no trees, the plan he put before the Board of Visitors in 1817 called for grass and trees on the Lawn. This same note appeared on a second sketch made soon thereafter. As rector of his new university, Jefferson paid $1.50 in 1823 for 100 locust saplings. Only one area could have accommodated this many. An engraving made forty years later shows sizeable trees on the Lawn, presumably these locusts. Two written accounts concerning this early period mention trees on the Lawn. One identified the trees as locusts; the other account by Robert Mills, an architectural student-disciple of Jefferson's, indicated their proper placement to avoid obstructing the view of nearby pavilions.

While the Lawn is lovely, the most charming landscaping is found to the rear of the pavilions where Jefferson designed small gardens in the space between the pavilions and the parallel line of buildings which form what are called the East Range and West Range. These housed six dining halls for students plus fifty-five additional living quarters. The gardens opposite each hotel were divided in two, the section closest to the pavilion was designed for beauty, while that closest to the hotel was planned for growing fruits and vegetables. Pavilions not opposite a hotel enjoyed an undivided garden space. These beautifully proportioned areas are architectural gems.

Just as striking as the garden designs are the seven-foot serpentine walls which surround them. Serpentine walls had been used in America before. Jefferson was familiar with them at Greenspring, Governor William Berkeley's residence, which he visited frequently when in Williamsburg. He would also have seen them in England. In addition to their aesthetic appeal of curved lines as opposed to straight, Jefferson was ever mindful of their economy of bricks. The walls served important horticultural purposes too. They guarded against wind and wandering hogs and other animals. They also trapped heat from the sun in early spring when blooming fruit trees and early vegetables were subject to frost.

Unfortunately the walls, only one brick thick, had some structural liabilities despite their strengthening curves and were subject to mortar disintegration from freezing water. The present reconstructed walls survive only through constant maintenance, the original walls having fallen down because of lack of care and outright destruction by humans and livestock.

The original planting plans for the gardens no longer exist, if they ever did. Jefferson died before the gardens could have been planted. Over the years the various occupants of the pavilions and hotels made changes in the plantings of their predecessors. Today we see the reconstruction efforts begun in 1948 by the Garden Club of Virginia. The location of the walks, trees, shrubs, and herbacious plants are based on known gardens of the period. Because they have been planned with such great care it is not difficult to believe Jefferson himself would have approved these masterpieces of design.

The designation of utility for the gardens opposite the hotels might suggest that these portions are somehow less aesthetic. They are not, for they include fruit trees. Because of the well-planned walks the effect is as elegant as the sections devoted to pleasure. The side wall privies which served both faculty and students, some now restored as tool houses, demonstrate that even utility buildings can add significantly to the decor of a garden. The use of decorative gates for entrances to the various garden compartments and the garden benches, tastefully located, add to the visual pleasure of the kitchen gardens as well as those devoted to ornamentals.

Jefferson was concerned that his university have a botanical garden too. Thus he wrote to the proctor, A. S. Brockenbrough in the late summer of 1825: "The botanical garden, after being laid off under the direction of Dr. Emmet [the professor of natural history], to be pursued at all spare time."[5] And just two and one-half months before his death on July 4, 1826, he wrote a lengthy letter giving Emmet details about the garden and also about establishing a school of botany.

Jefferson had previously consulted José Francisco Correa da Serra, Portugal's ambassador to the U.S. He described the Abbé as the most learned man he had ever met, with a particular interest in botany. The two men became good friends. After their first meeting the Abbé came to Monticello so frequently one room there was designated as his. From him Jefferson sought and received a plan for a garden at his university. Jefferson then chose a site he found suitable for two acres of trees and four acres of other plantings.

For the section to be devoted to non-woody plants Jefferson told Emmet he had a "special resource"—André Thouïn, superintendent of the National Garden at Paris. When he checked into this, however, he found Thouïn had died, and his successor was now sending the annual box of seeds from France to the Albemarle Agricultural Society. Less than two months before his death Jefferson wrote the Society asking that the last contribution just arrived in New York be sent to the University. This garden, however, was never constructed; other university considerations demanded its limited resources.

A major part of the University still required attention: the establishment of a school of botany. To this end in 1822 the Albemarle Agricultural Society, under the leadership of Madison, came up with an innovative idea. Each agricultural society in the state would be asked to support the cause. To show its own good faith the Albemarle Society resolved that $1000 in its treasury would be appropriated to establish a fund to support a professor of agriculture at the new school. Madison wrote a cover letter in which he spelled out the need for such a post. With sufficient funds even more could be accomplished. This included the establishment of an experimental as well as model small farm which would serve to teach students and visitors alike the best possible methods of farming, along with the plants and animals which could accomplish this goal.

Surry County responded to the plea by appropriating $100. The president of the Fredericksburg Society wrote a letter, but its contents were not recorded in the Albemarle minutes, nor do the minutes record responses from any other groups. An Albemarle member was later assigned the task of soliciting funds from throughout the state, but the results of that effort were not recorded either. Maybe the Albemarle group was the strongest in members and commitment. No doubt the lack of response was due in large part because of the poor financial condition of Virginia farmers.

For his part Jefferson was finding money and an appropriate professor a problem too. He chose Emmet, a chemist, for the position. Chemistry, as

Jefferson and Madison were both well aware, was beginning to unravel some of nature's mysteries, particularly in the area of agriculture. Until money could be found to support both, however, the chair of chemistry and agriculture would have to be combined. Jefferson wrote Emmet regarding the school of botany:

> Not that I suppose the lectures can be begun in the present year, but that we may this year make the preparations necessary for commencing them the next. For that branch, I presume, can be taught advantageously only during the short season while nature is in general bloom, say during a certain portion of the months of April and May, when suspending the other branches of your department, that of Botany may claim your exclusive attention. Of this, however, you are to be the judge, as well as of what I may now propose on the subject of preparation. I will do this in writing, while sitting at my table, and at ease, because I can rally there, for your consideration, with more composure than in extempore conversation, my thoughts on what we have to do in the present season.[6]

In a little over two months death intervened. Emmet was not enthusi-astic about adding botany to his already crowded schedule. When the chief proponent of the plan was gone Emmet was relieved of the duty. The post remained vacant until 1869 when John W. Mallett was appointed professor of analytical, industrial, and agricultural chemistry. Not until 1872 was John Page appointed professor of natural history, experimental, and practi-cal agriculture. The state's efforts in the agricultural field would be directed in time to a different institution, the Virginia Polytechnic Institute and State University.

Of all Mr. Jefferson himself planted, at this writing only these survive: at Monticello one sugar maple, two tulip poplars, a red cedar, a European larch and stump sprouts of linden and elm. At Poplar Forest there are some dozen tulip poplars which appear to date to his lifetime. Interesting as these trees are and as exceptional as his landscaping plans were for Monticello, Poplar Forest and the University of Virginia, the real legacy from this most extraordinary man was his dedication to the future of horticulture and farming. Jefferson also showed us the qualities needed to achieve his goals: a willingness to experiment and pursue practices to make the soil fertile for the future as well as for today. As a scholar of the classics Jefferson was well aware that soil erosion and degradation commonly reduce great cities and states to nothing. He did not want to see his beloved America succumb to the same fate.

Notes

Introduction

1. Thomas Jefferson, *Notes on the State of Virginia*, (1781; reprint, New York: Harper & Row, 1964), 157.
2. Andrew A. Lipscomb and Albert Ellery Bergh, eds., *The Writings of Thomas Jefferson*, (Washington: Thomas Jefferson Memorial Association of the United States, 1903), 5:93–4.
3. Thomas Jefferson to Samuel Vaughan, 1790, Jefferson Papers, Library of Congress.
4. Thomas Jefferson to Philip Tabb, 1809, "Glimpses of the Past," Jefferson Papers, Missouri Historical Society, 3:108–9.
5. Paul Leiscester Ford, ed., *The Writings of Thomas Jefferson* (New York: G. P. Putnam's Sons, 1892–99), 7:12.
6. Sarah N. Randolph, *The Domestic Life of Thomas Jefferson* (New York: Harper & Bros., 1871), 37–38.
7. Thomas Jefferson to Henry Knox, 1795, Jefferson Papers, Massachusetts Historical Society.
8. Lipscomb and Bergh, *Writings*, 9:302–4.
9. Merrill D. Peterson, ed., *Thomas Jefferson: A Reference Biograph* (New York: Charles Scriber's Sons, 1986), 385.
10. Randolph, *Domestic Life*, 210.
11. Ibid., 171.
12. Ibid., 241.
13. Ibid., 133.
14. Ibid., 137.
15. Thomas Jefferson Randolph, *Memoirs, Correspondence, and Private Papers of Thomas Jefferson* (London, 1829), 209.
16. Ford, *Writings*, 5:504–6.
17. Randolph, *Domestic Life*, 224.
18. Thomas Jefferson to Thomas Mann Randolph, 1793, Jefferson Papers, Library of Congress.
19. Thomas Jefferson to Henry Remson, 1794, Franklin Collection, Jefferson Papers, Yale University.
20. Lipscomb and Bergh, *Writings*, 9:297.
21. Thomas Jefferson to Horatio Gates, 1794, Jefferson Papers, Library of Congress.
22. Ibid.

23. Lipscomb and Bergh, *Writings*, 9:297.

24. Randolph, *Domestic Life*, 233.

25. Lipscomb and Bergh, *Writings*, 9:355–7.

26. Edwin Morris Betts and James A. Bear, Jr., eds., *Family Letters of Thomas Jefferson* (Columbia, Mo.: University of Missouri Press, 1966), 289.

27. Thomas Jefferson to Augustin Francois Silvestre, 1807, Jefferson Papers, Massachusetts Historical Society.

28. Lipscomb and Bergh, *Writings*, 11:182.

29. Thomas Jefferson to Timothy Matlack, 1807, Jefferson Papers, Library of Congress.

30. Lipscomb and Bergh, *Writings*, 11:137.

31. Ibid., 11:411.

32. Thomas Jefferson to Charles Willson Peale, 1809, Jefferson Papers, Library of Congress.

33. Lipscomb and Bergh, *Writings*, 12:260.

Chapter 1

1. Lipscomb and Bergh, *Writings*, 13:78–79.

2. For further information on Jefferson's lineage see Dumas Malone, *Jefferson the Virginian* (Boston: Little, Brown and Company, 1948), Chaps. 1, 2.

3. Julian Boyd, ed., *Papers of Thomas Jefferson* (Princeton, N.J.: Princeton University Press, 1950), 1:61.

4. Despite this avowal Jefferson has comparatively little to say in his correspondence about his building activities or his feelings for them.

5. Ford, *Writings*, 6:454.

6. James A. Bear, Jr., ed., *Jefferson at Monticello* (Charlottesville, Va.: University Press of Virginia, 1967), 18.

7. Percy Wells Bidwell and John Falconer, *History of Agriculture in the Northern United States, 1620–1860* (Clifton, N.J.: Augustus M. Kelley, 1973), 81.

8. Lewis Cecil Gray, *Agriculture in the Southern United States to 1860* (New York: Peter Smith, 1941), 197.

9. It should be noted, however, that the value of manure to improve the land was not uniformly understood then, any more than it is today. Indeed only a few groups of people, such as those in parts of Eastern Asia have over many centuries faithfully returned animal excrement to the soil, no matter how much work was involved.

10. Jefferson's solution to this problem is found in a 1794 letter to John Taylor: "Why could we not have a moveable airy cow house, to be set up in the middle of the field which is to be dunged, & soil our cattle in that thro' the summer as well as winter, keeping them constantly up & well littered?" *Jefferson Papers*, 7th ser., Massachusetts Historical Collection (Boston, 1900), 1:49–55.

11. U. B. Phillips, *Plantation and Frontier Documents (1649–1863)* (Cleveland, Ohio: Arthur H. Clark Co., 1909), 1:110.

12. Lynn Ceci, "Fish Fertilizer: A Native North American Practice?" *Science*, 188:26–30.

13. Fish fertilizer is still touted today, but now in liquid form and deodorized. It is one of the highest organic sources of nitrogen and has a wide range of trace elements.

14. Kelp in liquid, meal, or powered form has replaced rockweed. It too has a wealth of trace elements.

15. These include Dr. George Logan, Judge Richard Peters, and Chancellor Robert R. Livingston.

16. Thomas Jefferson to William Strickland, June 30, 1803. Jefferson Papers, Library of Congress.

17. Throughout this period most farmers used the ancient slash-and-burn system of agriculture. It was easier and cheaper than to replenish the soils with fertilizers or crop rotation.

18. Merrill D. Peterson, *Thomas Jefferson and the New Nation* (New York, Oxford University Press, 1970), 525.

19. Timothy Dwight, *Travels* (NewHaven, Conn.: S. Converse, Printer, 1821), 3:303.

20. *The Cultivator* (1838–39), 6:144.

21. *American Husbandry*, 1:134.

22. See Chapter 5 for the history of agricultural implements used prior to and during Jefferson's lifetime.

23. Upon the invention of inorganic fertilizers, experiments to maintain soil organically fell by the wayside except among the few farmers who looked beyond their immediate crop. Now that the "down side" of inorganic fertilizer is becoming increasingly obvious, particularly water pollution, more consideration to organic methods practiced by such farmers as Jefferson will inevitably be given.

24. This was a reflection of an increasingly urban population that required farm products and had the money to pay for them. At the same time agricultural knowledge of American growing conditions was increasing.

25. Salt was virtually beyond the reach of the average family except in favored locations.

26. Stores in rural areas carried little more than these basics until the twentieth century.

27. A description of these advances is found in Jethro Tull, *The Horse-hoeing Husbandry* (London, 1762).

28. See *Thomas Jefferson's Garden Book* (annotated by Edwin Morris Betts [Philadelphia: The American Philosophical Society, 1985], 655–62) for a list of books and pamphlets on agriculture, gardening, and botany in Jefferson's library.

29. Today Penn's estate, fully restored, is open to the public.

30. Bartram's home and garden are also open to the public.

31. The American Philosophical Society's headquarters in Philadelphia is open to the public.

32. For Eliot and other early agricultural writers see "Early American Soil Conservationists," Misc. Pub. 449, U.S. Soil Conservation Service. See also U. P. Hedrick, *History of Horticulture in America to 1860* (New York: Oxford University Press, 1950).

33. Thomas Jefferson to Thomas Mann Randolph, 1793, Jefferson Papers, Library of Congress.

34. Correspondence between Jefferson and Randolph can be found in *Thomas Jefferson's Garden Book* and *Thomas Jefferson's Farm Book*, annotated by Edwin Morris Betts (Charlottesville, Va.: University Press of Virginia, 1976).

35. Jefferson to Randolph, 1793.

36. See Donald Jackson, ed., *Diaries of George Washington* (Charlottesville, Va.: University Press of Virginia, 1976), and Walter Edwin Brooke, ed., *The Agricultural Papers of George Washington* (Boston: Richard G. Badger, Gorham, 1919).

37. Jefferson wrote Sir John Sinclair in 1803: "Our agricultural society has at length formed itself. Like our American Philosophical Society, it is voluntary, and unconnected with the public, and is precisely an execution of the plan I formerly sketched to you. Some State societies have been formed heretofore; the others will do the same. Each State society names two of its members of Congress to be their members in the Central society, which is of course together during the sessions of Congress. . . . The Central society was formed

the last winter only, so that it will be some time before they get under way. Mr. Madison, the Secretary of State, was elected their President." (Lipscomb and Bergh, *Writings*, 10:396–98). See Grey, *Agriculture in the Southern United States to 1860*, 782–92 and Bidwell and Falconer, *History of Agriculture in the Northern United States 1620–1860*, Chap. 14 for a detailed account of early agricultural societies, agricultural schools and farm papers.

38. See Lipscomb and Bergh, *Writings*, 17:404–10, for Jefferson's complete plan for the establishment of agricultural societies.

Chapter 2

1. This became painfully obvious after Jefferson left the presidency.

2. See account by the Duke de la Rouchefoucauld-Liancourt, *Travels Through the United States of North America, in the Years 1795, 1796, 1797* of his 1797 visit to Monticello, in which he gives a figure of 1120 acres.

3. Thomas Jefferson to Thomas Mann Randolph, August 18, 1795, Jefferson Papers, Library of Congress.

4. Ibid.

5. Lipscomb and Bergh, *Writings*, 9:286–88.

6. Bear, *Jefferson at Monticello*, 51.

7. Randolph, *Domestic Life*, 229.

8. The Jeffersons' share of the Wayles debt amounted to some £4000. As there were additional heirs under Wayles' will, this represents only a part of the unrecorded total. In 1776 ten or more Virginia planters owed more than £5000 to English creditors. Wayles was presumably one of these. Jefferson was fully aware of the enormity of the debt which was now his. His legal income in 1769 came to £370, a sum considered at this period to be a sign of success. In 1771 he cleared £10 per hogshead of tobacco. His Bedford crop swung between 20–29 hogsheads per year, with prices varying according to quality and the market. Thus paying off Wayles' debt, while formidable, would have proven feasible except for the problems Jefferson encountered with the transition to an American currency after the Revolutionary War. As he was a man of honor, he in effect paid the debt twice to satisfy his English creditors. See also T. H. Breen, *Tobacco Culture: the Mentality of the Great Tidewater Planters on the Eve of the Revolution* (Princeton, N.J.: Princeton University Press, 1985), 128.

9. Lipscomb and Bergh, *Writings*, 9:139–143.

10. Henry S. Randall, *The Life of Thomas Jefferson* (Philadelphia: J. B. Lippincott, 1871), 2:404.

11. Ford, *Writings*, 10:379.

12. Jefferson detailed his problems in this letter. He said an estate runs a planter into debt "if at a distance from him, if he is absent, if he is unskilled as I am, if short crops reduce him to deal on credit, and most assuredly if thunder struck from the hand of a friend as I was. Altho' all these causes conspired against me, and should have put me on my guard I had no suspicions until my grandson undertook the management of my estate and developed to me the state of my affairs, fortunately while yet retrievable in a comfortable degree." (Ford, *Writings*, 10:379; as it turned out Jeff could only delay disaster).

13. Ford, *Writings*, 10:383.

14. Lipscomb and Bergh, *Writings*, 12:389–91.

15. Jefferson was curiously indifferent to the details of his farming operations while abroad. See Chap. 7.

16. Thomas Jefferson to George Washington, September 1790, Jefferson Papers, Library of Congress.

17. See Tull, *Horse-hoeing Husbandry*.

18. See Washington Papers, Library of Congress.

19. Edmund Ruffin, *Essay on Calcareous Manures*, (Petersburg, Va.: J. W. Campbell, 1832), 12.

20. Lipscomb and Bergh, *Writings*, 9:139–43.

21. Thomas Jefferson to James Madison, June, 1793, Jefferson Papers, Library of Congress.

22. Thomas Jefferson to Thomas Mann Randolph, June, 1793, Jefferson Papers, Library of Congress.

23. Randolph, *Domestic Life*, 221–22.

24. Thomas Jefferson to George Logan, 1793, Jefferson Papers, Library of Congress.

25. Lipscomb and Bergh, *Writings*, 9:286–88.

26. Ibid.

27. Thomas Jefferson to Ferdinando Fairfax, April, 1794, Jefferson Papers, Library of Congress.

28. For example, to Philip Mazzei, General Henry Knox and George Wythe.

29. Jefferson, *Farm Book*, 45.

30. Lipscomb and Bergh, *Writings*, 9:305.

31. Jefferson, *Farm Book*, 119.

32. Randall, *Life of Thomas Jefferson*, 2:303–7.

33. Lipscomb and Bergh, *Writings*, 9:349.

34. On the other hand the very ancient combination of maize, squash, and beans is still used today, the difference being that this grouping developed in nature.

35. Randolph Jefferson to Thomas Jefferson, 1792, Carr-Cary Papers, University of Virginia.

36. Lipscomb and Bergh, *Writings*, 11:411–12.

37. Randolph, *Domestic Life*, 222.

38. Thomas Jefferson to Edmund Bacon, 1808, Jefferson Papers, Hunting Library.

39. Jefferson, *Account Book* 1775.

40. Randall, *Life of Thomas Jefferson* 2:303–7.

41. Lipscomb and Bergh, *Writings*, 10:11–14. Strickland wrote *Observations on the Agriculture of the United States of America* in 1801. It was in Jefferson's library.

42. Thomas Jefferson to Thomas Mann Randolph, 1793, Jefferson Papers, Library of Congress.

43. Even though much has been learned about plant nutrition since Jefferson's day, the debate between advocates of organic and inorganic fertilizers goes on.

44. Thomas Jefferson to Richard Peters, March 6, 1816, Jefferson Papers, Library of Congress.

45. Lipscomb and Bergh, *Writings*, 10:396–98. The "Loudon System" ultimately spread throughout the state and beyond. Before the close of the antebellum period northern Virginia had become one of the South's most important general farming regions—due primarily to clover, gypsum, lime and Mr. Binns.

46. John Sinclair to Thomas Jefferson, Jefferson Papers, Library of Congress.

47. Thomas Jefferson to Joel Yancy, 1819, Jefferson Papers, Massachusetts Historical Society.

Chapter 3

1. For the first 50 years of Virginia's history as a colony most frontier land was obtained by patent which allowed 50 acres for each person (a headright) brought into the colony. The tract was secured by a small quitrent with seating or planting of the tract within three years.

2. Issac Weld, though, added this reason: "It is not, however, so much owing to the great share of nutriment which the tobacco plant requires, that the land is impoverished, as to the particular mode of cultivating it, which renders it necessary for people to be continually walking between the plants, from the moment they are set out, so that the ground about each plant is left exposed to the burning rays of the sun all the summer, and becomes at the end of the season a hard beaten pathway." (*Travels Through the States of North America 1795–1797* [New York: Johnson Reprint Corp., 1968], 1:151).

3. Boyd, 11:656.

4. Jefferson Papers, Massachusetts Historical Society.

5. For a good discussion of this subject see Emory G. Evans, "Planter Indebtedness and the Coming of the Revolution in Virginia," *William and Mary Quarterly*, 3d ser. 19 (1962) 511–33.

6. Weld, *Travels through the States*, 1:138–39.

7. Jefferson indicated to his brother-in-law, Frances Eppes, that the Wayles debt was about £9000 sterling, but that there were some 420 hogsheads of tobacco already applied to it and the debt therefore would not be too formidable. See Boyd, 11:652. It was not to be that simple. See Malone, *The Virginian*, 443; Thomas Jefferson to Alexander Dodson, January 1, 1792, Jefferson Papers, Massachusetts Historical Society.

8. Boyd, 10:27.

9. John Rolfe, *Relation*, Virginia Historical Register, 1.105.

10. J. F. D. Smyth, a practicing Maryland farmer of the Revolutionary War period, recognized seven types: Oronoko, sweet-scented, Hudson, Frederick, thick joint, shoe string, and thickset. John Josselyn, an early English visitor to New England, mentions three kinds of tobacco sold: horse tobacco, having a broad, long leaf picked at the end; round-pointed, and sweet scented. The Indians, he said, used a small round-leafed tobacco "odious to the English."

11. By the mid-1700s a law provided that all tobacco for export had to be brought to warehouses established and maintained by the colony, where it was then viewed by bonded inspectors who graded and weighed it and stamped the hogshead.

12. Thomas Jefferson to Thomas Mann Randolph, 1801, Jefferson Papers, Library of Congress.

13. See Boyd, 7:209–12.

14. John Taylor, *Arator, or Agricultural Essays* (Georgetown, 1813), 232–35.

15. Until he began his house at Poplar Forest in 1806, Jefferson made the trip to Bedford only four times. After that he went three or four times a year. The record of visits to his Goochland and Cumberland County properties is so sketchy it is obvious he was dependent on his overseers there even more than at Poplar Forest.

16. Jefferson, *Notes*, 159.

17. Lipscomb and Bergh, *Writings*, 8:58–59.

18. Ibid., 10:63. This effort paid off when 30,000 plants (29 hogsheads) were marketed from Poplar Forest and 20,000 plants from Albemarle.

19. Thomas Jefferson to John Taylor, 1810, Jefferson Papers, Library of Congress.

20. Lipscomb and Bergh, *Writings*, 12:266–67.

21. Ibid., 11:121.

22. Thomas Jefferson to Martha Randolph, 1815, Jefferson Papers, Massachusetts Historical Society.

23. Thomas Jefferson to Bernard Peyton, 1823, Jefferson Papers, Massachusetts Historical Society.

24. Joel Yancy to Thomas Jefferson, 1820, Jefferson Papers, Massachusetts Historical Society.

25. Thomas Jefferson to Jeremiah Goodman, 1811, Jefferson Papers, Alderman Memorial Library, University of Virginia.

26. The Lynchburg market is still the largest in the state and was the largest in the world.

27. Jefferson, *Account Book 1775*, April 29 and March 12, respectively.

28. Thomas Jefferson to James Maury, 1815, Jefferson Papers, Library of Congress.

29. No doubt Jefferson was surprised to learn from his friend that Germans thought tobacco cleaned and invigorated the soil.

30. Thomas Jefferson to Thomas Mann Randolph, 1792, Jefferson Papers, Library of Congress.

31. Jefferson Papers, Yale University.

32. Thomas Jefferson to George Jefferson, 1801, Jefferson Papers, Massachusetts Historical Society.

33. Thomas Leiper to Thomas Jefferson, February 17, 1801, Massachusetts Historical Society.

34. Thomas Jefferson to Thomas Mann Randolph, 1791, Jefferson Papers, Library of Congress.

35. Thomas Mann Randolph to Thomas Jefferson, 1791, Jefferson Papers, Alderman Memorial Library, University of Virginia.

36. In Chester County, Pennsylvania, wheat, rye, oats, and barley were reported as the "principal productions" with maize held in so little esteem that many preferred to get what little they used from farther south. In Bucks County, Pennsylvania, maize was not attempted in large plantings before 1750; wheat was the cash crop.

37. Jefferson, *Notes*, 159.

38. Ibid.

39. Jefferson Papers, Library of Congress.

40. The mill, according to Thomas's statement in 1809, was established in 1757. As expenses for mill construction appear in Peter's account books as early as 1753–54. His plans for growing wheat, at least on an expanded basis, must have been formulated during this period.

41. Lipscomb and Bergh, *Writings*, 8:58–59.

42. Ibid., 14:260–63.

43. Thomas Jefferson to Thomas Mann Randolph, 1790, Jefferson Papers, Library of Congress.

44. Thomas Jefferson to John F. Mercer, September 5, 1797, Jefferson Papers, Library of Congress.

45. Ford, *Writings*, 5:325–26.

46. Thomas Jefferson to Thomas Mann Randolph, 1792, Jefferson Papers, Library of Congress.

47. Thomas Mann Randolph to Thomas Jefferson, 1792, Jefferson Papers, Massachusetts Historical Society.

48. Jefferson, *Notes*, 160.

49. Thomas Jefferson to Martha Randolph, 1811, Jefferson Papers, Massachusetts Historical Society.

50. Nevertheless flowers of both crops were memorialized in the capitals used in the small rotundas of the nation's capitol. Jefferson and Benjamin Latrobe were responsible for the design.

51. For an excellent description of Indian corn at the beginning of the 18th century see Robert Beverly, *The History and Present State of Virginia*, (1705; reprint, Chapel Hill, N.C.: University of North Carolina Press, 1947), 143–44.

52. The squaws, however, took pride in keeping their corn fields clean.

53. For a detailed discussion of this method by a practicing farmer of the era see J. F. D. Smyth, *A Tour in the United States of America* (reprint, New York: New York Times and Arno, 1968), 1:293–99 and 2:123–27.

54. George Washington to Thomas Jefferson, Jefferson Papers, Library of Congress.

55. Thomas Mann Randolph to Thomas Jefferson, 1792, Jefferson Papers, Alderman Memorial Library, University of Virginia.

56. Thomas Jefferson to Thomas Mann Randolph, 1792, Jefferson Papers, Library of Congress.

57. Lipscomb and Bergh, *Writings*, 10:11–14.

58. Randall, *Life of Thomas Jefferson*, 2:303–7.

59. George Washington to Thomas Jefferson, 1792, Jefferson Papers, Library of Congress. Growing cowpeas with corn continues in some southern gardens. They are planted after the corn is up. Jefferson's potatoes were also planted after the corn was up.

60. John Taylor to Thomas Jefferson, Jefferson Papers, Library of Congress.

61. Thomas Jefferson to Charles Willson Peale, 1815, Jefferson Papers, Library of Congress.

62. Thomas Jefferson to Thomas Mann Randolph, February 1796, Jefferson Papers, Library of Congress.

63. Thomas Jefferson to Joel Yancy, March 1817, Jefferson Papers, Massachusetts Historical Society.

64. Joel Yancy to Thomas Jefferson, May 1820, Jefferson Papers, Massachusetts Historical Society.

65. Joel Yancy to Thomas Jefferson, 1821, Jefferson Papers, Massachusetts Historical Society.

66. Jefferson, *Account Book 1774*.

67. Thomas Jefferson to George Washington, 1790, Jefferson Papers, Library of Congress.

68. Thomas Jefferson to John Wayles Eppes, 1803, Jefferson Papers, Alderman Memorial Library, University of Virginia.

Chapter 4

1. Jefferson carried on a spirited correspondence with Priestley. Ingen-housz sent Jefferson Volume 2 of his book *On Vegetables*. Jefferson may have met the Dutchman while he was abroad, as they were in Paris at the same time and corresponded as well. Jefferson dissected Ingen-Housz's views in a letter to the Reverend James Madison, President of William and Mary College (See Boyd 13:379–82). Taylor was a personal friend and agricultural confidant.

2. In many respects Jefferson was like the Englishman Arthur Young. Young, a practicing farmer most of his life, was never successful financially. However, he became an outstanding publicist for agricultural change.

3. Boyd, 18:97–8.

4. Jefferson, *Notes*, 37.

5. Lipscomb and Bergh, *Writings*, 12:204–5. Waterhouse lectured on botany, natural history, and minerology at Rhode Island College. He pioneered vaccination in America and sent sufficient smallpox vaccine to President Jefferson to inoculate about 200 persons.

6. Ralph Izard to Thomas Jefferson, 1787, Jefferson Papers, Library of Congress.

7. H. A. Washington, ed., *The Writings of Thomas Jefferson*, (Washington: Taylor and Maury, 1853), 174–76.

8. Lipscomb and Bergh, *Writings*, 12:204–5.

9. Thomas Jefferson to John Milledge, 1809, Jefferson Papers, Library of Congress.

10. John Milledge to Thomas Jefferson, 1809, Jefferson Papers, Library of Congress.

11. The mission cultivar is still a leading one in California.

12. Lipscomb and Bergh, *Writings*, 6:193–204.

13. Thomas Jefferson to Stephen Cathalan, 1804, Jefferson Papers, Library of Congress.

14. Lipscomb and Bergh, *Writings*, 13:204–5.

15. Thomas Jefferson to William Johnson, 1817, Jefferson Papers, Library of Congress. Jefferson had appointed the South Carolinian to the Supreme Court of the U.S. in 1801.

16. Worthington Chauncy Ford, ed., *Thomas Jefferson's Correspondence* (Boston: N.P., 1916), 269.

17. Thomas Jefferson to N. Herbemont, November 3, 1822, Jefferson Papers, Library of Congress.

18. Thomas Jefferson to Bernard McMahon, 1811, Jefferson Papers, Library of Congress.

19. Thomas Jefferson to John Milledge, 1811, Jefferson Papers, Library of Congress.

20. Lipscomb and Bergh, *Writings*, 8:58–59.

21. Thomas Jefferson to Edmund Bacon, December 1808, Jefferson Papers, Huntington Library.

22. Jefferson, *Farm Book*, 249.

23. Thomas Jefferson to Bernard Peyton, 1818, Jefferson Papers, Massachusetts Historical Collection, 1:269.

24. Lipscomb and Bergh, *Writings*, 7:465–66.

25. Ibid., 12:252–54.

26. William Bartram to Thomas Jefferson, 1808, Jefferson Papers, Library of Congress.

27. Lipscomb and Bergh, *Writings*, 12:90–93.

28. Thomas Jefferson to Benjamin Vaughan, June 1790, Jefferson Papers, Library of Congress.

29. Thomas Jefferson to William Drayton, May 1, 1791, Jefferson Papers, Library of Congress.

30. Ford, *Writings*, 5:326–27.

31. Thomas Jefferson to William Prince, July 1791, Jefferson Papers, Massachusetts Historical Society.

32. Joseph Fay to Thomas Jefferson, 1792, Jefferson Papers, Massachusetts Historical Society.

33. Ford, *Writings*, 5:508–10.

34. Lipscomb and Bergh, *Writings*, 12:90–93.

35. Lord Delaware, colonial governor at Jamestown, was the first to promote grape growing in the Colonies. He wrote in 1616 to the London Company suggesting this could be a source of revenue. Three years later the Company sent a collection of French grapes along with several French vignerons. This venture was short-lived. The Virginia Assembly in 1619, 1639, about 1660, and again in 1769 encouraged grape growing. Meanwhile Governor Alexander Spotswood in 1710 brought in a group of Germans to make wine on land he gave them in Spotsylvania County. Men in other colonies also made a concerted effort to make wine in America. These included Lord Baltimore, who in 1662 planted 300 vines at St. Mary's. John Bartram in 1762 appears

to be the first to recommend the cultivation of native grapes—or any of our native fruits.

36. Thomas Jefferson to Anthony Giannini, 1786, Jefferson Papers, Library of Congress.

37. Thomas Jefferson to William Drayton, July 30, 1787, Jefferson Papers, Library of Congress.

38. Lipscomb and Bergh, *Writings*, 6:193–204.

39. The Swiss John James Dufour who came to this country in 1796 with the intention of founding a wine industry spent three to four years visiting every part of the U.S., observing existing vineyards and sites where vineyards had been tried. He found only one location which seemed promising to him: Legaux's near Philadelphia, and only one grape, the Cape of Good Hope.

40. Thomas Jefferson to John Adlum, 1809, Jefferson Papers, Library of Congress.

41. Jefferson, *Garden Book 1810*.

42. Thomas Jefferson to John Dortie, October 1, 1811, Jefferson Papers, Library of Congress.

43. Bernard McMahon, to Thomas Jefferson, 1812, Jefferson Papers, Library of Congress.

44. Thomas Jefferson to John David, Dec. 25, 1815, Jefferson Papers, Library of Congress. The labrusca is known as the northern fox grape and the rotundifolia, as the southern fox grape or muscadine. Which species Jefferson had in mind is unclear. Both have had a major impact on American grapes. In 1819 Adlum introduced the Catawba grape to his old friend. A derivative of the labrusca, where it originated is not known, but it probably came from the Catawba River area of North Carolina. It immediately proved its superiority to all others in Adlum's vineyard and went on to dominate the field for table use and winemaking. At last Jefferson's goal was attained.

45. Thomas Jefferson to John Adlum, 1816, Jefferson Papers, Library of Congress. With the introduction of the Concord, a derivative of labrusca, in the 1850s, commercial grape growing finally began in the U.S.

46. Thomas Jefferson to William Johnson, May 10, 1817, Jefferson Papers, Library of Congress.

47. Ford, *Correspondence*, 270–71.

48. Sainfoin is sometimes referred to as a grass. The name sainfoin is also applied to any of several Western hemisphere legumes.

49. Thomas Jefferson to Thomas Mann Randolph, Jefferson Papers, Library of Congress.

50. Lipscomb and Bergh, *Writings*, 12:90–93.

51. Thomas Jefferson to John Dortie, October 1, 1811, Jefferson Papers, Library of Congress.

Chapter 5

1. Thomas Jefferson to Charles Willson Peale, 1813, Jefferson Papers, Massachusetts Historical Collection (Boston, 1900) 1:178–80.

2. For a full description see Thomas Jefferson to John Sinclair, March 23, 1798, Jefferson Papers, Massachusetts Historical Society.

3. Boyd, 16:370.

4. R. Worthington, ed., *Letters and Other Writings of James Madison* (1865; reprint, New York: U.S. Congress, 1884), 1:589.

5. Thomas Jefferson to John Taylor, 1794, Jefferson Papers, Massachusetts Historical Collection, 7th ser. (Boston: 1900), 1:49–55.

6. Thomas Jefferson to Charles Willson Peale, 1813, Jefferson Papers Massachusetts Historical Collection, 7th ser. (Boston: 1900), 1:178–80.

7. Thomas Jefferson to Harry Innes, Jefferson Papers, Library of Congress.

8. Randall, *Life of Thomas Jefferson*, 2:308.

9. Rittenhouse and Jefferson had worked together in the American Philosophical Society (APS). Jefferson had been elected a member in 1780 and was appointed as one of the Society's officers the following year. He was a member of the Society for forty-seven years and for seventeen, its president. After founder Benjamin Franklin died in 1790, Rittenhouse became president and Jefferson one of the Society's vice presidents. In 1791 the two men and two other members investigated methods for obtaining fresh water from salt water, indicating the breadth of scientific interest encountered in the Society. Rittenhouse was also involved in the political structure of his state. He served as a Pennsylvania state treasurer and director of the Philadelphia mint.

The APS roster was a prestigious international one. Its members included George Washington, John Adams, John Jay, Robert Patterson, and Dr. Caspar Wistar. Especially in its early years the APS was very loosely run for various reasons, not the least of which was due to the very busy lives of its members, men whose jobs were usually in fields not directly related to APS interest. Franklin, John Bartram, Rittenhouse and Jefferson were probably the only members to whom the term scientist could be applied. Nevertheless the Society was effective on a variety of levels and Jefferson was a tireless promoter of it.

10. Thomas Jefferson to Charles Willson Peale, 1815, Jefferson Papers, Library of Congress.

11. Robert Livingson held various posts for his country. He was, for example, a member of the Committee to Draft the Declaration of Independence, U.S. Minister to France, and President of the Society for the Useful Arts. Philip Tabb carried forward agricultural work of importance. Edmund Ruffin described him as "one of the earliest good farmers of Virginia and deservedly the most celebrated in his time for his judicious management, and for his success in improving his farm and its productions. André Thoüin was the Director the National Garden of Paris. Dupont de Nemours was a French economist and politician and father of the American industrialist E. I. Dupont.

12. Robert Patterson held the chair of math at the University of Pennsylvania, was a director of the Philadelphia mint, and president of APS.

13. In 1805 the English Board received a model incorporating the improvements Jefferson had made to the toe.

14. Society of Agriculture to Thomas Jefferson, 1807, Jefferson Papers, Library of Congress.

15. Thomas Jefferson to John Taylor, 1807, Jefferson Papers, Massachusetts Historical Society.

16. Thomas Jefferson to Charles Willson Peale, 1815, Jefferson Papers, Massachusetts Historical Collection, 1:233–35.

17. Columella was quite emphatic about this: "But especial care must be taken in the ploughing always to run the furrow crosswise to the slope." However, his reasoning was quite different from Randolph's, for Columella continues "for by this method the difficulty of the ascent is mitigated, and the toil of man and beast is thereby lessened most handily." Columella *On Agriculture*, trans. Harrison B. Ash (Cambridge, Mass.: N.P., 1941), 135.

18. Lipscomb and Bergh, *Writings*, 17:404–10.

19. Virginia, Board of Agriculture, *Report* (1842–43, Doc. 12), 63.

20. It is not to be supposed farmers everywhere have updated their farm implements. Wooden plows are still being used in the Alpujarras Mountains of southern

Spain. As for animals to pull plows, in this country, Sen. Huey Long of Louisiana remembered seeing his older brothers in the early 1900s hitched up and pulling a plow on the family farm.

21. These figures were reported in the *New York Farmer* in 1829. On the other hand, during the Colonial period Landon Carter of Virginia reported a worker could beat out about a bushel a day.

22. Jefferson, *Farm Book*, 46.

23. Jefferson Papers, Massachusetts Historical Collection, 1:233–35.

24. Lipscomb and Bergh, *Writings*, 9:214–15.

25. Ibid., 9:342–43.

26. George Washington to Thomas Jefferson, July 6, 1796, Jefferson Papers, Library of Congress.

27. See Betts, *Farm Book*, 314–15. The Duke de la Rochefoucauld-Liancourt provides a good description of the entire farming operation at Monticello. See Randall, *Life of Thomas Jefferson*, 2:303–7.

28. Thomas Jefferson to Thomas Mann Randolph, August 11, 1793, Jefferson Papers, Library of Congress.

29. Thomas Jefferson to Dr. Cunningham Harris, November 6, 1812, Jefferson Papers, Library of Congress.

30. Lipscomb and Bergh, *Writings*, 9:342–43.

31. Robert McCormick, father of Cyrus, invented a hydraulic hemp-breaking machine in this same period. He also invented a threshing machine and a reaper, the latter proving unusable.

32. Hemp is still used for clothing in parts of Asia as well as for twine. It is seldom grown in America today except as a source of marijuana.

33. Figures are in Jefferson's *Garden Book* entries for 1772 for the first, and his *Account Book 1772* for the second and third.

Chapter 6

1. Thomas Jefferson to Robert Gamble, May 19, 1793, Jefferson Papers, Library of Congress.

2. Jefferson, *Garden Book*, April 22, 1804.

3. Thomas Jefferson to James Walker, January 1807, Jefferson Papers, Massachusetts Historical Society.

4. Jefferson, *Garden Book*, 1814.

5. Betts and Bear, Family Letters, 71–72.

6. Thomas Jefferson to Edmund Bacon, 1819, Jefferson Papers, Massachusetts Historical Society.

7. Thomas Jefferson to James Madison, July, 1806, Jefferson Papers, Library of Congress.

8. Washington, *Writings*, 174–76.

9. By 1811 Jefferson called upon his sheep-raising friend E. I. Dupont in Delaware to provide him with powder from the new E. I. Dupont de Nemours and Co., established in 1802.

10. A second gristmill was planned near the dam in 1819. The canal to service it was completed at the end of that year. In August of 1819 Jefferson wrote Edmund Bacon from Poplar Forest: "I have engaged here the best millwright [I] have ever known to go and rebuild the sawmill [in operation since 1813] and the gristmill as soon as the canal is done." (Jefferson Papers, Massachusetts Historical Society). Jefferson wrote in Decem-

ber of that year: "I have just completed a canal for a mill at the West end of the dam." For a man now 76 this devotion to building for the future is certainly unusual. But then he was also busy supervising the construction of the University of Virginia.

11. Thomas Jefferson to Edmund Bacon, December 1806, Jefferson Papers, Library of Congress.

12. Martha Randolph to Thomas Jefferson, March 1809, Jefferson Papers, Massachusetts Historical Society.

13. George Jefferson to Thomas Jefferson, 1810, Jefferson Papers, Massachusetts Historical Society.

14. Thomas Jefferson to Jonathan Shoemaker, 1809, Jefferson Papers, Massachusetts Historical Society.

15. Ibid.

16. Thomas Jefferson to Edmund Bacon, 1806, Jefferson Papers, Massachusetts Historical Society.

17. Thomas Jefferson to Edmund Bacon, 1807, Jefferson Papers, Huntington Library.

18. Betts and Bear, *Family Correspondence*, 67.

19. Thomas Jefferson to Edmund Bacon, 1807, Jefferson Papers, Massachusetts Historical Society.

20. Thomas Jefferson to Oliver Evans, Jefferson Papers, Massachusetts Historical Society.

21. Thomas Jefferson to Peter Miner, November 18, 1813, Jefferson Papers, Library of Congress.

22. Thomas Jefferson to James Walker, 1811, Jefferson Papers, Massachusetts Historical Society.

23. Jefferson, *Notes on the State of Virginia*, 156–57.

24. Lipscomb and Bergh, *Writings*, 13:122.

25. Thomas Jefferson to Thaddeus Kosciusko, 1812, Jefferson Papers, Library of Congress. See also Jefferson, *Farm Book*, 152.

26. Thomas Jefferson to James Ronaldson, 1812, Jefferson Papers, Library of Congress.

27. Thomas Jefferson to William Thornton, 1812, Jefferson Papers Library of Congress.

28. Thomas Jefferson to Robert Livingston, 1813, Jefferson Papers, Massachusetts Historical Society.

29. The spinning Jenny had been invented in 1764, the first of three improvements which would revolutionize the art of spinning. The next followed soon thereafter in 1769, Arkwright's throstle machine, and then Crompton's mule spinner in 1779. The machine Jefferson discussed with Thornton was supposedly more simple than the Arkwright's. Jefferson was to find his workmen could not cope with repairs of either the Barrett or Herrick machines. Mules were also known in Jefferson's neighborhood, but had the same handicaps.

30. Thomas Jefferson to William Thornton, 1814, Jefferson Papers, Library of Congress.

31. Thomas Jefferson to Jeremiah Goodman, 1812, Jefferson Papers, Massachusetts Historical Society.

32. Thomas Jefferson to Jeremiah Goodman, March 5, 1813, Jefferson Papers, Library of Congress.

33. Thomas Jefferson to E. I. Dupont, 1812, Jefferson Papers, Massachusetts Historical Society.

34. Thomas Jefferson to Hugh Holmes, July 1813, Jefferson Papers, Massachusetts Historical Society.

Chapter 7

1. The llama was not domesticated as a beast of burden until 1000 years ago. It was confined to high elevations in South America.

2. Lipscomb and Bergh, *Writings*, 9:342–43.

3. The term field grass husbandry signifies the new importance of grasses in the cultivation system. Heretofore fields were held as separate units, divided into those on which crops were grown, those used for pasture and meadows, and those in fallow. Now, as the Romans had done before, all fields were treated the same way, in crop rotations with each phase being allowed several years.

4. George Jefferson to Thomas Jefferson, 1801, Jefferson Papers, Massachusetts Historical Society.

5. Quoted in Jefferson, *Garden Book*, 518.

6. Thomas Jefferson to Jeremiah Goodman, 1814, Jefferson Papers, Library of Congress.

7. Quote in Jefferson, *Garden Book*, 492.

8. As with most other Virginia plantation owners, Jefferson could not bring himself to split up slave families. Their natural increase over the years left him with a bloated work force with a significant proportion too young or too old to be prime workers. Issac Weld remarked that in Virginia: "The number of the slaves increases most rapidly, so that there is scarcely any estate but what is overstocked. This is a circumstance complained of by every planter, as the maintenance of more than are requisite for the culture of the estate is attended with great expense. Motives of humanity deter them from selling the poor creatures or turning them adrift from the spot where they have been born and brought up in the midst of friends and relations." Weld, *Travels through the States*, 150.

9. Thomas Jefferson to Craven Peyton, November 14, 1819, Jefferson Papers, Library of Congress.

10. Joel Yancy to Thomas Jefferson, 1819, Jefferson Papers, Massachusetts Historical Society.

11. Thomas Jefferson to Joel Yancy, 1816, Jefferson Papers, Massachusetts Historical Society.

12. Quoted in Jefferson, *Garden Book*, 535.

13. Lipscomb and Bergh, *Writings*, 9:139–43.

14. Stuart was a soldier in the Revolutionary War, a legislator and jurist, and a prominent leader of conservative Jeffersonian Democrats in Virginia.

15. Jefferson identified this breed as the Senegal sheep, which was also called the Bengal.

16. William Keough to Thomas Jefferson, February 1808, Jefferson Papers, Library of Congress.

17. Thomas Jefferson to William Caruthers, March 12, 1813, Jefferson Papers, Library of Congress.

18. Caleb Kirk to Thomas Jefferson, 1809, Jefferson Papers, Library of Congress.

19. Libscomb and Bergh, *Writings*, 12:389–91.

20. Joseph Dougherty to Thomas Jefferson, June 1, 1810, Jefferson Papers, Library of Congress.

21. Bear, *Jefferson at Monticello*, 58–59.

22. Thomas Jefferson to William Caruthers, March 12, 1813, Jefferson Papers, Library of Congress.

23. Thomas Jefferson to Joseph Dougherty, December 25, 1812, Jefferson Papers, Library of Congress.

24. Published in 1809, the book was in Jefferson's library.

25. Hamilton W. Pierson, *Jefferson at Monticello* (New York: Charles Scribner, 1862), p. 64.

26. Jefferson, *Farm Book*, 75.

Chapter 8

1. Jane Jefferson, as women of her era were expected to do, coped with plantation matters in the absence of her husband. Peter's job as a surveyor could have kept him from home for days at a time. Thus she was qualified to carry on after his death. Details are missing because when Shadwell burned in 1770 valuable records burned too. Fortunately some of the memorandum books were saved. (The *Garden Book* may have been at Monticello.) Peter's account book is now at the Huntington Library in California. Thomas's account books have been published as J. A. Bear, Jr., and L. C. Stanton, eds., *Jefferson's Memorandum Books* (Lawrenceville, N.J.: Princeton University Press, 1986).

2. Randolph *Domestic Life*, 24. Weld had this to say: "The large estates are managed by stewards and overseers, the proprietors just amusing themselves with seeing what is going forward" *Travels Through the States* 1:148.

3. Randolph, *Domestic Life* 24.

4. Lipscomb and Bergh, *Writings*, 9:286–8.

5. Ford, *Writings*, 6:475.

6. Thomas Jefferson to Nicholas Lewis, February 1786, Jefferson Papers, Library of Congress.

7. Bowling Clark and a Mr. Franklin, both listed as overseers, must have similarly been appointed by Lewis in Jefferson's absence in France.

8. Thomas Jefferson to Nicholas Lewis, 1786, Jefferson Papers, Library of Congress.

9. Thomas Jefferson to Nicholas Lewis, June 1791, Jefferson Papers, Massachusetts Historical Society.

10. Thomas Jefferson to Thomas Garth, 1790, Jefferson Papers, Massachusetts Historical Society.

11. Compare these with instructions by other plantation owners to their overseers.

12. These men were slaves hired from other owners.

13. Thomas Jefferson to John Strode, June 5, 1805, Jefferson Papers, Library of Congress.

14. Bowling Clark, probably due to his family background, had a special relationship with Jefferson. He served as the latter's attorney in 1792.

15. Jefferson's complaints regarding Bedford came later in an 1819 letter to Joel Yancey, his current overseer, when he blames Goodman and Darnell, his overseers from 1811–15 for poor management, including not applying manure to the fields. Yet these were precisely the years Jefferson spent the most time at Poplar Forest, when he should have seen what was going on and corrected the men.

16. The 1781 *Account Book* named Richard Gaines as overseer for all of Jefferson's lands on the north side of the Rivanna River. Chisolm was his replacement.

17. Jefferson was not alone in using slaves as overseers. James Madison during the same general period likewise entrusted one of his slaves as overseer on one of his farms, even giving the man authority to purchase goods on Madison's account with a Fredericksburg merchant.

18. Boyd, 1:41.

19. Betts and Bear, *Family Correspondence*, 8.

20. Other manumissions were recorded later.

21. Thomas Jefferson to Anthony Giannini, 1786, Jefferson Papers, Library of Congress. George would be remembered by the absent Minister as the person who discovered the "lilly of Canada" in the woods near the stone spring. Together they transplanted some roots for the flower border near the house.

22. Randolph, *Domestic Life*, 215.

23. Thomas Jefferson to Thomas Mann Randolph, 1792, Jefferson Papers, Massachusetts Historical Society.

24. Ford, *Writings*, 8:174–75.

25. Thomas Jefferson to William Temple, April 26, 1795, Jefferson Papers, Massachusetts Historical Society.

26. Lester J. Cappon, ed., *The Adams-Jefferson Letters* (Chapel Hill, N.C.: University of North Carolina Press, 1959), 1.258.

27. Both George, Jr. and his younger brother Isaac worked as smiths for Jefferson.

28. Ford, *Writings*, 9:66.

29. Jefferson, *Farm Book*, 46.

30. Thomas Mann Randolph to Thomas Jefferson, 1798, Jefferson Papers, Alderman Library, University of Virginia.

31. Ibid.

32. Thomas Jefferson to Thomas Mann Randolph, January 1798, Jefferson Papers, Library of Congress.

33. Thomas Jefferson to Thomas Mann Randolph, 1798, Jefferson Papers, Library of Congress.

34. Thomas Mann Randolph to Thomas Jefferson, 1798, Jefferson Papers, Massachusetts Historical Society.

35. Quoted in Jefferson, *Garden Book*, 466.

36. John Hemins to Thomas Jefferson, November, 1821, Jefferson Papers, Library of Congress.

37. Other blacks were also given positions of responsibility. These are the two most interesting cases. Burwell and John were two Hemings who were freed by Jefferson. Edmund Bacon said: "Mr. Jefferson had a large number of favorite servants that were treated just as well as could be. Burwell was the main, principal servant on the place . . . Mr. Jefferson had the most perfect confidence in him. He told me not to be at all particular with him—to let him do pretty much as he pleased, and to let him have pocket money occasionally, as he wanted it . . . He stayed at Monticello and took charge of the meat house, garden, &c., and kept the premises in order." Betts and Bear, *Family Correspondence*, 99. Burwell was also a fine painter who painted the carriage, the house and also painted at the University. John Hemings learned his trade under white carpenters and joiners and ultimately was given the responsibility for doing the finishing work at Monticello and Poplar Forest because of his excellent abilities.

38. Ford, *Writings*, 9:85.

39. The French botanist Andre Michaux after his arrival in America in 1785 to collect plants for the King of France complained about the perennial shortage of labor he found as a result of westward migration and the lack of inclination to work of those who remained. He said he could have accomplished ten times more if American free workers had the same work habits he was accustomed to in France.

40. Boyd, 11:653.

41. Quoted in Jefferson, *Farm Book*, p. 39.

42. The lot the free black was not an enviable one even in the north. A news item from the *American Sentinel* in part said: "The Woodbury *Herald* of yesterday says, that the upper part of Gloucester, New Jersey, 'is literally overrun with blacks, driven by the violence of an infuriated mob, from their homes and property in Philadelphia, to seek

shelter and protection among the farmers of our country. Their numbers previous to this influx had become in some places troublesome—in others a burden and a nuisance. A temporary sojourn among us, considering the circumstances of the case, may be borne with—but the first indication of a permanent residence should, and we feel confident will, call forth a rigid enforcement of the statue against the admission of blacks into our boundaries" (Reprinted in the *Federal Union* [Milledgeville, Ga., Sept. 17, 1834]; see in Phillips, *Plantation and Frontier Documents*, 159).

43. Boyd, 14:492–93.

44. Ellen Wayles Coolidge, *Memoirs* (Coolidge Papers, University of Virginia). The notion that slaves were commonly brutalized, at least in Virginia, is not borne out by on-sight, disinterested foreign observers. See, for example, Hugh Jones, *Present State of Virginia* (reprint, Chapel Hill, N.C.: University of North Carolina Press, 1956), 130; Robert Beverley, *History and Present State of Virginia*, 271–72, and Weld, *Travel Through the States*, 1:148–50.

45. Quoted in Jefferson, *Garden Book*, 482.

46. Ibid., 492.

47. Randall, *Life of Thomas Jefferson*, 2:303–7.

48. Betts and Bear, *Family Correspondence*, 13, 23.

49. Ibid., 97, 103.

50. Ibid., 103.

51. Thomas Jefferson to Thomas Mann Randolph, Jefferson Papers, Library of Congress.

52. Thomas Jefferson to Thomas Mann Randolph, Jefferson Papers, Massachusetts Historical Society. For early records regarding treatment of slaves by their owners see Phillips, *Plantation and Frontier Documents*.

53. Thomas Jefferson to Reuben Perry, Tucker-Coleman Papers, Colonial Williamsburg, Inc.

54. The hired slaves came from counties other than Albemarle.

55. The nine-year lease which began in 1800 included these terms: "With respect to the negroes he will feed & clothe them well, take care of them in sickness, employing medical aid if necessary" (Jefferson Papers, Massachusetts Historical Society).

56. Thomas Jefferson to Henry Clark, October 18, 1820, Jefferson Papers, Massachusetts Historical Society.

Chapter 9

1. By 1767 in the *Garden Book* there are numerous references to "sowing" and "planting," presumably by Jefferson himself.

2. Lipscomb and Bergh, *Writings*, 14:201.

3. Jefferson's plans for his water supply appear in his *Weather Memorandum Book*, 1776–1820, and are reprinted in Jefferson, *Garden Book*, 629–31. Gravity-fed water systems are still used in rural Virginia, with pipes running from a dependable spring to the house.

4. He had in fact been growing fruits, nuts and vegetables at Shadwell as indicated in the *Garden Book* entry for 1767.

5. George Wythe to Thomas Jefferson, 1770, Jefferson Papers, Massachusetts Historical Society.

6. His mother and unmarried siblings apparently continued to live at Shadwell but in another building.

7. Jefferson Papers, Huntington Library. Such underplanting had been done in apple orchards in England. *The Compleat Cyderman*, written in 1754 by experienced

fruit growers, recommended tillage instead of grass under the trees as a method of promoting tree growth. Although famous for its apples at this time, farmers in both Devonshire and Herefordshire reverted to pasture before the end of the century. Progress is not always in a straight line.

8. Thomas Jefferson to Ferdinand Grand, December 28, 1786, Jefferson Papers, Library of Congress.

9. Although pears were a favorite fruit in New England, if not in other colonies, seedling pears are the poorest of all seedling fruit trees. Therefore, grafting (or use of suckers) is imperative. Thus, unlike apples and peaches, new pear varieties are few and the farmer needed to know how to graft or had to buy his pear trees.

10. Interestingly in 1813 sixty-seven peaches were transplanted to Monticello from Poplar forest. Bedford County today has commercial peach orchards and Jefferson undoubtedly found peach growing satisfactory in his day.

11. Ford, Correspondence, 190. Nurseryman William Prince offered pecans after planting 30 nuts in 1772. They yielded ten trees, eight of which were sold in England. Pecans were offered regularly by Prince thereafter.

12. The one exception this author has found is boxwood. This shrub, used so extensively in England and Virginia during this period, does not merit mentioning on Jefferson's part—let alone planting.

13. One hundred acres was a fairly large holding in English eyes, the lesser gentry and yeomen of the period averaging but 150 acres, which was shared with the local aristocracy. The threat of widespread starvation in England was ever present whenever the weather did not cooperate. Such a famine occurred in the winter of 1623. A worse seige prevailed from 1630 until 1633. The motives for immigration to America were considerable and the need for self-sufficiency very real.

14. Jefferson had his first vegetable garden at Shadwell. It included peas, asparagus, celery, onion, lettuce, radish, broccoli, cauliflower, and cucumbers.

15. Robert Beverly, History and Present State of Virginia, remarks, "And yet they hadn't many Gardens in the Country, fit to bear that name" (316).

16. These triangles were later discarded.

17. Betts and Bear, Family Correspondence, 47.

18. Landreth's son David began a second establishment in Charleston, South Carolina and took over the Philadelphia store in 1828. Another Landreth, Thomas, was in charge of the nursery branch.

19. Margaret Bayard Smith, First Forty Years of Washington Society (New York, 1906), 68. The National Intelligence was founded in 1800. The Smiths were good friends of Jefferson.

20. There were twenty-four squares by 1812.

21. In 1794 in the Garden Book he merely listed the vegetables and fruits he intended to plant. He also recorded a list of seeds saved.

22. Thomas Jefferson to Bernard McMahon, 1810, Jefferson Papers, Library of Congress.

23. Vegetable breeding, except for New World species, did not occupy the attention of American breeders until the 1900s.

24. Jefferson may have been referring to the husk tomato (Physalis) grown by North American Indians. George Washington grew the "love apple" (what we call tomato today) at Mount Vernon.

25. Boyd, 12:343.

26. This was an English practice. In 1639 one observer recorded a "greatt store of good Fruit trees on the hedges in and by the high waies" (quoted in Carl Bridenbaugh, Vexted and Troubled Englishmen 1590–1642 [New York: Oxford University Press, 1968], 70).

27. Bernard McMahon, *American Gardener's Calender* (1806), 65.
28. Remains of the pavilion were discovered during reconstruction.
29. Plans, 1804, Jefferson Papers, Massachusetts Historical Society.

Chapter 10

1. When Margaret Bayard Smith and her husband, Samuel Harrison Smith, visited Monticello in 1809, Jefferson showed her where he meant to place this Gothic building as well as other such improvements.
2. The full plan is in Jefferson, *Account Book 1771.*
3. Lipscomb and Bergh, *Writings*, 19:19–20.
4. An indication that little came of it all can be found in an 1806 letter to William Hamilton, Jefferson Papers, Library of Congress.
5. Jefferson, *Garden Book*, November 12, 1772.
6. Memoranda, 1807, Jefferson Papers, Massachusetts Historical Society.
7. Thomas Jefferson to Edmund Bacon, 1808, Jefferson Papers, Massachusetts Historical Society.
8. Four years later Mrs. Thornton returned and found the house and grounds much improved. Mrs. Smith found this road tolerable when she visited in 1809 — at least on the way up. On a later visit in 1828, two years after Jefferson's death, deterioration had set in. She commented: "The road was so rugged and broken, that the carriage passed it with difficulty." Smith, 233.
9. Smith, *First Forty Years*, 68.
10. Ibid., 73.
11. Jefferson's sister, wife, and daughter were all named Martha.
12. Also known as sweet shrub, strawberry bush, sweet Betsy, and bubby flower.
13. *Magnolia tripetala.*
14. *Melia azedarach*, the chinaberry tree, native to the orient and widely planted in the southern U.S.
15. Randall, *Life of Thomas Jefferson* 1:447.
16. Lipscomb and Bergh, *Writings*, 17:236–44.
17. Jefferson was hardly the first to foster such exchanges, which date from the first settlers of Jamestown. It is doubtful, however, that anyone else took such pains to get European plants established in America.
18. Jefferson, *Notes*, 37.
19. Randolph, *Domestic Life*, 221–22.
20. Lipscomb and Bergh, *Writings*, 19:185.
21. The handwriting of Jefferson and Latrobe is remarkably similar, especially in the fact neither man consistently made certain key letters like "n" and "d" in the same manner. Jefferson's capital "G," however, is consistent as is Latrobe's, and they are not the same. Furthermore, the White House plan, compared with other plans Jefferson is known to have produced for Monticello, is in a free-flowing professional style, quite unlike those of Monticello. While Jefferson was brilliant in his planting designs, his artistic representations of them, while adequate to establish his point, are not impressive.
22. That the ample grounds to the north should be landscaped to become a public pleasure garden was an idea held by many from the beginning. It was envisioned that private mansions bordering this park-like area would form a stylish foil to the great house itself.
23. Pennsylvania, Connecticut, Vermont, and New York.

24. This was finished by March of 1808 and torn down in Andrew Johnson's term as President.

25. Betts and Bear, *Family Letters*, 55.

26. Smith, *First Forty Years*, 11.

27. With its double row of trees on either side of the long, narrow expanse of formal gardens, the Jardin des Plantes in Paris bears a striking resemblance to Jefferson's choice of plants. The Lombardy poplar was a recent introduction to America, and it had taken the country by storm.

28. Identified by Mrs. Smith as willow oaks; she called it a favorite tree of Jefferson's.

29. Thomas Jefferson to Thomas Munroe, March 1807, Jefferson Papers, Library of Congress.

30. *Letters of the Presidents of the U.S. to the Commissioners of Public Buildings and Grounds*, Manuscript Division, Library of Congress.

31. John H. B. Latrobe, *Capitol and Washington*, (N.P., 1881), 25.

32. Subscribing to the venture, among others, were: George Washington (who headed the list with $100), Jefferson (who gave $50), John Adams ($20), James Madison ($20), Alexander Hamilton ($50), and Robert Morris ($80).

33. Jefferson probably had met Michaux in Paris in 1785. André Thoüin was a mutual friend. Michaux had come to the U.S. on assignment of the king to explore American trees, shrubs, and herbaceous plants for possible French use.

34. By April of 1805 the number was increased to a company of thirty-two for the final push to the Pacific.

35. Lipscomb and Bergh: *Writings*, 10:366–68.

36. The initial plans were made in Jefferson's office at the White House with his personal participation and leadership. While Jefferson left no day-by-day record of his activities while President, he was a committed planner whose attention to details is legendary. The Lewis and Clark expedition was of prime importance to him for political and personal reasons. This thirst for knowledge was insatiable.

37. McMahon got seven varieties of currants, two of gooseberries and about twenty other new species, as well as five or six new genera of plants—a real bonanza, of which he was truly appreciative.

38. Thomas Jefferson to André Thoüin, 1813, Jefferson Papers, Library of Congress.

39. Thomas Jefferson to Bernard McMahon 1813, Jefferson Papers, Library of Congress.

40. *Mahonia nervosa*.

41. Smith, p. 394.

42. Weymouth pine is the European designation for our easter white pine. Lord Weymouth planted them more than 200 years ago on his English estate. Why Jefferson used the name Weymouth is not clear as he undoubtedly got his pines in America.

43. Jefferson Papers, Library of Congress.

44. Thomas Jefferson to William Hamilton, 1806, Jefferson Papers, Library of Congress.

45. Jefferson had planted lilac as early as 1767 at Shadwell and refers to these shrubs regularly thereafter. He first mentions the golden willow in Philadelphia in 1791. He asked Edmund Bacon to plant some in 1808. Anne mentions they looked fine in April of that year. After that he planted numerous specimens at Poplar Forest.

46. Jefferson's first recorded flower garden dates to 1767 at Shadwell. His *Garden Book* entries for that year show he tried a respectable number of species. The entries for the preceding year, the first in his new book, consist of native flowers plus imported bulbs which someone else probably had planted in some earlier year.

47. Thomas Jefferson to Anne Randolph, 1807, Jefferson Papers, Massachusetts Historical Society.

48. Betts and Bear, *Family Letters*, 292.

49. Thomas Jefferson to Madame de Tessé, 1803, Jefferson Papers, Library of Congress.

50. Betts and Bear, *Family Letters*, 294.

51. Thomas Jefferson to Ellen Randolph, April, 1808, Thomas Jefferson Papers, Massachusetts Historical Society.

52. Betts and Bear, *Family Letters*, 312–13.

53. Ibid., 328.

54. Anne Bankhead to Thomas Jefferson, November, 1808, Jefferson Papers, Massachusetts Historical Society.

55. Randolph, *Domestic Life*, 330–31.

56. Betts and Bear, *Family Letters*, 351–2.

57. Ibid., 400.

58. Ibid.

59. Randall, *Life of Thomas Jefferson*, 47.

60. Thomas Jefferson to Samuel Harrison Smith, 1810, Jefferson Papers, Library of Congress.

61. Thomas Jefferson to Bernard McMahon, April, 1809, Jefferson Papers, Library of Congress.

62. Ibid.

63. Thomas Jefferson to Samuel Harrison Smith, August 1813, Jefferson Papers, Library of Congress.

64. Betts and Bear, *Family Letters*, 46.

65. Francis Eppes, Jefferson's only surviving grandchild by his youngest daughter Maria (who died when Francis was a young boy), reacted to a similar situation very differently, although he was in close contact with his grandfather while growing up. As Maria's share of Jefferson's estate, Francis was given the house at Poplar Forest and most of the land there. Within two years of Jefferson's death Francis sold out.

66. Carnations.

67. The yucca, Adam's needle.

Chapter 11

1. See Merrill D. Peterson, ed., *Writings of Thomas Jefferson* (New York: Viking), 1149–53.

2. Lipscomb and Bergh, *Writings*, 15:123.

3. Ibid., 15:248.

4. Ford, *Writings*, 12:263.

5. Thomas Jefferson to A. S. Brockenbrough, 1825, Jefferson Papers, Library of Congress.

6. Lipscomb and Bergh, *Writings*, 16:163–67. As early as 1803 Jefferson told a friend: "In every College and University, a professorship of agriculture, and the class of its students, might be honored as the first. Young men closing their academical education with this, as the crown of all other sciences, fascinated with its solid charms, and at a time when they are to choose an occupation, instead of crowding other classes, would return to the farms of their fathers, their own, or those of others, and replenish and invigorate a calling, now languishing under contempt and oppression" Lipscomb and Bergh, *Writings*, 10:430.

Index